Telesthesia

For Christen Diane Clifford, with love.

Telesthesia
Communication, Culture, and Class

McKenzie Wark

polity

Copyright © McKenzie Wark 2012

The right of McKenzie Wark to be identified as Author of this Work has been asserted in accordance with the UK Copyright, Designs and Patents Act 1988.

First published in 2012 by Polity Press

Polity Press
65 Bridge Street
Cambridge CB2 1UR, UK

Polity Press
350 Main Street
Malden, MA 02148, USA

ISBN-13: 978-0-7456-5398-3
ISBN-13: 978-0-7456-5399-0(pb)

A catalogue record for this book is available from the British Library.

Typeset in 11 on 13 pt Sabon
by Toppan Best-set Premedia Limited
Printed and bound in Great Britain by the MPG Books Group

The publisher has used its best endeavours to ensure that the URLs for external websites referred to in this book are correct and active at the time of going to press. However, the publisher has no responsibility for the websites and can make no guarantee that a site will remain live or that the content is or will remain appropriate.

Every effort has been made to trace all copyright holders, but if any have been inadvertently overlooked the publisher will be pleased to include any necessary credits in any subsequent reprint or edition.

For further information on Polity, visit our website: www.politybooks.com

Contents

Acknowledgments

My thanks to John Thompson, Jennifer Jahn, Neil de Cort, Helen Gray, and everyone at Polity.

Previous versions of some of these essays appeared in the journals *Arena, Cultural Studies, Dissent, Mute, New Formations, Theory, Culture & Society, Theory & Event, Rhizomes, Transition.*

My thanks to invitations to present versions of some of these essays at Ars Electronica, Albert Einstein Center, Aspen Institute, Biennale of Sydney, Simpson Center for the Humanities at the University of Washington, Carnegie Museum in Pittsburgh, Sarai Media Center in Delhi, DeRoy Lecture Series at Wayne State University, Tate Britain, University of Plymouth, McGill University, American University in Paris, Dartmouth College, Laboral in Gijon, Pompidou Center, Brown University, New Museum, Cal IT2 at UCSD, Microsoft Research in Redmond, and elsewhere.

Special thanks to Joshua Clover for the epigram, which is from a work in progress, and to Trevor Paglen for the cover image, a detail from *Detachment 3, Air Force Flight Test Center, 2008 Groom Lake, NY, Distance ~26 Miles.*

The real movement is nothing but the laws of motion through which capitalism realizes and abolishes itself. This then is not a party or political form but the law of value as such: the dynamic which it sets loose and by which it is then borne along ineluctably toward that undiscovered country from which no value returns.

Joshua Clover

1

How to Occupy an Abstraction

Zuccotti Park, New York

It started with a small and motley band, who took over a little park in downtown Manhattan and declared they had "occupied Wall Street." The occupation wasn't actually on Wall Street, of course. And while there is actually a street called Wall Street in downtown Manhattan, "Wall Street" is something of an abstraction. So what the occupation did involved taking over a little (quasi-) public square in the general vicinity of Wall Street in the financial district, turning it into something like an allegory. Against the abstraction of Wall Street, it proposed another, perhaps no less abstract, story.

The abstraction that is Wall Street already has a double aspect. On the one hand, Wall Street means a certain kind of power, an oligopoly of financial institutions which extract a rent from the rest of us, in exchange for which we don't seem to get very much. "What's good for General Motors is good for America" was the slogan of the old military industrial complex. These days the slogan of the rentier class is: "What's good for Goldman Sachs is none of your fucking business."

This rentier class is an oligopoly that makes French aristocrats of the eighteenth century look like serious, well-organized administrators. If the rhetoric of their media sockpuppets is to be believed, this rentier class are such hothouse flowers that they won't get out of bed in the morning without the promise of a fat bonus, and their constitutions are so sensitive that if anyone says anything bad about them they will take their money and sulk in the corner. They had, to cap it all, so mismanaged their own affairs that vast tracts of public money were required to keep them in business.

The abstraction that is Wall Street also stands for something else, for an inhuman kind of power, which one can imagine running beneath one's feet throughout the financial district. Let's call this power the **vectoral**. It's the combination of fiber-optic cables and massive amounts of computer power. Some vast proportion of the money in circulation around the planet is being automatically traded even as you read this. Engineers are now seriously thinking about trading at the speed of light.[1] Perhaps we should welcome our new robot overlords, who might as well be from outer space.

How can you occupy an abstraction? Perhaps only with another abstraction. Occupy Wall Street took over a more-or-less public park nestled in the downtown landscape of tower blocks, not too far from the old World Trade Center site, and set up camp. It was an occupation which, almost uniquely, made no demands.[2] It had at its core a suggestion: what if people came together and found a way to structure a conversation which might come up with a better way to run the world? Could they do any worse than the way it is run by the combined efforts of Wall Street as the rentier class and Wall Street as the computerized vectors trading intangible assets?

Some commentators saw the modesty of this request as a weakness of Occupy Wall Street.[3] They wanted a list of demands, and they were not shy about proposing some. But perhaps the best thing about Occupy Wall Street was its reluctance to make demands. What remains of what was once called "politics" in the United States is full of demands: to reduce the debt, to cut taxes, to abolish regulations. Nobody even bothers with much justification for these demands any more. Somehow it is just assumed that only what matters to the rentier class matters at all. It's not that the rentier class buys politicians in America. Why bother when you can rent them by the hour? In this context, the most interesting thing about Occupy Wall Street was its suggestion that the main thing that's lacking is not demands, but process. What is lacking is politics itself.

It may sound counterintuitive, but there really is no politics in the United States. There is exploitation, oppression, inequality, violence; there are rumors that there might still be a state. But there is no politics. There is only the semblance of politics. It's mostly just professionals renting influence to favor their interests. The state seems no longer capable of negotiating the common interests of its ruling class.

Politics from below is also simulated. The Tea Party was really just a great marketing campaign.[4] It made the old rentier class demands seem at least temporarily appealing. Like fast food, it seemed delicious until the indigestion started. It's the Contract on America, its Compassionate Conservatism, but with new ingredients! The Tea Party was quite successful. But you can't fool all of the people all of the time, and there is always a new marketing campaign waiting in the wings for when the current one runs out of steam.

None of this is anything but the semblance of a politics. So the genius of the occupation is simply to suggest that there could be a politics, one in which people meet and propose and negotiate. This suggestion points to the great absence at the center of American life: a whole nation, even an empire, with no politics.

Wall Street is a name for an abstraction with the double sense of a rentier class that uses vectoral power to control resources, bypassing political processes that at least had to negotiate with popular interests. Against this, the occupation proposed another abstraction, and it too has a double aspect.

On the one hand, it's a physical thing, a taking of space. Anticipating the occupation, the NYPD put the space around Wall Street under heavy control. Zuccotti Park was actually the fifth on a list of possible sites for the occupation. A lot of people only found the site via cellphone message. This cat-and-mouse game confused the NYPD initially, so it responded with clumsy tactics. It just couldn't figure out what to do with an ongoing occupation that remained peaceful and mostly content to camp out, but which swelled on the weekends to thousands of people.

Occupy Wall Street had the rentier class a bit spooked.[5] In the absence of any real competence at managing the growth and refinement of the economy, the rentier class basically decided to loot and pillage from what is left of the United States and to hell with the consequences. They just don't want to be caught doing it.

Not that they would be too bothered by a few anarchists, but they do fret about this catching on. The taking of a tiny square in downtown New York hardly impinges on the power of the vector. It doesn't much inconvenience the minions who work in the surrounding offices, but the actual occupation is connected to a more abstract kind of occupation, and the slightest hint that it could spread disturbs the fragile constitutions of the rentier sensibility.

The occupation extended out into the intangible world of the vector, but not in the same way as Wall Street. The cop who was stupid enough to pepper-spray some women who were already cordoned off behind orange mesh was quickly identified by hackers, and his information appeared on the Internet for all to see. The incident on the Brooklyn Bridge where the police let people onto the roadway, and then arrested them for being on the roadway, is on the Internet from multiple angles. The occupation is also an occupation of the social media vector.

The so-called mainstream media didn't quite know how to deal with this when it started.[6] The formalities of how "news" is now made are so baroque that news outlets initially resorted to obtuse debates about whether the occupation was "news." It didn't have top-tier publicists. It didn't issue free samples. It didn't buy advertising space. It started without any celebrity spokesmodels. It had a nice poster, but still: how could it be news? These events exposed the poverty of reporting in America. And that in itself is news.

The abstraction that was the occupation was a double one, an occupation of a place, somewhere near the actual Wall Street; and the occupation of the social media vector, with slogans, images, videos, stories. "Keep on forwarding!" might not be a bad slogan for it. Or: "Link arms; link urls!" Not to mention keep on imagining the actual language for a politics in the space of social media. The companies that own those social media vectors will still collect a rent from all we say and do – not much can be done about that – but at least the space can be occupied by something other than LOL cats.

At a time when progressive intellectuals were in the habit of talking about "The Political," the occupation proceeded by creating a lower-case-politics which was abstract and yet at the same time completely everyday. It's no accident that it started with what we might broadly define as "anarchists," who had been working on both the theory and the practice of a lower-case politics for some time.[7]

The organized labor movement started paying attention when it looked like the anarchists and the following they drew would not be easily dissuaded by bad weather or the NYPD. It is as if organized labor woke up one morning, saw that the occupation was still going strong, and said to itself "I must follow them, for I am its leader!"

From the first day, the occupation had the makings of what I would call a **weird global media event**. It was an event in that nobody knew what would happen next. It was a media event in that its fate was tied to the occupation of the double space of Zuccotti Park and the media at the same time. It was a global media event at least since the moment when the NYPD arrested 700 people on the Brooklyn Bridge and handed the occupation great free publicity. (Thanks, guys!) And it was a weird global media event in that it had unprecedented elements that set it outside the staple stories of how boredom, dissent, utopia, and all that other stuff is usually managed and assuaged.

For example, commentators tied themselves in knots over whether it was a social movement or not. It was an occupation. It is in the title in case you missed it: Occupy Wall Street. Those who had been paying attention might notice it is part of a global wave of anarchist-inspired occupations, big and small. My own university, the New School for Social Research, was occupied in 2008, however briefly. This is a tactic that has been tried and refined over many years.

An occupation is conceptually the opposite of a movement. A movement aims for some internal consistency within itself but uses space just as a place to park its ranks. An occupation has no internal consistency, no "rank" or "file," but chooses meaningful spaces that have significant resonance into the abstract terrain of symbolic geography.

That an occupation just doesn't do some of the things social movements do is part of why it worked, at least for a while. It is remote from The Political, but it is also different from the Social Forum politics of the recent past as well. For those who want a theory to go with the practice, you will have to look elsewhere than to Negri or Badizek (Alain Badiou and Slavoj Žižek).[8] There's no multitude; there's no vanguard. It was like Tiananmen Square in 1989 or Tahrir Square in 2011, in spatial logic, if completely different in scale and class composition.

If the occupation was a little confusing for us intellectuals, take pity on our poor billionaire mayor! Bloomberg suggested that the occupation was inconveniencing the regular bank employees struggling on a mere 40k–50k per year.[9] The average household income in my neighborhood, which is quite a nice one, is just under 40k per year – and that's *household* income. The "poor bankers!" line seemed only to exacerbate the underlying issue of class polarization. The occupiers adopted the slogan "we are the 99%!" with some success. One sign I saw in Zuccotti Park said LET THEM EAT CAKE. That seemed a nice historical irony.

Nobody knew how it would play out. That's how it is with weird global media events. The actors in such a situation discover what's what usually by experiment, by trial and error. And perhaps, sometimes, some social science. Whatever other motives might have been involved, I'm guessing that arresting 700 people on the Brooklyn Bridge creates a great data sample set for police intelligence. I'm sure they were very curious to know what kinds of people showed up at the Occupation: from which boroughs, with what kinds of jobs, etc. While most attention was on a certain pepper-spray-wielding police officer, there's another, more modern, side to the NYPD. Since Commissioner Bratton modernized the force, it has become more "data driven." The police know the power of abstractions also.

The pages of books turn too slow to avoid the iceberg of time. It's a pleasure to be able to write the opening words of this book from Zuccotti Park, from occupied territory, tiny though it is. Around me I can see people who have come, at least for this moment, to entertain the possibility that even in this curiously doubled world, at once both concrete and abstract, another kind of world might be possible. There could be another politics other than the sideshow of professional operatives licking their lips over the spoils of electoral office. It's a rare pleasure to write these opening words from this place – before the laptop battery runs out.

Making another world possible might require, among other things, a politics and even a culture that can occupy both its concrete and abstract dimensions, and doing that might require both a critical theory and an experimental practice alive to just such a terrain. Such a practice has to start, for instance, from the recognition that the abstract is just as real as the concrete, and perhaps more so. Modernity is the abstract made real. Occupy Wall Street was just such an experimental practice, if only one of many. What follows is the theory, also just one of many. If a politics is to be possible at all, perhaps both new theories and new practices might be the order of the day.

> It may be, sir, that the politicians of the United States are not so fastidious as some gentlemen are, as to disclosing the principles on which they act. They boldly preach what they practice. When they are contending for victory, they avow their intention of enjoying the fruits of it. If they are defeated, they expect to retire from office. If they are successful, they claim, as a matter of right, the advantages of success. They see nothing wrong in the rule, that *to the victor belong the spoils of the enemy*.[10]

Senator William Learned Marcy of New York had Andrew Jackson in his sights in these remarks. When Jackson became president he purged the government and employed an unprecedented number of his own supporters. Since the Post Office was the biggest branch of government, most of the fruit Jackson had to offer was to be found there. Jackson found work for over 400 new postmasters. To the victor, the spoils.

This spoils system of government turned out to have short-term advantages and long-term disadvantages. Jackson secured loyalty but hardly competence. When President Garfield was assassinated in 1881 by a disgruntled spoils-claimant, reform was not long coming. It is curious, though, that of the 900 sinecures Jackson had to hand out, nearly half of the spoils were at the Post Office.

Curious, also, is this word "spoils" itself. From the middle English *spoilen*, from the old French *espoillier*, from the Latin *spolium*, spoils means always both ruin and beauty. The spoils of war are the glorious token of victory but at the same time are mere fragments of an even greater whole that this victory has itself destroyed. When one social form subsumes another, perhaps it can only do so by reducing the prize possessions of the defeated to mere fragments, to be revalued and patched back willy-nilly into a new regime.

For one party to contest against another presupposes a relation between them, be it electoral politics or the battlefield. Suppose what was victorious was not one party over another, but this relation itself? What if its victory was not over a particular party but over all of them? To the **vector**, the spoils. And what is this vector? Well, in Andrew Jackson's times: the Post Office. In the early twenty-first century, the vector takes a different form. The Post Office is now the spoiled fruit of an ageing communication system. A new infrastructure replaces the Post Office, experienced in everyday life as wireless telephony and the Internet, up to and including financial trading at the speed of light. Jackson's triumph might have enabled him to put his cronies in the Post Office, but the vector triumphs over the old forms of party politics, and much else besides.

Any social form resides within a communication infrastructure that gives it a certain shape, a certain tempo. This infrastructure is usually somewhat invisible. It is taken for granted, except when it fails, or when something unprecedented seems to happen within the space it defines. One way to map it is to stay tuned for these seemingly unprecedented effects. That is what this book is about: mapping the contours of what a given infrastructure of the vector makes possible.

When occupations took over symbolically resonant spaces in Tunisia and Egypt in 2011, they were sometimes announced as the "Twitter revolutions," as if the popular social networking site could be assigned a causal role.[11] This would then ritually be denounced by other commentators, who assign the real cause to the hearts and minds of the activists involved. The problem with both of these positions is that they make a fetish of one aspect or other of the vectoral: either the technical link or the human node. There is no vector without humans; there are no humans without vectors. One can't separate one from the other.

A more subtle problem is that it doesn't help overmuch to try to discern the specific vectors involved in a particular event. A curious property of the vector is that it is a relation between particulars that takes an abstract form. It lifts the particular into the abstract. The hard thing to discern is this abstraction. Take the Post Office, for example. It works by making all of physical space **addressable**. Your house is qualitatively different from your neighbor's house. But the Post Office doesn't care about that. You are at number ten Railway Street, in between numbers eight and twelve. The Post Office abstracts from particulars to make space abstract. Even, in a sense, a digital space.

When Guy Debord and his friends practiced the *dérive*, or drift through the streets of Paris, they were trying to sense the passing ambiences, mapping the "psychogeography" of how particular streets could make you feel.[12] They charted the contours of what the abstract space of the street grid made possible which was not digital, which had nothing to do with the addressable space which coordinated who and what was supposed to own what and reside where.

They were not trying to revive a past world, as if modern forms of addressable space could be wished away. Rather, they were interested in how that which cannot be made an object of calculation and distribution was recreated at a new level, within an addressable space. Of course, radio and telephony already existed, and television was on its way when they conducted these experiments. The Internet was just a gleam in some hacker's eye. The kinds of addressable space made possible by the evolution of the vector were becoming more complicated. Their essential premise was right, however. Every evolution of the vector produces spaces that afford kinds of situations, moments, occupations, or events that were not anticipated in their design and are discovered by accident or experiment.

This book is about a certain method of reading off from how events happen certain underlying properties of the kinds of abstract spaces that the vector defines. It's a book about method, then, but one that explains the method by performing it. The examples range across the last 20 years and across the planet, but it doesn't pretend to be global in its findings. This vectoral analysis can be performed anywhere, but the results will vary. It's not culturally neutral, but it does tend to point toward the space underlying particular cultural differences rather than reifying those differences themselves.

This book, then, recounts some particular intellectual travels, of a particular journeyman-theorist. It's a journey that starts with questions of **postcolonial** space, space that has a metropolitan center "there" and a provincial periphery "here." It ends with a quite different kind of space, that of a ruling class "above" and of subordinate classes "below" – and a relation between. This kind of abstract space was once called, and without embarrassment, **postmodern**. The origins of both phenomena are – pardon the pun – postal; or, rather, vectoral.

How can these two kinds of space be thought together? And thought from the inside, as something experienced rather than merely posited? Perhaps it would require a translation, out of the distinct languages within which the postcolonial and the postmodern are experienced, to find the terms whereby both can be thought as aspects of the same historical development. The development that both have in common is of what I call the vectoral. The vector is a term that, just for starters, we might think of as denoting the possible uses of a particular technology of relation, from the sailing ship to telecommunications.

No matter which axis of space is under consideration, postcolonial or postmodern, these essays have a consistent method, what I would call **antipodality**, which begins from the experience of being neither here nor there. It's about drifting along a moving and variable line, and of thinking and writing from within that experience. Antipodality is not quite the same thing as "hybridity," or "becoming-minor," nor is it the boundary-troubling experience of the "cyborg."[13] Such approaches tend to concentrate on what the relation of the vector produces, and consequently lose sight of that relation itself. Likewise, it is not the same as the "transnational."[14] It is about the relations with which the transnational is produced.

These essays elaborate their own jargon. Theory-writing is full of jargons, of course. If one is attempting to describe the world differently, then one has to push language against its own grain a bit, make it feel the strain. There's a role for jargons, then, but they can become commonplace – spoiled. Sometimes they need to be cooked up fresh. These essays elaborate a shifting lexicon: **vector, telesthesia, third nature**, the **weird global media event**, the **military entertainment complex, game space**. (The last chapter is a glossary that collects and coordinates the range of senses covered by these terms.) These essays speak of and speak to distinctive kinds of persona, which are different from, but coexist with, those of race or gender: the **antipodal**, the **gamer**, the **hacker**. All these are speculative terms, keys to possible realities.[15]

If a good fact is very, very true but about one thing in particular, then a good theory is only *slightly true*, but about everything. The aim of these essays is to be slightly true, or possibly true, and no more. A thick description for ethnographers is one that explains an aspect of a culture and also the local context that gives rise to that aspect. Clifford Geertz:

> The important thing about the anthropologist's findings is their complex specific-ness, their circumstantiality. It is with the kind of material produced by long term, mainly (but not exclusively) qualitative, highly participative, and almost obsessively fine combed field study in *confined contexts* that the mega-concepts . . . can be given the sort of sensible actuality that makes it possible to think not only realistically and concretely about them, but, what is more important, creatively and imaginatively with them.[16]

And a wonderful thing this thick description is, when there are confined contexts.

What if the principal object one wishes to know something about is precisely the *un-confining* of contexts? What if one found oneself "in the context of no context," what then?[17] Perhaps then what might do the trick is **thin description**, which might work by subtracting from thick description its sense of having as context the very idea of a context. In thin description, one might not be terribly interested in whether a wink is caused by a tic, an infection, or an intention, but rather that the gesture is communicable across space and time to an observer, who writes it down and communicates it to another, in contexts unknown, far away.

Telesthesia starts out on the periphery, the antipodes, and works toward a center, or rather to the absence of one. It pursues the antipodal feeling of being neither here nor there – as a tendency. Each essay is a relay in the attempt to think antipodality to the limit. This kind of speculative thinking is somewhat anathema to the empirical bent of anglophone thought, perhaps even to the English language. We are not a theoretical people, or so we are told. We want the static fact, not the dynamic event. We want a writing that circumscribes a thing, rather than one that delineates a force. This book documents a 20-year attempt to write theory in English, and about experiences one can have of certain particular parts of the anglophone world.

Ironically, even writing *about* theory in English tends to approach it empirically, as sets of proper names and sets of statements attached to proper names, to be gathered and arranged as facts. In English, theory is more written *about* than written.

Telesthesia does not want to represent what other theory is "about." Rather, it appropriates concepts, sometimes from recognizable sources, high and low, and puts them to use.

There are two kinds of theory. The better known is High Theory; the lists of proper names: Michel Foucault, Jacques Derrida, Gilles Deleuze. While not exactly establishment types to start out with in the provincial world of Parisian letters, they nevertheless acquired a certain centrality, not least to anglophone writing.[18] *Telesthesia* is by contrast an instance of **low theory**. Here too are some well-known names, but of figures who were hardly ever embraced by institutional knowledge: Paul Virilio, Jean Baudrillard, Guy Debord. They have nothing in common other than their marginal institutional status, even if it was a highly visible one, and certain key elements of the practice of writing.

Low theory is practiced somewhere in the margins between institutional forms of writing. Even if written in the heart of Paris, low theory is in its own way antipodal. It is not quite of the academy or the art world, or journalism. It always has some relationship to the exigencies of political time, the time of the event, the time of indeterminacy. It does not get written in the even, calendar time of semesters and sabbaticals. It works in and against the unruly tempo of events, or even of occupations. The essay or tract, rather than the paper or thesis, is its preferred form.[19] It is speculative, playful, tactical. It is not built to last.

All the essays in this book began life as such temporary and temporal interventions. They are nevertheless concerned with a long-term and slow-moving development in postmodern and postcolonial spaces. It is no longer fashionable to be "post" anything. The gesture exhausted itself. Yet the problem of thinking in and about the tempos of these spaces persists. This is particularly so if one takes the question of the vector to be central to the production of the experience of the postcolonial or the postmodern in the first place. Centrally preoccupied as they are with the effects of the vector, these essays resist the temptation to think of communication and media always under the banner of the new. They are not about "new" media. The role assigned to media within the rhetoric of a not-yet-dead modernity is always to be the very sign of the new.

Telesthesia is about thinking historically but it is not a history book. It is concerned with how long-unfolding transformations in the form and qualities of relations come to be experienced, cumulatively, in the present. Or, rather, particular presents. While there is a strong sense here of the emergence of a connective, abstracting kind of relation – that of the vector – it is not for all that a universalizing or homogenizing one. What the psychogeography of the vector comes to feel like, when mapped over a century or two, is a turbulent and wildly differentiating space.

While there are recognizable intellectual keys to this way of writing from a metropolitan High- and low-theory discourse, there are also some antipodean ones. This book includes writing indebted to Australian writers from whom I have learned a great deal: Bernard Smith, Ross Gibson, Eric Michaels, and particularly Meaghan Morris.[20] All are antipodean writers keenly engaged with writing of the center, from Marxism to late twentieth-century High Theory. This book takes Australian experience as only a particular instance of an antipodean experience.[21] We are all antipodal, in that the vector puts most everybody on a slippery line, neither here nor there, at some point in their lives.

In *Culture and Power: A History of Cultural Studies*, Mark Gibson identified my writing as belonging to the "republican school" of cultural studies, inspired by John Hartley and developed by Catharine Lumby and myself:

> If, as the media republican argument suggests, power is not continuously distributed; if it comes into view only sometimes, perhaps even as an exception; then we are subtly led to think not of a general phenomenon but of specific and discrete *phenomena*. We are led to think not of "power" but of "*powers*" . . . The way is opened to a grittier recognition of violence and conflict where they occur, but a recognition that does not extend to a prejudicial view of all social relations as conforming to some universal pattern.[22]

Indeed, but where I diverge from Hartley and Lumby is in opening up a more speculative dimension as to what might hypothetically constitute the conditions of existence of phenomena and the powers that animate them. In the Australian context in which our "republican school" was created, politics seemed still to exist. Intellectuals and scholars have their roles in the constitution of the *res publica*, the "public thing." In the United States, where I emigrated in 2000, the existence of the "public thing" seems less reliably given. It seemed useful to think, not about "universal patterns," but underlying conditions of possibility.

The first group of essays examines the "horizontal" axis of abstract space, or the relation between centers and peripheries. The last few essays are more interested in "vertical" abstract space, or the relation between base and superstructure in social formations, and in particular class relations. In the later essays the focus shifts from the experience of the vector as a relation of empire to the experience of vector as a relation of class. The persona of the hacker takes the place of the persona of the antipodean, but performs the same conceptual role, of being neither here nor there, neither ruling class nor proletariat. This book finds a certain virtue precisely in the ambivalence and ambiguity of these liminal personas. In between the essays on horizontal space at the beginning and vertical space at the end are some about "temporal abstract space," or history. How does the vector change relations of past to present?

This book is a panorama, then. A landscape unfolds here, a psychogeography. It makes no effort to take possession of this vast tract of time and space. It is not very interested in ownership. It is not about thinking of writing like a real-estate developer, taking a tract and turning it into disciplinary fields and subfields. This panorama is rather of spaces within which one might want to journey, with a writing that might "assay" the territory rather than plant a flag in it.

Veni, vidi, vici, as Julius Caesar allegedly said after the battle of Zela.[23] I came, I saw, I conquered. Used as a line of force, as a kind of power, the vector has things rather the other way around: *vidi, vici, veni*: I saw, I conquered, I came. It's the opening of a space to perception that creates the possibility of domination. But all vectors have their antipodal slippage. To try to use them as an instrument is to experience this. The moral of the story is: to the vector, the spoils. The vector is, as Bernard Stiegler puts it, a "pharmakon," at once poison and cure, ambivalently available for quite contradictory purposes.[24] It is cause neither for Heideggerian lament nor corporate boosterism, but rather for drift, mapping, for the recording of provisional results.

In the nineteenth century the congestion of the roads within Paris made it increasingly difficult to deliver letters by express post. So an alternative system was built, which used pneumatic tubes.[25] The tubes ran along tunnels created by hydrologists for water pipes and sewer pipes. Along the vectors of water under the city sped brass canisters filled with express letters, written on a distinctive blue notepaper. Hence the expression, "to catch a blue," meaning to receive an express communication. Similar systems existed in other major cities. In some cases these systems lived on well into the twentieth century, when telephony was making a lot of physical mail obsolete. The "blue" is a curious example of a vector that moved information faster than most other things moved at the time. It's a precursor to a strange fold in social space to come.

Pneumatic tubes are vectors, roads are vectors, sea lanes are vectors; so too are railway lines, along all of which move commodities, people, arms, letters, and packages. A somewhat different class of vector might include the telegraph, telephone, television, and all that comes after them. These are the vectors of **telesthesia**, of perception at a distance. They double and complicate the spaces made possible by transport vectors. Telesthesia means the movement of information at a faster rate than things. The Post Office moves a box of soap and a magazine at the same maximum speed. The telegraph moves information faster than any box of soap. Telesthesia opens up a space with strange properties. Charting those properties via their effects is the task to which we now attend.

2

Fresh Maimed Babies

Sydney, Australia

What should we say then of that noble and generous Epicurean pleasure that prides itself on nourishing virtue tenderly in its bosom and letting it frolic there, giving it disgrace, fever, poverty, death and tortures as toys to play with?

Michel de Montaigne

The most innocent-looking media images are sometimes the most sinister. Take Somalia, where in the early nineties United Nations forces found themselves buried up to their bright blue bonnets in cynical *realpolitik*. How did it all start? With pictures of starving children. Poor innocents with frail limbs and big brown eyes and flies crawling up their nostrils. They stared at us out of smudgy newsprint or pixelated satellite news feeds, but always with a resolution hard enough to make my heart leap into my mouth. Who would not want to help them, these blameless victims, as soon as possible, no questions asked?

When I see these images, it is I who becomes childlike. I want someone to make it all better. The child occupies such a sacred place in our structures of feeling that one cannot help but feel *something*.[1] Advertisers know this. It is why kids figure so often in ads that are really about cameras or toilet cleaners. In the camera ad, children are not only the subject, being shot, but armed with the camera, doing the shooting. See how easy it is! One's complete innocence of everything connected with image-making is no obstacle. Just point and shoot! A child can do it! Or the toilet cleaner ad, with that hair-raising moment when the little girl's hand reaches out to touch the toilet. Thank goodness Mommy made it nice and clean!

I think about all this while standing in line at the toy store. I'm buying Christmas presents for my niece and nephew. I'm staring at the pretty colors on the Lego boxes I'm holding. Distracted, I faintly register the sounds of the checkout up ahead, and the distant report of gunfire. Somewhere nearby a roomful of video console trial machines battle it out with a gang of youngsters for their hearts, minds, and brand loyalties.

They make pink Lego now. It's called *Paradisa*. Little yellow-faced Lego people stand around under palm trees, dressed in resort wear, pushing pink baby carriages, mixing pink drinks. A plastic red parrot perches on the edge of a carnival wheel-of-fortune. Lego sure looks different from when I was a kid, but the basic premise is still the same. A utopian world of many colors, laid out on a regular modern grid. Snap-together heaven for children to make and unmake.

Lego people remind me of another advert, one I saw on a bus shelter in Sydney once. It showed hundreds of little Lego people. "Spot the refugee?" it asks. I imagine children playing refugee games with Lego internment camps, razor wire, questionnaires, and quarantine. Maybe they'll make a Lego set called *Quarantina*.[2] Snap-together hell for little Lego people cast adrift in a toy-box world of loose Lego pieces, a jumble of jaggy-colored shapes.

There are forces at work in the world even grown-ups don't understand. On television I see a mess of jaggy-colored Lego shapes – the Vance-Owen peace plan for the former Yugoslavia. Not even Lord Owen seems to understand it. I stare blankly, trying to grapple with too much exposure to too little information. A war in my living room; a sullen guest uninvited. Give me a bright image to which I can cling.

There was such an image: Bosnia's own baby Irma. Dr Edo Jaganjac, who tried in vain to treat her, was no fool. He gave up begging the UN to save his fatally wounded little patient and went to the BBC. The BBC's Irma story aired only once back home in Britain, on the midday news. Then the bureau chiefs thought better of it. They thought the story was "emotive" and of "limited news value," but these rational reflections came too late. The story sparked a forest fire of public feeling. Folks who had not spared a second thought for Balkan suffering became anxious for the life of one small Balkan child. Prime minister John Major and the tabloid editors outbid each other in public displays of compassion. The editors threatened to charter planes. Bring the babies out to safety! The government airlifted Irma out of Bosnia and whisked her into a London hospital for a life-saving operation. This will no doubt be written up in *The Lancet* as the first case of post-modern medicine. Diagnosis: innocent shrapnel victim urgently needs expensive care. Prescription: a short, sharp dose of TV news exposure.

Not wanting to be bested by the tabloids' displays of baby-saving zeal, the prime minister ordered an airlift of suitable orphans, a gesture doubtless designed to fill the "compassion gap" in British politics of the moment. The hitch was that very few of the refugees waiting forlornly for a ticket out of hell had that wide-eyed look that comes across so well in medium close-up, shot against a background of dirt or dinge. Being certified refugees, they were for the most part adults who had done something to make themselves refugees. Some, Lord help them, had vainly struggled for peace.

The refugees were more than a little annoyed that British baby-hunters passed them over to get on with pinching a few infants. Like old toys, they were rejected in favor of the new season's hit doll. Bosnian babies had an extra feature – innocence. It makes them a most satisfying gift for yourself when you work up a hankering for feeling good in Michael Jackson's ingenuous "We Are the World" sort of a way. Dollar for dollar, adult refugees are nowhere near the value. There's always the suspicion that they may be adulterated with impurities – such as politics.

Practical ethics is, like the essay, out of style. These things may not be unconnected. Michel de Montaigne, following in the footsteps of the Platonist plutarch, the Stoic Seneca, and with a bit of the Epicurean Lucretius on the side, essayed that only those who have been tempted by evil and resisted it are truly virtuous, and that this is a more worthy thing than being merely innocent and untested.[3] In the moral economy of TV news, we prefer the innocent and untested, lest it reflect on our own untested virtue. We respond, as if in all innocence, to innocence.

As the media become increasingly global, so does our anxiety at the troubling images it portrays. This fuels a conscience industry of global proportions. It's a barter trade: the world's "trouble spots" send us images of fresh maimed babies and we send truckloads of food and medicine in return. That was the deal in Bosnia and Somalia. It's the most abstract kind of relation between the image of suffering and our response. Somewhat less abstract, but invoking the same relation, are the adverts for those schemes where you sponsor a particular child in a particular place. There's a great one narrated by a young African boy, who we see moseying about his home village with a stick, talking about cattle dip and how it stops the cows getting sick. This slightly abstracted relation to the fostering of innocence draws on a more familiar relation, the one that brings me into the toy shop every Christmas. I am my niece and nephew's distant, loving, Lego-giving uncle, sponsor of the makings of new worlds for the innocents.

Is this too callous a thought to have in a toy shop? Perhaps, but I feel more sorrow for those poor people who lack the means or the wit to supply CNN and Reuters with pictures of their crying, wounded children than for those who do. To those we see, we send presents, which is at least better than nothing. Others get nothing, and die not only unaided, but unknown. If an ailing child falls in a forest and the media aren't there to record it, does she make a sound?

Propagandists have long known how to exploit our desire for innocent-seeming stories. Stories of German soldiers bayoneting Belgian babies in 1914 were given the authoritative stamp of a committee of lawyers and historians. These myths were not laid to rest until an inquiry in 1922, which failed to substantiate any of the hearsay claims or unsworn testimony passed off as evidence during the war.[4] Such is the pre-history of at least one aspect of what might more expansively be described as the **military entertainment complex.**[5]

Compassion has no memory. After Saddam Hussein invaded their little pocket monarchy, the Kuwaiti government paid the public relations firm Hill & Knowlton US$10.8 million to persuade the American public of the necessity of a war to restore its property to it. One would think pointing up the squalid violence of the Iraqi regime an easy task, but American lawmakers and the public are bored quickly by human rights talk. They flip channels.

Human rights abuse is not enough. Nothing short of a massacre of the innocents will do. And so Hill & Knowlton had a 15-year-old "hospital volunteer" called "Nayirah" tell the Congressional Human Rights Caucus a tall tale of evil Iraqis pitching babies out of incubators and leaving them on the cold floor to die. This young woman later turned out to be the Kuwaiti ambassador's daughter.[6]

Even George Bush ran with the sham baby story – no fewer than five times – and for the same reason as the English disinformation about the infanticide of the Huns: to persuade a reluctant public to go to war. Stories of wounded innocence can provoke us into sending food or medicine, which does no harm and perhaps some good. It can also lead to sending in the troops, and that's another story. Babies died all the time in Iraq from the score-settling and "ethnic cleansing" of Saddam Hussein. Only there were no pictures, and America sent nothing. Until, of course – it did. But that is another story, featuring different children.

In all of these stories, there is an inverse ratio between clarity and significance. In the absence of clarity about who has power over whom, a story appealing to feelings will have to do. And what better story than that someone is doing something vile to children? The only problem is that doing stories about children is not much less vile than doing vile things to them. It's a sort of banal vileness. With the globalization of the media vector, what Hannah Arendt called the "banality of evil" becomes an everyday thing, a glimmer of sentiment with few real effects.[7] Occasionally it motivates us to stare into the abyss of unfathomable suffering, caused by obscure designs, just for a bit. We glance at the face of horror in the mirror of the media for a while, muse on holocausts and pogroms, and take a station break.

There was a separate pile of tiny skulls . . .

To "pilger" is a journalist's verb, meaning to use sensationalism in a good cause. No one pilgers as good as John Pilger, from whom the expression was coined, and none of his pilgering has ever been quite as good as his use of children with bits of limbs blown off by landmines in Cambodia. Who planted the landmines? The Khmer Rouge. Who trained them in their use? British SAS officers. Who funded this guerrilla war against the government in Phnom

Penh? The United States.[8] Pilgering often starts with images like "tiny skulls." In Pilger's hands they become moral totems, motivating the search for the injurers responsible for the monstrous injury. His TV show about those children and the landmines prompted the Swedish prime minister not to flip channels, but to change his country's vote at the UN.

If we see a stranger touch a child on television we need instant reassurance that this adult is one of "us" and can be trusted. If not, strange things happen. I remember watching television back in 1991, when Saddam Hussein took child "hostages" and displayed them on television. The Iraqi dictator appeared in a Western suit and tie with a little white handkerchief neatly folded in his left breast pocket. He claimed that the Western media misrepresented the situation. "In the past few days," he said, "I have come across articles published in the Western papers urging President Bush to strike Iraq and actually use force against Iraq despite your presence here." Responding to a mother's worries about her child's education, he offered to send "experts from the Ministry of Education." Putting his hand gently on the head of seven-year-old Stuart Lockwood, he remarked, "when he and his friends, and all those present here, have played their role in preventing war, then you will all be heroes of peace."[9]

The British foreign secretary Douglas Hurd called this the "most sickening thing I have seen for some time." This same Douglas Hurd denounced John Pilger's television show about British SAS officers training Khmer Rouge guerrillas with landmines. Hurd claimed his government was amongst the first to denounce the Khmer Rouge. This was not quite so. The British government was a reliable supporter of the coalition to which the Khmer Rouge belonged. Pictures of wounded innocence call forth statements from our leaders, for they feel that they must act. They are not induced to act in any coherent way, merely to appear to act on behalf of innocence with a memorable display of compassion, which is of course promptly forgotten.

Saddam Hussein patting that child unwittingly triggered an old myth about "Arabs." A myth that can be understood in terms of what Slavoj Žižek, a philosopher from the former Yugoslavia, calls a threat to our sense of "national enjoyment." "We always impute to the 'other' an excessive enjoyment," says Žižek, "s/he wants to steal our enjoyment (by ruining our way of life) or has access to some secret, perverse enjoyment."[10] When the Western news carried the close-up of Saddam Hussein's hand stroking the boy's head, he changed characters in what Edward Said calls the "Orientalist" vision the West has of the Middle East. Saddam did not appear to be a Muslim "fundamentalist," a denier of pleasure. In the absence of any other cultural memory of images of the Middle East, the focus on the gesture of touching encouraged the viewer to read it in terms of the other strand that Said identifies in Orientalism.[11]

From Wilde's *Salome* and Flaubert's *Salambo*, to Trocchi's *Carnal Days* in the sultry sun, there is another string of Orientalist stories: of *excessive* enjoyment, of harems, slaves, veils, dancing girls – and boys. Not least of which, the myth of the Arab peder-ast, who turns up closer to home in the film *Gallipoli*. A scene contrasts "our" ANZAC soldiers buying prostitutes ("normal enjoyment") with the hint of Arabs buggering little boys (excess).

When Saddam opened a **vector** of communication to the West he obviously did not have these Orientalist fantasies and fears in mind. According to Egyptian journalist Mohamed Heikal, Iraqi television frequently pictured him kissing babies during the war. "This had succeeded in Iraqi terms, and officials thought they could make it work internationally, but they were wrong." Akbar Ahmed, a Muslim scholar at Cambridge, likewise reads the image in terms of how he thinks the dictator's own people would respond. "In his culture an elder, or figure of authority, often displays affec-tion to children by patting the child or tousling the hair. It is socially approved and appreciated." Even a dictator must practice the political arts of affect.

Only at home he gets feedback on how his message goes over – from the secret police. In the international arena, there is no such closed loop to confirm and confine meanings. The Western media portrayed him as no longer one of "us" (an Arab "moder-ate") but one of "them" (an Arab "extremist"). His touch became not patronizing, but licentious.[12] The threat to the innocence of "our" children is often localized as somewhere "out there," far from home. This spatial way of structuring and narrating the world outside is, however, highly unstable. The bad keeps creeping up close to home. Since we must think only good thoughts about our children, it is convenient to find other remote figures who think – and do – the bad.

EVIL VIDEO insists the headline of the *Telegraph Mirror*.[13] The subhead is more circumspect: DID CHUCKY INSPIRE JAMIE'S MURDER? "Chucky" is a child's toy possessed by evil from the movie *Child's Play* and its sequels. "Jamie" is Jamie Bulger, the two-year-old murdered by a pair of ten-year-old children, Jon Venables and Robert Thompson. There is a superficial similarity between some scenes in *Child's Play 3* and details of the murder. While Venables' father had hired the video, there was no evidence that either of the murderers had seen it. No evidence connecting Venables' and Thompson's behavior to videos was entered during the trial at all.

The only word to describe the attribution of evil influence solely to a popular video for such a singular crime is "fetishism."[14] Needing to localize the evil influence in something, it is **abstracted** and extracted out of every context and bottled up *in video*. The family context, the social context, the educational context – all these distill away, so that we are left with innocent children enthralled by the evil influence of *Child's Play 3*. There is a certain wonderful circularity to it all. The media show images of evil and violence in the world. Therefore the media must be the *cause* of the evil and violence in the world that the media then picture in still more images.[15] Presumably what's wrong with all those Khmer Rouge killers who leave as their press release "separate piles of tiny skulls" is that they watched the *Child's Play* videos in cadre training camp.

Behind this fetish lies the problem of our relations of **telesthesia** – perception at a distance. In our everyday life we think about ourselves and our family and our loved ones and our friends and our neighbors. Yet this everyday life is shot through with images from afar. Turn on the TV and the first thing you see is the light of a different day. As Willard Scott, the avuncular weathercaster on *NBC Today*, used to say, "Now's here's what's happening in your world, even as we speak." What's happening in my world, in your world, right in the home and televisual hearth, is images far beyond the scope of our everyday frameworks of propriety. We see images of bodies violated, bodies sexualized, but these images don't respect our sense of what belongs where. They won't be partitioned off, relegated to adults-only times or public spaces. They're beaming into private spaces, into children's unconscious lives. Images radiate everywhere, ubiquitous and thus obscene.[16]

Distant crises, complex and obscure, are presented as if they were family dramas, reduced to the scale of one-on-one. But at the other end of the media vector, at the receiving end of telesthesia, we're getting very uneasy about this rendering mundane of a big and frightening wheel-of-fortune world. We want to reject it, so we fetishize the media itself as the evil. It must be the thing that is dangerous, mysterious, bad – but also fascinating. We are drawn and repulsed by the seductive spectacle of other places, other worlds. Sometimes we respond by demanding that the media present only nice things, pretty pink fetish images. Like a gleaming white toilet bowl, we want TV clean and safe for kiddies. Secretly we want it safe for us too, safe from tiny skulls staring back at our conscience. Let's go online and look at videos of kids falling off bicycles, or saying spacey things on the way home from the dentist.

It's all a matter of distance and power. What power do we have in relation to these images? Not much, yet we see power enacted in them, power that is sometimes too strong or too weak, sometimes too intimate or too distant, and occasionally just right. We see lords and patrons, nurses and agents, generals and parents, siblings and lawyers, doctors and pederasts, murderers and uncles – all hovering over the image of the child. Some of these can be trusted; others not. Sometimes you just can't tell. We implicitly count ourselves among the trustworthy. We know what is best – the right distance, the right benevolent power, the right gift for the young.

To my niece and nephew, I am probably still a fuzzy image, but I hope a trustworthy one. I'm the uncle from afar who brings gifts of Lego – a small pink world where my niece and nephew can make something for themselves. I'm also the writer who worries about the wrongs done in the world and what we can know and do about it. So I write my *essais*, my "trials," my "valuations" – to find the right distance between reason and compassion, between memory and forgetting. This is an essay about abstract things, but I wrote it thinking about the future of two very particular little people and the world they will come in part to inhabit, in part to build.

3

Neither Here Nor There

Taipei, Taiwan

There is quite a particular view of culture and the world that comes with growing up by the sea. Since this is an essay about how media technologies have remade the surface of the world in general, and about how one might grasp this from a particular vantage point, it seems appropriate to start by the sea.

When I was a kid growing up in suburban Newcastle, Australia, in a little weatherboard house perched between the railway line and the highway, I loved to pore over the pages of our *Reader's Digest World Atlas*. I layered tracing paper over its maps of Australia and traced the outlines, making maps of my own. First I would draw the contours of nature. In green and blue and brown I projected an image of the ocean, the land, and the mountains. This was a jaggy mass of impassable terrains, each unique and tortuous.

Then I filled those contours with dots of various sizes, all enclosed with jagged lines that divide the land mass up into a patchwork of spaces. Unknowingly, I drew the geography of places, of our second nature. The dots mark out cities and towns of various sizes; the borders mark out the territories these towns were able to bring under their control in the modern period. The railways and the newspapers between them defined spaces that were integrated economically, politically, and culturally. Regionalism gave way to nationalism.[1] This tendency breaks down the separation of places and aggregates them into bigger, more **abstract** units. Thus the natural barriers and contours of the land were overcome with a second nature of productive flows.

Next I took out a big red magic marker and started to join up all of the dots. Big fat lines between the big towns; smaller ones between the regional centers. From the telegraph to telecommunications, a new geography has been overlaid on top of nature and second nature. This, it seems to me, is one way of reading what most Australians were and probably still are taught in school.

In the house I grew up in, a model ship took pride of place on the mantle. It was a model of the *Cutty Sark,* one of the greatest of the clipper ships. It's nothing but a brand of whiskey now. The first time I went to China was in 1987. I went to the Shanghai museum to look at the classical paintings. There wasn't much to see there. But there is a model of the *Cutty Sark*. Its famous record-breaking run was from my home town of Newcastle, in the state of New South Wales, on the east coast of Australia – to Shanghai, China.

By the early twenty-first century, Newcastle became one of the world's biggest coal ports, and one of the biggest destinations for that coal was China. It is transported as bulk cargo, on giant ships. If you have stuff that was made in China, in a sense you have a little piece of my home town. That's where the coal came from that fired the plants that made the electricity that powered other plants that made your stuff, shipped as containerized cargo, from China to the world.

Some of that stuff is just stuff, plastic toys, kitchenware, and so forth. But some of that stuff is of a different kind: cellphones, Smartphones, laptops. This stuff is made with the same electricity as all the other things. There is something different about these things, at least potentially. The difference becomes clear when you plug them in, not just to power but to the infrastructure of networks, whose lines I drew in red on those tracing-paper maps. These devices and their networks make a space that has peculiar properties of a quite different order.

I lived by the sea, in Ultimo in Sydney, for many years after I left Newcastle. My apartment was just behind all of the old abandoned wool stores that kept mysteriously burning down. They were relics of rather more than a lost wool-exporting economy and a fading pastoral culture. They were the residues of a regime of power now surpassed. A new regime of power has taken hold of the byways of the planet. A regime not of sea-lanes and ship-lore, but of comsats and data flows.[2] We all increasingly come to live now, as Manuel Castells says, not in a space of *places* but a space of *flows*.[3] This is a task for a kind of critical framing which, in this case, tries to find some resonance still in the idea of the local.

We live in a "global village," as Marshall McLuhan famously said. That new stuff, made with my home town's coal, brings the global village home. It is no longer clear what the boundary is between local and global. And when boundaries can be drawn, they do not necessarily map neatly onto geographic space. The local can be far; the global can be very present. Not for nothing did McLuhan describe this experience with an oxymoron. Global village – like virtual reality, living dead, open secret, postmodern, or even **cyberspace** – is a term where the modifier and the noun don't belong together. That we lose sight of the strangeness of all these terms speaks to an acclimatization to what was once a new and paradoxical kind of space.

I think I can say this: "we" are subjected to certain abstract forces at work in the world. That's a speculative statement and the reader simply decides for herself or himself whether they accede to such a claim. Yet I cannot say "we" in the affirmative sense, as nominating a community with a will, which acts in its own name. So for the time being I prefer to consider how the new relations of communication can be thought more specifically from Ultimo in Sydney, Australia.

You see some strange things from Ultimo – like a great flock of sailing ships, gliding through the heads. Ultimo was a good place from which to watch this symbolic passing from the naval regime of power to a new matrix of vectors, on January 26, 1988. It was a strange experience, watching those sailing ships, simultaneously entering Sydney Harbor and entering my living room – and many thousands of others via the live TV broadcast. It was a re-enactment of the white invasion of the Australian continent, performed 200 years later for the cameras. As with the first arrival of the First Fleet, on this second coming the invaders parked their boats and thanked their sponsors.

Paul Virilio asks: "when we can go to the antipodes and back in an instant, what will become of us?" This question fruitfully combines a temporal and a spatial problem about our experience of everyday life. The temporal dimension is: what are these times we are living in? The spatial dimension is: what space is this that makes us what we are? I think an answer on both counts can come from the antipodes. Australia is only one of the antipodes in the regime of spatial relations, but an interesting one.

In his video work *Night's High Noon: An Anti-Terrain* (1988), Peter Callas shows an image of an Aboriginal man standing on the beach, watching the First Fleet arrive. Cut to an image of the same headland, some time later. A white figure stands on the beach, watching a mushroom cloud rise on the horizon. Callas manages to portray a place that is always in a relation to an elsewhere, which is always defined by its relation to a powerful other. First the British came and colonized. Then the Americans came and coca-colonized.[4] This is that place. We are no one, whoever we are, always oscillating in **antipodality** with plural elsewheres. This is one of the necessary conditions of making art or criticism in Australia. That is a condition which even low theory can only transcend by acknowledging it.

To talk about antipodes is to talk very centrally about the regimes of vectoral technology via which the imperial powers created a relation to an antipodes. These relations now have a life of their own. This is why I want to talk about what Raymond Williams called emergent, as opposed to dominant and residual, cultural forms.[5] To do that means to talk about the vectors of relation between places and people rather than to talk about the identities of the people themselves. This essay is not one of those ethical statements about intersubjective relations of class, race, gender, or ethnicity. These things are very important, but so too are the social relations which subordinate the people of one *place* to another, or which organize the exploitation of nature *as space itself*, through the extraction and movement of value.

This is an essay about people's connections to sailing ships and comsats. It is about what Bernard Steigler calls grammatization, only it is about that aspect of it that he tends to neglect.[6] Grammatization breaks variable flows up into equivalent units. Language does this, but so too does the Post Office, or an assembly line, or bulk cargo and containerized shipping. A flow – of phonemes or letters or coal or Lego sets – is chopped up into equivalent, exchangeable bits. What kinds of spaces does this make possible? What kinds of relations flourish? Antipodean ones.

Given a will to think historically about cultural change and to use the media as a foil, two problems arise in thinking about the emergent, grammatized forms of culture. One is the problem of access to knowledge about new techniques. The other is the problem of generalizing from specific experiences. In other words, we confront a limit to what we know of time and of space. We know least about what is nearest in time – the emergent present; and what is most distant in space – the forms of culture of our antipodean others. What compounds the issue is that the things we want to critically examine – emergent media forms – are precisely what appear to overcome these problems for us with their childlike faith in certain images and stories. This is a problem that calls for experimental practice and for critical theory; for intuitive visualization and speculative conceptualization; and in particular for **low theory** and media art.[7]

No matter how global and how abstract the analysis wants to be, it can never extract itself from its quite specific cultural origins. Hence this writing takes the form of an essay and asks the essay's classic question: "What do I know?" I want to begin with my own experience of this planet of noise we now live on. The result is a very abstract essay, but also a very self-consciously partial one, tied to quite particular experiences of sailing ships and television. In it I rephrase Montaigne's self-questioning from "What do I know?" to the more suitably antipodean: "From where am I addressed?"[8]

For a long time Australian culture manifested a desperate attempt to fix a few things in consciousness between two great abstract terrains of movement. The first is the sea. The sea, as Hegel says, "gives us the idea of the indefinite, the unlimited, and infinite: and in feeling his own infinite in that Infinite, man is stimulated and emboldened to stretch beyond the limited: the sea invites man to conquest and to piratical plunder, but also to honest gain and to commerce."[9] Thus, ambivalently, did this first regime of the vector traverse the globe.

The cultures that invaded Australia did so using a naval technology. This technology turned the space of nautical dangers into an abstract space of movement, migration, trade, and, above all, strategy. This history was a history of the transformation of the space of the oceans into a space of flows. The project of transforming the antipodes through invasion and settlement presupposes a world of material flows. The "conquest" of nature and the creation of the second nature of built environments presupposes this abstract space of flows. From the First Fleet to the fast clippers, its development is central to the project of modernity.

Yet overlaid on top of this second nature of material flows there is now another abstract space that produces another feeling of the unlimited. The passage from modernity to postmodernity seems to me better described as the passage from one form of abstraction to another – from the second nature of abstract social spaces created by sea and rail vectors to the abstract communicational spaces created by the telegraph, telephone, television, and telecommunications. These are the techniques of **telesthesia**, of perception at a distance. Since the telegraph, the time of communications has run at a faster speed to the time of transport, and indeed these two synonymous terms begin to diverge in meaning as they diverge as terrains of abstraction.[10]

Second nature emerges out of the struggle to wrest freedom from necessity. It is an overcoming of the tyranny of nature, achieved through the social organization of labor. As we know only too well, the process of creating second nature creates new tyrannies as well. Freedom from nature becomes the elimination of nature. The social organization of second nature is, among other things, a class relation. The division of labor makes every function – including art – partial and fetishized.[11]

The decline of modernity is in many respects a loss of faith in second nature. The division of labor brings with it fragmentation, anomie; the compulsions of discipline and the anarchy of the market. The redemptive vision of second nature withered in both its Marxist and bourgeois forms. Yet this does not stop the projection of the fantasy of redemption. Redemption is always around the corner in virtual reality, hypertext, cyberspace, Web 2.0, mobile media, social networking, or the "cloud." Although the terrain is different, the projection of a vectoral field of total communication extends and completes the projection of a vectoral field of extraction and production. Such is the new fantasy of wresting freedom from necessity – for those at least who are at the very heart of the relations of power that struggle in and against second nature, in the process making of it a new kind of terrain.

Sitting on the dock of the bay, the question concerning technology looks a little different. Viewed from the antipodes, the fundamental thing about modernity is the creation of the globe as an abstract space of movement, exploitation, and strategy. It is not what happened in Europe that is fundamental to modernity, it is Europe's relation to its many antipodes. It is not what is happening in the United States or Japan or China that is fundamental to postmodernity, but what is happening in their relations to their antipodes.[12] In both cases, that relation is only secondarily intersubjective. It is primarily the encounter of vectoral techniques of power premised on a radical abstracting of space, overcoming prior modes of dwelling on the earth.

From the perspective of the antipodes, or at least from a harborside flat in Ultimo, one can contrast Foucault's notion of disciplinary technologies with a genealogy of what one might call vectoral technologies. It is not the Panopticon but the British navy that in this latter view emerges as a key technological regime of power in the early modern period. Let's not forget that Bentham's famous pamphlet was called *The Panopticon or New South Wales?* Vectoral power was not based on close disciplining and inspection of the social body, but on a purging of the social body. The vector vents its spleen on an other that is partly mapped but still mostly imagined.[13]

Yet there is a link between the disciplinary, panoptic strategy and the vectoral strategy of transporting surplus, criminalized people to the antipodes. Both are characteristic forms of producing a second nature. Both are regimes that combine a field of visibility, a technology respectively for enclosing or traversing it, a discourse and its executors. Where the panoptic strategy is one of intensive techniques, subdividing, scrutinizing, and enclosing space within the city, transportation was an extensive vector, based on a technology that can project, plan, and traverse the globe. The world becomes the object of the vector, of the potentiality of movement. Bodies, cargoes, weapons, information: this principally naval technology produced, almost as an afterthought, the settlement of Botany Bay, the city of Sydney, the colony of New South Wales, and eventually the country known as Australia. The vector brings the nodes so named within its addressable space.

The antipodes are not the other of empires. While the idealized mythologies of the exotic still haunt global media exchanges (and the arts), they are subsidiary to the management of the antipodean other via techniques of assay and appraisal which see in the antipodes not the noble savage or the evil demon, but a resource to be managed and mobilized along the lines opened up by the vector. The sublime antipodean other becomes enmeshed in an abstract grid capable of more mundane valuations of economic and strategic advantage. The other becomes a resource, not a double, for the project of the West.[14]

In the development of the vectoral regime of power, everything depended on the development of technologies of perception. In the naval regime, techniques for finding a ship's longitudinal position were decisive.[15] This is what enabled Captain Cook to chart the east coast of Australia in 1770, and Captain Phillip to guide the First Fleet back to that same address. This made possible a much more productive relation between the abstract space of maps, charts, and solar calculations, and the places through which ships passed on their travels. Gradually, every movement becomes equivalent and interchangeable with any other movement. Gradually, any destination becomes equivalent and interchangeable with any other place. As with physical movement, so too with information. Information no longer knows its destination.

In his remarkable book, *European Vision and the South Pacific*, Bernard Smith shows how the rise of British naval imperialism precipitates the fall of neoclassical representation.[16] The neoclassical style pictured landscapes in terms of the *ideal*, and this aesthetic was institutionally enshrined in the Royal Academy. The Royal Society, on the other hand, favored an aesthetic based on the representation of the *typical*. Through its connection with scientific naval expeditions to the Pacific, the Royal Society saw to it that the more productively useful representation of the typical became the technique of representing what explorers like Captain Cook and Joseph Banks found. The new mode of art became an organic part of the most advanced edge of modern social relations. The old form of representation was preserved – as if in aspic – as a traditional but no longer living form. This split has troubled modern art ever since.

Fine art develops out of the Royal Academy model of picturing the ideal. The Royal Society's techniques of perception, based on types, is the precursor to what Virilio calls a logistics of perception. The modern extension of the fine art tradition will critique this logistics of perception from the sidelines, but cannot really counter it as a form of power. The key question of aesthetics moves from a preoccupation with the formal properties of the content *in* images to the relations of production *of* images.

Contemporary artists may use certain kinds of video cameras, which they may or may not notice work remarkably well in low light conditions. It never seems to occur to ask why. At the heart of the video game is a charge-coupled device, or CCD. These were designed for use in satellites, put in orbit with the principal purpose of detecting the flare of Russian intercontinental ballistic missiles.

One of the ways the Americans knew the Russians intended to station missiles in Cuba was because they had built a telltale diamond-shaped installation on Cuban territory. This shape was what a camera mounted on a satellite could make out of the anti-aircraft battery that the Russians typically built around missile installations. These had not been all that hard to find via satellite, for while the Soviet Union was a big place, the Russians generally built their missile silos along the lines of the major railways. So photo intelligence here is really a matter of looking for two kinds of the typical: the typical sites of the missiles, and the typical form in which the Russian military–industrial complex built them. When one of these typical forms showed up somewhere else, in Cuba, it was one of the pieces of evidence that set in train that weird global media event that is the Cuban Missile Crisis.

Today we appear to have gone beyond technologies which enframe the world, in Heidegger's sense.[17] We live not with the discrete framing of the continuous space of the world but with the temporal editing of its multiple and continuous times into a singular rhythm of cuts and ruptures. The edit becomes the device for regulating, not static pictures or singular texts but constant flows of information. Information about markets, products, consumers, events, forces, and resources – above all, information about other information – now has to be organized in the exercise of far more extensive powers. Vectoral power is not the Panopticon, which is the sense of being visible from one central point, whether a guard tower in a prison or a satellite in space. Vectoral power is a **transopticon,** or the sense of the editability of multiple flows of intelligence into a continuous feed.

The naval vectoral regime created a new role for the artist in framing and inscribing the typical. The typical became the mode of assessing the relative worth of projects designed to exploit what the typical pictured. This process could result in miscalculation, as it did notoriously in the decision to colonize Botany Bay, Australia. The land itself did not live up to its representation.[18] Nevertheless, the pursuit of the vector has also been the endless process of refining and verifying information about the world and hence increasing its openness to development and transformation into second nature.

Today sophisticated techniques are gathering to make ever more complex projects instantly and constantly comparable and assessable – from refinancing News Corp. to invading a country to selling sneakers. The development of vectoral flows of information is what makes possible the space of flows, in which jobs, troops, money – anything – can be redirected from one interchangeable address to another. The aesthetic is part of this emergent terrain of third nature whether it likes it or not. The vector enables an ever more rarified **aesthetic economy**.

The development of **third nature** overlaps with the development of second nature – hence the difficulties of periodizing the modern and postmodern. The salient point is the development of the telegraph. What is distinctive about the telegraph is that it begins a regime of communication where information can travel faster than people or things. The telegraph, telephone, television, telecommunications – **telesthesia**. When information can move faster and more freely than people or things, its relation to those other movements and to space itself changes. No longer a space of places, we move on to a space of flows.

If there is a qualitative change in the social relations of culture that deserves the name of postmodern, perhaps this is it. Or perhaps we could call this state of affairs *third nature*. Second nature, which appears to us as the geography of cities and roads and harbors and wool stores, is progressively overlaid with the red lines of a third nature of information flows, creating an information landscape which unevenly but almost entirely covers the old territories. While this process has been going on since the telegraph, it reaches critical mass in the late 1970s. The "postmodern" emerged as a catalogue of its temporal symptoms; "cyberspace" as a description of its spatial effects. Both the postmodern in theory and cyberspace in literature were explorations of a landscape of third nature.

We can see now, very clearly, what the terminal state of third nature would be, at least as a concept. Deleuze and Guattari ask provocatively and more than once: "Perhaps we have not become abstract enough?"[19] What would it mean to become ever more abstracted from the boundedness of territory and subjectivity? One can imagine a delirious future. Not the future of Marx's communism: from each according to their abilities, to each according to their needs. Rather the future of the rhizome made concrete: where every trajectory is potentially connected to every other trajectory, and where all trajectories are potentially equal and equally rootless. We no longer have roots, we have aerials. We no longer have origins, we have terminals. We no longer have antipodes, we have antipodality.

This fantasy has appeared in different guises, also, among the Californian technofreaks, the postmodern wing of the green movement, in the corporate improvisations of Rupert Murdoch, and among the high-frontier hegemonists in the Pentagon.[20] The struggle over the relations of communication and the making of third nature are every bit as intense as the struggles over the relations of production and the shaping of second nature – but many of the old rules no longer apply.

The perception of third nature differs from place to place. The vector may be abstract but it is hardly universal. Even when attempting to think it in the abstract, one always does so starting from local modes of perception. In thinking the vector in its abstraction, one way to retain a sense of locality is to try to discover the relations of **antipodality** lurking within them. Antipodality is the feeling of being neither here nor there. It is an experience of identity in relation to the other in which the relation always appears more strongly to consciousness than either the identity it founds or the other it projects.

Experiencing antipodality is always very unsettling, sometimes a little schizophrenic. There is nothing uniquely Australian about it, although it is a very common anxiety in Australian culture.[21] This is a place which is always in a relation to an elsewhere, which is always defined by its relation to a powerful other. We are no one, whoever we are, always oscillating in antipodality with elsewheres.

These days the anxiety of antipodality is growing ever more common. The globalization of trade flows and cultural flows made possible by the vector reopens the old wounds of identity, breaking the skin at unexpected places. The volume and velocity of cultural product in circulation on the planet of noise keep rising. Popular music, cinema, and television, the raw materials of popular culture, are increasingly sold into global markets in accordance with transnational financing and marketing plans.[22] Suddenly cultural identity looks like it is in flux.

The relations and the flows are more clearly in view than the sources or destinations. Cultural differences are no longer so tied to the experience of the particularities of place. These "vertical" differences – of locality, ethnicity, nation – are doubled by "horizontal" differences, determined not by being rooted in a particular place but by being plugged into a particular circuit. We vainly try to preserve forms of difference that are rapidly reorganizing themselves along another axis.[23]

This new experience of difference is an experience of an active trajectory between places, identities, and formations, rather than a drawing of borders, be they of the self or place. This is antipodality. Antipodality is the cultural difference created by the vector. The acceleration of the vectors of transnational communication makes the antipodean experience more common. With the Internet connecting every part of the globe that can afford it, many people are experiencing antipodality as the feeling of being caught in a network of cultural trajectories beyond their control.[24] In what the Situationists calls the **overdeveloped** world, both the culture of everyday life and the culture of scholarly thinking about the present seem to me to betray traces of unease, if not downright paranoia, about antipodality.[25] Yet it is undoubtedly the emergent axis of technocultural struggle.

The anxious, nauseous side of antipodality throws off – or throws up – its own kinds of political (or pseudo-political) reactions. On the one hand, it leads to attempts to shore up identity against the flux. The various resurgent nationalisms and faith-based fantasies of political community, whether Islamicist, born again or Hindu-nationalist, seem to have elements of this reactive return to an imagined core of immutable identity and community. On the other hand, the kind of coalition-building involved in counter-globalization movements presents the paradox of using the experience of antipodality as the ground for a positive politics in and against third nature.[26]

Now the point about this is that any attempt to create community of necessity excludes something or someone. Community only forms as a struggle against something other, be it nature, other communities, or the vector. While struggles still of course take place in relation to nature and second nature, they now have an added dimension: the struggle, not for natural space, not for social space, but for information space. Every community "de-informates" certain spaces within itself and creates certain barriers to the flow of information from without. Every community, by definition, requires some degree of "correctness" from would-be members. Hence I want to signal a certain moral ambiguity about the concept of community and identity. They are necessary, perhaps, but as intellectuals we need to keep a critical distance.

To return to Deleuze's question, "What if we have not become abstract enough?," out of the course of this analysis some answers begin to suggest themselves. Whether we like it or not, cultural differences cannot be preserved from the impact of telesthesia. New forms of difference are emerging out of the struggle with the vector; others succumb and become extinct. The abstraction of social relations from identity and place is not something that technologies achieve of their own accord. It results from the dialectic between communities and the technical regime of the vectors of telesthesia. Innovative forms of autonomous communication give the planet of noise, so to speak, something to suck on. The dialectic of autonomy and antipodality structures an emerging politics of relationality and flow rather than of identity and locality. Our communicational interventions (for that is what both art and writing are) have to be rethought for this world of third nature we have made, which is very rapidly remaking us.

New technology cannot be used to preserve cultural differences. Traditional culture, reified as museum interactives, does not constitute preservation so much as mummification. New technology can be used to create new differences and new forms of autonomy and community, but it cannot be used to "preserve" old differences in any meaningful sense. Traditional forms of cultural difference are not independent of the techniques used to maintain them.

The work of Eric Michaels and Francis Jupurrurla in the Warlpiri Aboriginal community is interesting precisely because Michaels thought video could be used to *create* a viable community which would grow organically out of traditional information practices[27] (even though, as Tim Rowse points out, Warlpiri social organization does not traditionally take the form of anything remotely like "community" at all).[28] This was not preservation; it was a creative process. It was not ethnography – it was art.

Naturally, it was a far more morally ambivalent project than simply preserving a form of communication assumed to have always already been there. Michaels thought that only by becoming abstract – by incorporating the information-managing relations of third nature – could the constraints on knowledge, so vital to the oral information economy of the Warlpiri, be developed and sustained. That may be at least slightly true for us all.

When Captain Phillip and the First Fleet arrived and thanked their sponsors, it was the beginning of the end of one version of indigenous culture. When the First Fleet re-enactors arrived 200 years later and thanked their sponsors, live on national television, it was less clear then that something too was passing. The national-cultural-media space that many thought the Bicentennial was supposed to affirm was already a thing of the past.

4

Speaking Trajectories

Sydney, Australia

Experiencing a world made over by the vector is one thing, but how then to write about it? Can there be ways of putting words together, sentences together, which in their grammar grasp what grammatization has wrought? Theory is a kind of writing, after all. Its claim to be doing something, to have some reason to exist, has to lie at least in part on the claim that it finds methods of working with language that have a particular kind of grasp on the world. What it is that theory grasps is distinct from what, say, the novel grasps. Its claim is to be able with some asperity to know something about the abstract dimensions of everyday life. While the novel might be good at the concreteness of quotidian details, and the subtle variations of structures of feeling, theory is about something else. It's about the nuances of how abstract forces create experiences.

The following two essays concern themselves with two exemplary practitioners of low theory – one Australian, one French – to whom I apprenticed myself, as a writer: Meaghan Morris and Paul Virilio. Their writing appeared, in the 1980s, to be describing particular kinds of experience in quite particular ways. They both used the essay form, but shorn of its commonplaces, and expanded to encompass new categories of experience. They were both **low theory** in the sense that their sites of publication and circulation were interstitial, circulating between academia, the art world, architecture, and other "applied" fields. The circulation of this writing was itself vectoral rather than disciplinary, at least for a time. Both had a knack for seizing upon particular events as the vehicles for a writing which nevertheless did not content itself with the enumeration of particulars, which is what the essay in the anglophone world has devolved into.[1]

Let me start with a passage from a classic Meaghan Morris essay on a quintessentially "popular cultural text," *Australia Live*, the four-hour transcontinental "celebration" which appeared as television's contribution to the Australian Bicentenary of 1988. Morris's first move is to place the event in a genre, the genre of "panorama." She then distinguishes two variants of the panorama, the imperial and the touristic. Where the former constructs the act of seeing as possessing, in the latter seeing is a "passing by." These two modalities of the panorama, it should be noted, have a particular resonance in the Australian context, as both are genres in which the antipodean experience of landscape has been historically encoded. This essay will return to the difference between these two modalities of panorama, and hence explore a trajectory opened up in its opening move. But before coming to that, the panorama has a couple of other jobs to perform.

First, Morris includes an account of the critical response to *Australia Live* in magazines and newspapers within her definition of its genre. For example, many criticisms drew attention to the lack of historical depth in *Australia Live* when in fact this was simply a feature of the panorama as a genre: its relinquishment of historical continuity in favor of spatial grasp. The full significance of this move will become apparent later, but for the moment it is worth noting that Morris manages to bracket the "doxa" surrounding the event in the media with the event itself, thus extricating herself from the conventional criticism of the event. Morris sidesteps doxa by defining the object differently: the "*Australia Live* effect" is not an effect of television, but of panorama – a genre which has both a current televisual form, but also prior ones to which it can be compared. Sidestepping the obvious (in order to sneak up on it from behind) is crucial to Morris. "The true violence is that of the self evident," and her method builds on that of the Barthesian essay: the paradox, which shows that, "in fact," things are otherwise.[2]

Having accounted for the lack of historical resonance in *Australia Live* in terms of its generic properties, Morris can go on to say what role, in fact, it performs: "*Australia Live* had no commemorative, or even 'nostalgic' aspirations whatsoever. It produced Australia as a space for visiting, investing, cruising, developing. Its basic theme was (capital) mobility. Comprehensive notes on the risks – drought, grasshopper plagues, restless natives – were included." The video cameras' panoramic gaze produced "a landscape without shadows: a surveillance – space where nothing secret, mysterious, troubling or malcontent could find a place to lurk or hide."[3] The panorama is a genre through which Morris makes us see a changing modality of power. If the imperial panorama presented the image of the dominions as a possession to its imperial administrators, the touristic panorama shows off the acreage to potential real-estate developers. This relation to the land is fundamental, for it is at the centre of both the antipodean relation as a relation of political–economic power and the culture of the antipodes as a lived relation to that power.

Lest this seem overdrawn, compare Morris's acerbic parody above with this straight-faced remark from *The Financial Review*: "It all sounds a trifle cold and calculating but facts are facts: one Japanese tourist is equal to 10 tonnes of wheat or 15 tonnes of coal, 5 tonnes of sugar, 7 tonnes of aluminia or 60 tonnes of iron ore in real dollar terms."[4] In other words, Australia is a site for the most primary and most tertiary of industries, for the extraction of raw rock and the distraction of pure allure, of ore and awe. Imports – and practically everything in Australia is imported, from cars to cultural theories – have to be financed on the back of these precarious activities. Hence the pointed irony of Morris's remarks – and her interest in tourism.[5] The tourist's gaze is the original **transopticon**, culling snapshots from different times and places into the expected narratives.

Lest all this seem out of place in an essay about culture, which the division of academic labor tends to treat as a domain with a relatively absolute autonomy from the economic, it should be pointed out that only in a metropolitan country could the economic be separated from the cultural and the local from elsewhere.[6] The antipodean relation is one where no such separation is possible, for the national always hinges on a *problematic* relation to the international, and the cultural to a crisis-prone antipathy to the economic. Morris finds a writerly solution to this tight coupling in the antipodes of what the metropolitan discourses keep distinct by making a virtue of necessity. Her essays shift position and modality between the national and the international. They unerringly find the points at which power manifests itself in its absence, where its effect creates a void in discourse, where identity hangs precariously on the edge of an absent power.

As antipodean low theory, a Morris essay on *Australia Live* cannot help but address leading metropolitan theories on the spectacle of the media event, in this case those of Baudrillard and Jameson. The *Australia Live* Bicentennial spectacle lent itself easily to such readings, as Morris points out. Critical distance was indeed foreclosed. The past did appear as nothing more than a genre of the present. It would be too easy to import these rhetorical tropes and apply them locally, to play the provincial-popular off against the metropolitan-theoretical. Easier still to critique this oh-so very antipodean need to import the big picture theory to organize and interpret the local "scene." This seems all to accord with the neocolonial scheme of things.

After showing the relevance of foreign theory for local events, and a mastery of both the theory and the act of interpreting the local through its lens, Morris shifts the roles – and the rules. The relevance of the local event is established and legitimated by its neat fit with the theory from the centers. Having established the local event as the minor, antipodean pole in relation to the theory, Morris has nevertheless established a relation, and can begin to construct a theoretical vector that might work back in the other direction, from the antipode back again.

Since the antipode is not a fixed address but a relational node, Morris makes Jameson and Baudrillard, "postmodern theory," into an antipodean destination against which to orient this writing. Unlike Baudrillard's dazzling reversals and contaminations of paired terms, this reversal is not symmetrical.[7] As in the classic rhetorical tradition that Jean-François Lyotard appeals to, reversal is a tactic for building up the lesser term temporarily, "making the weaker case appear the stronger," just enough to turn it against the dominant term in a binary pair.[8] The degree to which one can reverse the vector of a theory is ultimately not a question of will but of institutional power, but one can temporarily take up a speaking trajectory, back along its line, by looking for the gaps in its transmissions.

Thus Morris says of *Australia Live* that it enacts a certain critical dilemma that is not at all unique to High Theory. High Theory is as symptomatic of a certain befuddling complexity as *Australia Live*. In either case, it is a question of how to read the discourse – not just the text – and the possibilities it opens out in the complex institutional matrix of discourses, sites, and vectors. Morris states the problem, then, in these terms:

> There is no single "source" making sense of the world in communication with a captive audience. Complaints about collapsing standards (in aesthetic quality, in reality values, or in degrees of critical distance) are side effects of this process. It is not that aesthetic standards cannot be stated, historical reality asserted, or distance maintained (critics do these things all the time) – but that there is no guarantee of "a" public who will care to validate the outcome, or be "mobilized" by the result.[9]

This experience of a lack of common narrative, central authority, unity of place and time is, as Morris is slyly aware, an antipodean experience as much as it is a postmodern one. Critical theories of each and every genre have responded to this scenario by pondering and problematizing the problem of the relationship of text to subject. This experience even has a peculiarly Australian modality: "if it is now conventional for feminist essays to begin by questioning the place from which one speaks; it has also long been customary for Australian essays to pose the question of speaking of place."[10] The proliferation of vectors of telesthesia is making the experience of the problem of textuality – rendered as a problematic relation to place – an increasingly common experience. The gaps and silences in metropolitan discourse – including theory High and low – occur when it confronts this proliferation of relations to others. It is in this break in transmission that the space exists for antipodean theory.

Every vector creates a new antipode. As the volume and velocity of vectors being made and unmade increases, the *tyranny of difference* proliferates. Not only are new antipodes created and reached, their promise and danger realized only too soon, they also disappear more rapidly as well. The other comes . . . and goes. The old reciprocities between the imperial strategy and the antipodean counter-site, the old uneven dialogues that gave the appearance of community and communication, disperse into a myriad of lines: good, bad, crossed, and engaged. There is something lost here; hence the theory of nostalgia and the nostalgia of theory, which is one of the common modalities of the postmodern. Yet there are also possibilities here. It is the possibilities that Morris chooses to respond to. The imperial mode of discourse really has nothing to offer its antipodes; hence the mourning and nostalgia might set the tone at the centre, but at the end of the line it can only be cause for celebration.

All authority in antipodean experience is either too close and too shallow or too distant and too obscure to have any real effects. One either worships imperial power or resents it – both relations at a distance. In the essays of Meaghan Morris, there is a playful, self-conscious version of this dilemma of authority as it appears from the antipodean end of the line. Indeed, there is an ironic version of the whole antipodean neurosis about identity in these texts. Morris writes in a manner which is self-consciously antipodean, but which does not necessarily have anything to do with being Australian. It is antipodean in the sense that Morris writes from the perspective of the minor term in any and every vectoral equation. She writes in what appears to be the first person, but a first person that is clearly presented as a rhetorical construct, for all the apparently revealing and seductive intimacy of the voice. It is writing that is very concerned with discovering what spaces in language can be enacted besides a *staging* of authority, that is, besides what Paul Carter calls imperial writing.[11]

What she does not do is position herself as the great "other," the great excluded, oppressed, unloved, unwashed other term which resents and berates the master discourse. Rather, Morris approaches writing tactically. Her essays are premised on the assumption that there are always a great number of possible trajectories that can be opened up at will within the imperium of discourse. Not all of these positions are equally possible or equally effective. This is not a call to a liberal pluralism, a well-meaning multiculturalism. As Ghassan Hage shows, such a move tends to reinstall a certain kind of privilege. Those who once spoke on behalf of the homogeneous norm of the old cultural order just switch codes and speak for the new heterogeneous one instead. The marginal find their place in this order, but its old masters get to speak on behalf of its new rules.[12]

For example, in discussing the problem of "identity" in both feminist and antipodean writing, Morris finds a connection between the two in opposition to an American figure of Identity:

> Identity – for many Australians – is a concept invested with the sanctity that Americans can accord to the Self. It can have a similar function in feminist discourse, defining both an object of quests and a site for scrutiny. But Identity has a social, rather than a psychological, resonance – evoking mysteries of sex, class, race and place rather than those of ego and individuality. Identity is a cohesive, gregarious force. Yet Identity is assumed to be fictitious; to talk Identity is to indulge in (not necessarily frivolous) acts of improvisation.[13]

Here Morris juxtaposes a number of trajectories that give rise to antipodal formations: American imperial vs. peripheral; phallocentric vs. feminist. She problematizes them by showing how they intersect, how each and every experience of an antipodal relation and an identity that stands at one or other pole of it suffers from the irruption of other points of difference within it. There can be no speaking "position" now that so many discourses intersect so frequently, only speaking trajectories.

In discussing theories of female spectatorship in feminist screen theory, Morris observes that the concept of female spectator had a useful tactical significance in relation to the imperial conception of the male gaze. "In these contexts, 'female' has polemical force rather than essentialist significance." Thus the female spectator intersects and interrupts the male gaze–female body line of thought. Having made this interruption, the female spectator concept can be used to plot a new line, a new antipode – the feminist film text. At this point in the text, Morris improvises a move that interrupts the new female spectator–feminist film trajectory. About the female spectator, she notes that:

> I am uncomfortable with two other developments related to the use of this term. One is the notion of the female spectator as a strategy for feminist cinema. I find it hard to say why I am wary of this, and so I'm certainly interested in it. It's partly a matter of the American-ness of the contexts in which it so often appears, and of an intimate or intimist American-ness, which disturbs me when

even the slightest gesture is made toward specifying a value (no matter how abstract or "hypothetical") for "female". "Disturbs me" is probably too strong: I have a sensation of distancing similar to the bemusement I feel in other contexts when American feminism speaks of "the self" (or properties like "personal space") – and I'm fairly sure I don't have one of those and I'm not sure I want one.[14]

The other thing Morris is uncomfortable with in the term "female spectator" involves a quite different interruption along a quite different axis. In the work of John Fiske, for example, the "female spectator" is something which derives pleasure from the consumption of certain genres of television such as soap opera.[15] Where she would interrupt the passage from female spectator to feminist film by pointing out how the dominant pole of "Americanness" is implicated in it, she would interrupt another line which passes from female spectator to consumptive pleasure by pointing out the masculine assumption that the female spectator is simply the consumer on the end of a different genre of products. Hence each trajectory has a multiple of adjacent points which begin and terminate, often in the same object or subject, but which can be tactically differentiated out from each other.

Almost all of her essays have points at which the speaking position, the I of the text, slips from one tactical beach-head to another. Indeed the whole text can sometimes be composed to make these slippages of address *possible*. In "Politics Now" – a paper originally given at a conference with a decidedly "political" flavor – Morris positions herself as a petit bourgeois intellectual, pitting her faint-hearted persona against the militants who would speak the part of the working class, but also differentiating herself from the ruling class. She speaks as the antipodes' antipode. An antipode, after all, exists relative to some vector from a site of power and presence. As the sites of discursive power multiply, so too do the antipodean points each identify as the other pole, toward which it orients itself. These traceries intersect and overlap, making possible a mobile, antipodal strategy – in theoretical practice at least.

The petit bourgeois figure is a refreshingly candid one.[16] It makes excellent use of the ambivalence created by the oscillation between theoretical trajectories. Neither too "privileged" nor too "popular," and certainly not so powerful as to be capable of strategic control over the space of culture and its technologies, the petit bourgeois "makes the best of things," and, as Michel de Certeau points out, is capable of heroism in small affairs.[17] The essayistic style of Morris, like the tactical tricks de Certeau discovers within the space of disciplinary power, has a certain irreducible and singular way of insinuating itself into the discipline. The reading of de Certeau that Morris offers is a radical one, in that the minor, tactical mode is not just its object of disciplinary study but its method.

Like Ross Gibson's reading of the *Mad Max* films, this would be a "new beginning," in that it does not reify any particular vector.[18] It does not concentrate solely on the spatial antipode of Australia, or the gendered antipode of the feminine, or the class antipode of the petit bourgeois. Nor is it a matter of pulping all of them together in a plural soup. It is a question of moving tactically along one cultural trajectory and then off on another. In this manner, Morris traverses the fragments and detritus of academic discourses just as Max negotiates the remnants of old movies and Australian myths littering the desert. In either case, a strategy for movement, a joyous circulation, is posed as a writerly response to the proliferation of media vectors and its effects.

I think historically this response arises from the development of vectors which breached the distance between Australia and its old dominant pole, the "mother land," which ended the "tyranny of distance."[19] Rather than an oedipal rupture with the source, as in the old radical national formations, the proliferation of vectors in the late 1970s and 1980s called for the exploration of any and every multinational line in and out of the place. In place of the search for a speaking *position*, Morris constructs speaking trajectories: the I of the text moves tactically across the lines constructed in the text by the crossed wires which are the result of a myriad of vectors traversing the same ground.

As the media vector which brought us *Australia Live*, the Gulf War, and the Tiananmen Square massacre demonstrates, the age of the instant vectoral connection between the antipode and its other had already arrived by the late twentieth century. The instability between these poles oscillated nightly on TV, even before broadcast TV was displaced as the dominant vectoral form. What becomes of cultural identity when the breathing spaces that regulate the paranoid reaction of cultural identity to its external bearings collapse into the time of the televisual edit? What becomes of meaning when there are no shared codes and conventions? The answers, I think, ought to come *from* the antipodes. From the antipodean point of view, Morris gives us a way with the other's grammar in which to phrase a response other than silence, resentment, paranoia, and the fixed stare into mirrors which are no longer fixed but electronically mobile. This condition predicates a new mode of inquiry. It requires that we write differently.

If there is a limit to the Morrisonian style of writing, it would not be in the subtlety with which it plays with speaking trajectories. It would be with its habit of bracketing off the materiality of those trajectories themselves. For example, what kind of petit bourgeois are we talking about? (And talking as?) What is its stock in trade? What is its relation to that which defines any species of bourgeois – property? This is a question I want to come back to. Another line of questioning might be: rather than the abstract space of a national culture, what might one say about the more tangible spaces of the city? How are the concretely felt surfaces of built space also traversed by telesthesia? I found an approach to this through the writings of another exponent of a distinctive low-theory style – Paul Virilio. While of variable quality, at their best, his writings essayed another useful approach to what a sentence might be and do, when it is in and of third nature.

5

Cruising Virilio's Overexposed City

Sydney, Australia

A city made for speed is made for success.[1]

For Le Corbusier this meant principally a city made according to a rational use of space. He was also acutely aware of the chaos caused by the motor vehicle:

> In the early evening twilight on the Champs-Élysées it was as though the world had suddenly gone mad . . . . Day after day the fury of traffic grew. To leave your house meant that once you had crossed the threshold you were a possible sacrifice to death in the shape of innumerable motors. I think back 20 years, when I was a student, the road belonged to us then.

Poor Corbu! Walking his straight lines around Paris like an accident waiting to happen. One can imagine him being run over by a cement mixer.

Corbusier's *City of Tomorrow* was very much a project for reorganizing space under the conditions of modern transport and industry. From a rational organization of space would flow an economy of time: "a model city for commerce!" Yet even in this there is at least a hint of the possibility of something working against such a rational space, from within it. Concentrated within Corbusier's skyscrapers are not only workers but the "apparatus for abolishing time and space" – telephones, cables, and wireless.

Where Corbusier projects an optimism about the future of the modern city, based on a new spatial order, Paul Virilio turns this dream on its head, and sees the modern city in our time as being disorganized by technologies "for abolishing time and space," technologies which produce a new and more elaborate temporal order, but which irrupt within the spatial order of the old city. From a new economy of time comes a break in urban space. This is Virilio's "overexposed city."[2]

Perhaps Virilio himself is something of an accidental mouthpiece for certain observations about the city, which are themselves the product of being exposed to just such a city and its intersecting histories. Certainly Virilio's cadence and style are consequences of his relation to the city – this city, the city of speed. Virilian writing pursues a tendency only so far, to the point at which its vector becomes evident, then disappears, off on another peregrination.

The **vector** is a key term for Virilio. It describes the aspect of technology that interests him most, and also the style of writing he employs to capture that aspect. It is a term from geometry, meaning a line of fixed length and direction but no fixed position. Virilio employs it to mean any trajectory along which bodies, information, or warheads could potentially pass. Vectors are potential trajectories, possible dangers. The vector in Virilio *is* power, a terminal power beyond metaphors of structure, with which writing must find ways to keep pace.[3]

If it was typical of postmodern thinking to question the model of the subject as an enclosure of interiority, of consciousness, then it is left to Virilio to question the parallel notion of the architectural structure as an enclosure of interiority, of bounded space. He does this by questioning the very notion of "boundary." He points to the way "the boundary surface has been continually transformed," particularly by vectors of telesthesia that pass through physical boundaries: "the urban wall has given way to an infinity of openings and ruptured enclosures" and "the surface-boundary becomes an osmotic membrane, a blotter."[4]

Considered from the point of view of enclosure, of structure, the city presents itself as something static, monumental. One thinks of the most familiar forms of representation of the city: the map, the plan, the elevation. One thinks of a synchronic combination of architectural elements, arranged in space. When considered from the point of view of openings, the city takes on a different aspect. One thinks not of discrete entities in space, but of relational pathways, circuits, frequencies, "interruptions."[5]

The beauty of Virilio's writing is that it restores the temporal aspect of urbanism – with a vengeance. The architect Manuel de Solà-Morales has compared urbanism to dance, in that both are concerned with the relationship of the spatial to the temporal, ideally coming together in an Aristotelian unity.[6] He sees certain modern tendencies in architecture as having a spatial bias when applied to urban planning – Le Corbusier, for instance.

Far from rectifying the imbalance, as Morales would wish, Virilio shows how "technological time" has destroyed the dance of urban space and the whole aesthetic of urbanism.[7] Architectural space has been invaded by technological time. The tragedy of architecture for Virilio is that its geometric "capacity of defining a unity of time and place for activities now enters into open conflict with the structural capacities of mass communication."[8]

In the place of a discrete boundary in space, demarcating distinct spaces, one sees spaces co-joined by semi-permeable membranes, exposed to flows of information in particular ways. Virilio sees the spatial difference of the boundary as having been partly superseded by the temporal differences of the frequencies with which information passes through a city permeated by networks. Superimposed on the wall, the building, and the street are those other differences: a phone call begins or ends, two databases swap information from opposite ends of the city, an edit in the evening news switches the viewer from Angola to Afghanistan. A "montage of temporalities which are the product not only of the powers that be but of the technologies that organize time."[9] Passing through the surfaces of architecture is "architexture." The architectonic technologies of space are intersected by an "architectronics" of information time.

That the transopticon's edit or montage of information in time supersedes the boundary or form in space is a radical critique not only of modern architecture, but of its postmodernist styles as well. Virilio sees the recourse to history in postmodernism as a sham: a last resort to a false sense of time instead of coming to grips with the effects of technological time upon the city.

"Where the polis once inaugurated a political theatre, with the agora and the forum, today there remains nothing but the cathode ray screen, with its shadows and specters of a community in the process of disappearing."[10] Which sounds like Robert Venturi's remark that Americans don't need piazzas – they should be home watching TV.[11] But Venturi still managed to conjure up a sense of optimism: "The most urgent technological problem facing us is the humane meshing of advanced scientific and technical systems with our imperfect and exploited human systems."[12]

Virilio's critique of modernism goes beyond Venturi's "learning from Las Vegas." Virilio would have us see Scorsese's movie *Casino*, not Vegas itself, as the "place," or rather the time, to learn from: "Hollywood, much more than Venturi's Las Vegas, merits a study of urbanism," for "here, more than anywhere," advanced technologies have converged to create a synthetic space-time. The Babylon of film "derealization, the industrial zone of pretense."[13]

The city, says Virilio, is a gearbox full of speeds, a hierarchy of speeds, like a video interface equipped with play, fast forward, rewind, slow motion. Some city speeds are all but extinct, like the speed of the pneumatic tube, or the speed of democracy. Some are alive and well and producing something quite other than the space of urbanism, like the speeds of what Virilio calls *dromocracy*. The vector becomes a power over and against the social. Yet the problem of speed is not simply an abstract one which the writer or the artist or the architect can sit back and contemplate. The problem of speed is a constitutive one for art, as well as for writing. It has caught up with art and writing, overtaking them.

Marinetti attributed his baptism in the spirit of Futurist technology to overturning his motor car in a drainage ditch. He and his pals had interrupted their decadent, bourgeois, European boredom to race motor cars in the street in the dead of night. Marinetti didn't quite see Ballard's "nightmare marriage of sex and technology"[14] when he rolled his beautiful motor in the mire, but he came damned close. "Time and space died yesterday," he emerged saying. "We already live in the absolute, because we have created eternal, omnipresent speed."[15]

Virilio generalizes Marinetti's "political vision of speed," including his championing of the transient at the level of philosophical critique; his hostility to discourses with moral alibis for not confronting the realities of power – while at the same time turning these things back against Marinetti himself. "Every tech-

nology produces, provokes, programs a specific accident."[16]
Virilio introduces a melancholic note quite foreign to Futurist
megalomania.

Stress on the accident as the unintended effect of applied
rationality seems like a good starting point for a "media archaeology."[17] An older school of study of science and technology
tended to project backwards (in the name of "history") from the
materialized technological hardware to a conscious political or
commercial interest. The irony of technology lies rather in its
irrationality. Hence Virilio's ideas for the museum: "Every technology, every science should choose its specific accident, and reveal
it as a product . . . as a product to be 'epistemo-technically'
questioned."[18]

The *Powerhouse Museum* in Sydney, Australia, achieves precisely this, but in an unintended, ironic mode. The original building is a rather Gothic nineteenth-century electricity generating
station. This brick cathedral to the productive economy of nineteenth-century industry now houses an ossuary of the golden
age of Australian manufacturing, and doubles as a temple to the
new-age industry of Sydney: tourism. It is also a monument to
Aldo Rossi's observation that architectural forms persist while
"functions" come and go with history and technology.[19] Form
decays at a much slower rate than the history it originally monu-
mentalizes and the technologies it houses.

Both Virilio and Rossi, being fans of the cinema, would also
appreciate the fact that the stripped and gutted shell of the powerhouse, prior to renovation, was the set for the last scene of
Mad Max Beyond Thunderdome, where it features as the derelict
abbey to apocalyptic hope.[20] Thus this is a site at the crossroads
of a number of accidents and collisions: between form and function, between old and new industries, between decay and "destructive reconstruction." It is a ruined monument to the interruption
as a theory of how the vector progresses, as it digresses, through
time.

Given that the practice of critical writing itself takes place as
part of the overexposed city, under the sign of the accident, under
the flight-path of the vector, what are the forms and speeds of
writing appropriate to it? A question that perhaps we can defer
for the moment. "There comes a time when new questions are
more useful than ready-made answers."[21] Perhaps a place to start

is with the chronograph, the arrested impression, that the vector leaves as an after-image on the sensorium.

One of the paradoxes of the reception of Paul Virilio's work is that such a conservative, in some senses even reactionary, thinker could achieve such a fan base among seemingly forward-thinking writers and artists. It is as if he so well described that which he abhorred that even those who loved it felt obliged to acknowledge the pertinence of the description and make it their own. It is quite clear, for instance, that Virilio sets himself outside the leftist currents of his time. He spent May '68 conducting experiments in a research facility on a non-orthogonal architecture.[22] His disdain for Marxist theory is clear.

And yet it might be possible, even enabling, to cross-breed the Virilian vector with something closer to a Marxist view of how such abstract relations become the basis for the accumulation of economic power. In the essay that follows, I want to cathect Paul Virilio to Paolo Virno, and his variant of the category of the multitude, to steer a writing about third nature out of the reactive cul-de-sac to which Virilio would consign it. The category of multitudes presents its own problems, and later I want to take a closer look at how the vectoral might yet give rise to a distinctive way of thinking about class – and not least of the class of us seemingly petit bourgeois writers. The ostensible subject matter is the one that Morris identifies as so productive for thinking about telesthesia: tourism.

6

Architectronics of the Multitude

New York, New York

There is a hotel shaped like a crocodile. It's in the Kakadu National Park, in the Northern Territory of Australia. You can stay there for $169 Australian dollars a night – in the off season. The crocodile shape might refer to any of the things that one might journey there to experience. There are the Nourlangie and Ubirr Aboriginal rock art galleries. There are the Yellow Water Billabong and the massive sandstone escarpments above it. There are, in other words, all flavors of what was once the "exotic" – animal, vegetable, and mineral.

The exotic is what hails us from an elsewhere. It's a spatial notion, and since architecture as a discourse makes itself at home in all things spatial, it comes as no surprise that the exotic is a recurring point of reference for architecture – especially for the architecture of tourism. But there's a problem. It should also come as no surprise that the exotic, as such, in itself, no longer really exists. There is no place outside. The whole space of the planet is "inside" **third nature**. There are only interiors. The space of exploration is closed.

This is not a new proposition. But what might push it a bit further is to turn it around, and consider its consequences for architecture. What if, in the extinction of the exotic, architecture also ceased to exist? Can there be an architecture without an elsewhere, a pole against which it can ground its edifice? Perhaps not. And so, rather than seeing the Gagudju Crocodile Hotel as the epitome of an exotic architecture, or architecture of the exotic, it is rather the end of architecture and the beginning of something else, some other way of building.

It's common in thinking about architecture to think it historically, as a succession of styles. Or perhaps one could say it is a succession of built relations to the passage of time. Not only European architecture has this historical consciousness. Postcolonial architectures also grapple with the form they might give to the beginning of new, modern, built histories. They construct their own historical forms in parallel to European architecture's historical times.

What is **postcolonial** architecture but an attempt to commandeer, and overcome, the status of the exotic? Starting from exoticism, it re-centers building on what was once consigned to the status of the peripheral. One makes a claim for a new centrality. This was the first, rather slow and incomplete way in which the exotic began to disappear – under the monumental weight of architecture. The atemporal space of the exotic is replaced by a proliferation of historical times.

The search for the exotic had to push on, beyond the frontier of the modernization of the postcolonial and non-metropolitan world. This very process of searching out the exotic exhausts it. Each node of exoticism that is identified, mapped, linked by transport, communication, and infrastructure to the non-exotic world, tends to become, in the process, less and less exotic. What is built, on the ruins of the exotic, is architecture. Architecture which, while it may incorporate some of the details and features of the exotic, ends up subsuming them within its practice of building.

The exotic only exists when it confronts architecture as a pure, immediate singularity. It is outside the chain of signification. That is its very appeal. The pleasure and danger of the exotic is that it might touch the real. In the process of developing on its contact with the exotic, architecture cannot but assimilate it into the chain of signification. Sure, what was there remains different. Not everybody has a hotel shaped like a big crocodile, where you enter through its jaws, and check in where its teeth meet. But this is no longer exotic. It is just different. Architecture incorporates the really exotic within the symbolic order, thereby canceling its difference.

These days both architecture and the exotic, those co-dependent poles, have a common enemy in **telesthesia**, which tends to cancel out both the historical space of architecture and the atemporal space of the exotic. Since the telegraph detached the flow of information from the movement of people and things, it has been all over for architecture. The very last form of architecture on the planet was the construction of telegraph offices – some of which were very beautiful structures. But they are architecture's mausoleums.

The telegraph, telephone, television – telesthesia, the communication vector – puts core and periphery in touch with each other: at the latter's expense. Globalization begins in earnest with the telegraph. All of space becomes potentially a space of communication, an interior space. The historical space and the exotic space are in immediate contact. The former dominates the latter, while the exotic infiltrates and dissimulates. It yields up its pure otherness to the play of signs.

The telegraph is also the beginning of the age of tourism. There is no tourism without the telegraph, only travel. Tourism, aided and abetted by the telegraph, is the great extinguisher of the exotic. Of course, cultured types abhor the idea of tourism. They think they are still travelers, but really there are just different kinds of tourist now. Only the homeless are travelers. Only the homeless depart without a destination.

The whole point of tourism used to be that travel was an experience of something other than the home world to which one was otherwise permanently tied. The architecture of tourism was then the antithesis of the norm. It was everything that was expelled from the mundane world, a landscape of fantasy and splendor.

Tourism was the means by which a people could take a safe step or two outside the bounded space that formed a home world. A people could step into the exotic world of some other people – or, at least, into an image of this other maintained for this very purpose. One toured, on occasion, to maintain this relation between a people and its other.

Yet these are times when movement has become the norm. The boundaries defining a home world become porous, ambiguous. In place of a people bounded in space and bordered by an other, we find ourselves among a *multitude*, a heterogeneous continuum that constantly escapes from the identity of a people with its home.

More and more this multitude is on the move, sometimes by choice, often not.

A fine cinematic account of the multitude is *Dirty Pretty Things*, where the night concierge and a cleaner are brought together by the discovery of a human heart, stuck in a hotel toilet. It peels back the layer of multitude that is hotel guests to find another, hotel workers, then peels that back to posit another, darker, more desperate layer, yet a layer of the same substance – multitude.

One of the signs of the subtle transformation of peoples into multitudes is that what was once the architecture of tourism has become the norm. All architecture is now tourist architecture. Hotels look like condos, and condos like hotels. Malls dabble in the signs of the exotic, while formerly exotic locales become malls. All the tracks are beaten to within an inch of their lives.

To think further about this architecture of the departure lounge, we can turn to Paolo Virno's *Grammar of the Multitude*, where the distinction between a people and a multitude is given a particularly clear expression. He contrasts Hobbes' people, sheltering within the bounds of the state, with Spinoza's multitude, refusing to converge into any kind of unity or stay within any bounds.

The multitude is something that the Hobbesian aspect of the contemporary state fears and represses. It is, among other things, the relentless flow of refugees, "boat people," and trans-migrants, seeping through the pores of the state and its territories. The state finds it troubling even within its borders. Here the multitude appears in what Michel de Certeau calls the tactics of everyday life, always avoiding and evading surveillance and control.[1]

In liberal thought, the quirky, proliferating differences of the multitude are relegated to the sphere of the private. The public aspect of the citizen is a universal attribute, something amenable to unification. The private is the remainder. Difference is OK so long as it remains private. But just as communication undoes the gap between architecture and the exotic, so too it undoes the gap between public and private.

Nowhere is the breakdown of the distinction between public and private more evident than in the way the multitude organizes itself with its constant cellphone calls, blithely talking, in earshot of anyone, even about anal warts or erectile dysfunction. With the cellphone, the multitude finds its tool for creating its own spatiality – **cellspace** – inserting its differences into public space, refusing to keep the details private.

The multitude refuses the ready-made unity of state and nation. It prefers wandering out of bounds, and composes its own open-ended wholeness, one encounter at a time. No wonder states have discovered a newfound fear of it. The obsessive rituals of security checks at airports are the symptom of a state apparatus that finds itself bypassed at every turn by a multitude in motion, yet on which it comes increasingly to depend.

The multitude refuses the separation of public and private, and has no use for the separation of work from leisure. Its work is increasingly a matter of the management of immaterial codes and connections. This is the case not just with the "cognitariat," who trade in signs, but also with the less lucky transmigrants, those escaping from failed states. Their working assets are a multitude made of communal and familial ties, stretching across continents.

The new landscape of transit thus has many classes and comfort levels. You might be sipping piña coladas by the pool or holed up in a detention center for illegal immigrants, but either way it's the same landscape of holding pens seeking to capture, by force or by seduction, an itinerant multitude with no interest in staying put.

The multitude refuses the arbitrary alienation of one aspect of its being from another: work from leisure, private from public. It also refuses more than a temporary capture of its interests in any one place, in any one use of its time. Virno: "The many, in as much as they are many, are those who share the feeling of not feeling at home."[2] Or as an old Gang of Four song has it: "at home he feels like a tourist."[3] And on tour she feels perfectly at home.

The multitude comes into its own when it acquires the tools and techniques for making space habitable on its own terms. Its architecture is wireless hotspots, corner stores selling pre-paid cellphone cards, the laundromat with Internet access, the cafe with last week's newspapers in your mother tongue. Wherever the multitude is in motion, someone will find a way to capture some value from it as it flows by.

Marx, writing about colonial labor in *Capital*, already discovered the multitude in motion. "So long, therefore, as the laborer can accumulate for himself – and this he can do so long as he remains possessor of his means of production – capitalist accumulation and the capitalistic mode of production are impossible."[4] So long as labor can find a line along which to escape, and find the resources to realize its own value, it avoids becoming subsumed within capital. In the old world, one aspect of the emergent working class digs in, creates unions and political parties, transforming the liberal into the social state. The other aspect takes the first boat to the antipodes. It might work for a while in the factories there, but it wants nothing but to take off again, try its luck at prospecting, or maybe open a bar. It escapes from the prospect of being a people to become a multitude.

To this day the movement of the multitude creates and recreates a building without qualities. It is all over for the architecture of the state and its people. Go to any old mill town in the northeastern United States and you will most likely find a boarded-up main street with a grand police station and court house facing each other, a lawyer's office or two, all surrounded by nothing. Everybody took off for somewhere else.

Maybe the multitude is in a trailer park now, or some instant suburb – the kind architects hate but that has the virtue of pure impermanence. The multitude isn't kidding itself about stability and propriety. It has given up on civilizing capital, and has decided to try the opposite tack – being even more feral than capital itself. Forget about scenes of tender violence in Eminem's movie *8 Mile*, just put the word "Juggalo" into your search engine.[5]

All building is temporary now, and knows it. It's all box stores and strip malls, office parks and prefab "developments," each replacing the next like slash-and-burn agriculture. One can celebrate it as the new suburban anchor à la David Brooks, or condemn it as the soulless blighted world of the "middle mind" à la Curtis White.[6] But what's usually lacking is an understanding of the multitude's growing tactical competence. It no longer expects to "settle down."

Architecture and communication were always two aspects of the same phenomenon. Architecture is communication through time using space; communication is architecture through space using time. What is characteristic of our time is the reversal of priority between them. After a long struggle, communication now trumps architecture. The time-binding techniques of built form are now subordinated to the space-binding techniques of the communication vector.[7] With this reversal comes the rise of the multitude, which uses its competence in communication to escape from the enclosures and spatialized alienations of architecture.

If the state is at a loss for how to capture and stabilize the restless flux of the multitude, capital is on the case. Perhaps the ruling class is no longer exactly capitalist.[8] The factories and forges are now in the underdeveloped world, and ownership of the means of production is increasingly subordinated to the ownership of the patents, trademarks, and copyrights – "intellectual property" – that governs all production. As the overdeveloped world is hollowed out and its working class cast on the scrapheap, the new ruling class cares less and less about its care and feeding. "Welfare reform" is the first step toward abandoning the state's responsibilities to its people, now that its people need no longer be stabilized and managed as a working class.

The ruling class does not particularly care about "biopolitics" any more.[9] It senses no obligation to maintain the bodies of any particular population as potential recruits for its factories or armies. The revolution in military affairs replaces foot soldiers with pilotless drones, or, when that fails, with mercenaries. When it has used up the labor of a particular region, it can always source more, from somewhere else. In Alex Rivera's movie *Sleep Dealer*, workers from the South labor by telerobotics on the building sites and farms of the North. Meanwhile a pilot from the North shoots at people in the South who try to "steal" from the privatized water supply near their village. The narrative symmetry neatly unfolds the asymmetry of power.

While the new ruling class abandons its responsibilities to the working class, setting it loose as a dispossessed multitude, it cares more and more for quite another aspect of the multitude – its ability to generate what Jean Baudrillard used to call sign value.[10] It needs the restless productivity of the multitude to constantly create and recreate the image and the language of desire – one which it can capture and use as the attractive wrappings for the commodities it has made by the old capitalist method in the underdeveloped world.

The whole of the overdeveloped world becomes a new kind of factory for the production of signs of value and value for signs. New York, London, Paris, Los Angeles – each is a giant shop floor for making art, cinema, fashion, fiction, or philosophy. Each attracts a new kind of tourist, one who works for the privilege of seeing its sights. They come in the thousands, to be models or office assistants, turning whole city blocks into hotels, rented by the month or year rather than the night. Many are not even paid, but work as "interns."[11]

All of the separations that once held – between architecture and the exotic, between public and private, between work and leisure – are in each case effaced by the same development, the coming into being of the vector of telesthesia. It reorganizes space according to its own lights. Where once the portal was subordinated to the wall, now it is entirely the other way around. Space loses its qualities. Everyday life is determined by tempos of movement and relation.

This is hardly a utopian scenario, however. One tension remains, even if in a new form – the class tension of ownership and dispossession. The basis of this new tension is in a multitude coming into being, that overcomes the separation of public and private, work and leisure, and that adds incessant movement to its arsenal of strategies. The struggle for the future moves to a new terrain, leaving behind it, as a charming residue, what was once architecture. Meanwhile, up above, beyond the superstructures, at a metaphorical height reached only by pilotless drones, capital mutates, freeing itself from the ownership of things and fetishizing the control of information. All that was solid state splits into digital bits.

Just walking down the street nowadays is a kind of media archaeology in itself, a tour of the ruins of that media that is architecture, that vector through time. But this gaze through the **transopticon** adheres to the fragments of what passes. It is through the prism of the event that one glimpses the shape of things as they come.

7

Weird Global Media Event and Vectoral Unconscious

Newcastle, Australia

For anyone who is a regular checker of news feeds, one of two things can happen when you check. Usually, most of the news is things you could have predicted in advance. There is a ritual quality to news. It is like saying your prayers to some earthly wannabe god. The god of routine, perhaps. So you check. Stocks go up and down. One political party scores a point off the other. Somebody wins that day's match, and somebody loses. Somebody releases a new product or discovers something. A cat got stuck up a tree. Certain storylines exist in advance, and the facts are inveigled into those they best fit.

Every now and then, there's news of another kind: some raw outbreak of apparent facticity that does not fit any of the templates of news script. Or which could fit more than one, and is undecidable as to which. This can happen on any scale. Sometimes these news anomalies are local and the resolution of the peculiar facticity back into a storyline is local. Sometimes they're not. One of the features of these anomalies at their most intractable is that they seem to traverse the sense of scale in news.

Usually, what is local matters more than what is not. A cat stuck up a tree in your neighborhood is news. We are not terribly concerned with anyone else's cats. If someone gets run over on our block, that's news, but it would take a tsunami of death to make the news from far away. But there are anomalies to this sense of distance and scale in news. TOO UNFIT TO RUN:

TWO-YEAR-OLD WHO SMOKES 40 CIGARETTES A DAY PUFFS AWAY ON A TOY TRUCK.[1] A chain-smoking toddler is news even if he is far away. It's an interesting enough anomaly, and, as we have seen, children are a whole special category of mediated image.

There is another kind of anomaly, what I call the **weird global media event.**[2] Here are two – very different – examples that I would call "local" when I am a New Yorker, and something else when I'm not. The occupation of Wall Street in 2011 was such an event. What we now call "9/11" was such an event. As the mere fact of putting these two examples together hopefully shows the weird global media event as a category is beyond good and evil. It's just something that happens because the vector opens up possibilities for how things can occur.

Take 9/11 as a singular example: it is a *weird* global media event in that at the moment it happens, it appears outside the frame of conventional news narratives, and considerable work is involved in finding the narratives into which it fits. One of the signs of this is that initially a lot more images are shown, but through the iteration of the editing, the image-set winnows down to a more or less stable set. For example, images of "jumpers" from the towers were broadcast, but quickly edited out, as the image repertoire stabilized.

It is a weird *global* media event in the sense that it calls a world into being. It isn't global in the sense that it is of equal importance to everyone. There are probably vast tracts of the world where nobody really paid all that much attention to 3,000 people getting killed in New York City. What is that compared to a tsunami? But it is global in the sense that for some people it does call into being a sensation of the connectedness to a world, even though it does not call the world equally into being for everybody. It is a particular event, yet one which appears to unveil an abstract, connected world. It is a global media event because it calls a world into being. It is a weird global media event because it defies explanation (at least for a while). It subsumes every explanation as mere ripples and eddies in its wake.

It is a weird global *media* event because media, or more broadly speaking the vector, is not something external to it, looking on. That it is mediated is part of the structure of how the event itself unfolds. In the case of 9/11, the hijackers' aim was not just to destroy some buildings and kill the people in them. It was to generate images of this destruction of symbolically charged places.[3]

It is a weird global media *event* in its apparent singularity. It is not an event in the sense of a planned spectacle, like a royal wedding, the Olympic Games, or the annual opening of the UN General Assembly.[4] These could more properly be called conventional planetary media rituals, and are the opposite of weird global media events. Such rituals are staged with a clear set of narrative lines already in place, which can be more or less strictly managed. For instance, the BBC refused to allow its video feeds of the 2011 royal wedding to be used by *The Chaser*, a satirical program broadcast in Australia.[5] The range of acceptable interpretation of such rituals is, officially at least, narrow and defined in advance.

By contrast, the weird global media event always begins in the middle. Something happens for which there is no ready-made story instantly to hand. If only for a few moments, news media has to present the troubling images while it casts about for a story, inventing a beginning and positing an end. In the weird global media event what happens is always contrary to expectation. A new narrative trajectory has to be created to accommodate its singularity, while it is happening. But in the moment when it happens, the weird global media event announces the presence of an unstable, ineffable world – a world immune to interpretation. For an instant, we gape and gasp, confronted with the inexplicable.

Adorno: "The almost insoluble task is to let neither the power of others, nor our own powerlessness, stupefy us."[6] How are we to avoid being stupefied by an event, in which it is not even clear who or what just had the power to do what to whom? By being prepared, when the event happens, not to look at the lightning strike of images; nor to just wait for the thunderclap of explanation.[7] Rather, one looks toward the *horizon* of the event, to see what it illuminates. In the moment of the event, one can see the shape of the space that makes the event possible. One can glimpse the network of *strategic* and *logistic* vectors that create the event space within which any and every event now unfolds. One searches for the narrative horizon abstract enough to explain not just a particular weird global media event, but the abstract space within which any such event is possible.

When I say "September 11," or "9/11," like most New Yorkers I have before me the memory of an event that flashed as lightning in the dark, illuminating the space of the vector. There were the vectors of the planes, guided by air traffic control beacons.[8] There were the vectors of news information, spreading their own debris around the world. Of course, the range of things that "September 11" might signify is itself a cloud of dust, settling differently in one memory to the next, but designating a dispersal of differences, created out of nothing, instantaneously.

Of course this cloud of associations won't last. A lot of people remember where they were on 9/11. A lot of people still remember where they were when President Kennedy was assassinated. That event is in some respects the prototype of the weird global media event. And yet, when talking to students, I sometimes have to explain who Kennedy was and why this event matters. Fewer and fewer people remember. Nobody now remembers the assassination of President Garfield. The whole thing has passed from living memory.

The distribution of people who knew of the assassination of Garfield within, say, 24 hours, would be smaller and more geographically specific than the distribution of people who knew about the assassination of Kennedy. One imagines that in both cases such a map would look like a network, with thick lines joining major centers and smaller ones heading off into the provinces. The maps would both be transnational – these were both significant events – but one imagines the Kennedy assassination was more effectively communicated within the first 24 hours across the globe.

Such a map for 9/11 would stretch around the planet, sending shoots off into many provincial quarters. Including the city of Newcastle, on the east coast of Australia. My father awoke me in the middle of the night, to say he had a phone call from a friend of mine in Iowa, who said he had received a phone call from my partner in New York, saying that she was alive and well – and that I should turn on the news. She had been unable to place an international call, but got through to the Midwest. This might be another effect one could trace on these weird global media event maps: the effect of saturation. The phone lines flooded with calls, most of which could not get through, only adding to uncertainty. When we feel we most need to know about something inexplicable, it is often the case that the vector is jammed with traffic, or even that the collapse of the vector itself is part of the event.

What the vector communicates is unknowable, a cloud of dust. What it is that communicates is knowable, but only in the abstract. At the moment the event happens, most of those within its distant crowd can't know what lies behind the images and stories. There may be pictures of world political leaders, or of wreckage and disaster, of mobs and crowds, or an abandoned child. If the event is economic in nature, the images will be particularly obscure: the predictable pictures of corporate headquarters, or anxious floor traders yelling into phones. These images are meant to signify the fall of a currency or a bank or a once supposedly sound corporation. We cannot know the economy that fascinates those bizarre business news channels, with their scrolling stock quotes, and their experts who narrate the current events seamlessly – provided you don't check up on their predictions. But we can know the nature of a world in which such events are possible.

This is the world of the **vector**. Or more precisely, it is the world of the splitting of the vector into two different speeds. Paradoxically, the revolution of speed, which is the revolution of the vector, is a slow-moving one. The crucial moment of transformation was the development of the telegraph. Since the telegraph, information has moved faster than bodies, faster than commodities, faster than warheads. The Internet is really just a refinement of the telegraph; the telegraph was the "Victorian Internet."[9] Since the telegraph, the vector of information, with its superior speed, creates a geography within which to organize the distribution of people and things. This geography is a space within which all the possibilities for the organization of other spaces come together. It is where objects are brought together with subjects, and where the categories of object and subject exist as real, yet abstract, entities, each **addressable** to the other.

The space of the communication vector emerges as the promise of a space where the contradictions of second nature can be resolved. Second nature here means that space of the material transformation of nature by collective labor. Second nature is a space of a certain modernity: fragmentation, alienation, class struggle. In many ways, the space of the vector really is a third nature, from which the second nature of our built environments can be managed and organized, as a standing reserve, just as second nature treats nature as its "standing reserve."[10]

However, this third nature does not emerge as a rational and transparent space, with a homogeneous and continuous time. It emerges as a chaotic space, an event space. To the chaos of nature, history responded by building a second nature in which to dwell. To the chaos of second nature, history responded with a third nature, which in turn is producing yet more chaos. The angel of history, propelled by the blast of these two historical phases, can no longer look back at a point of origin and observe the disaster. The mounting disaster of the layering of one nature over another presses the angel of history forward into oblivious oblivion. Heiner Müller: "The past surges behind him, pouring rubble on wings and shoulders thundering like buried drums, while in front of him the future collects, crushes his eyes, explodes his eyeballs like a star wrenching the word into a resounding gag, strangling him with its breath."[11]

While it may be hard to perceive temporally, historically, when confronted by the weird global media event, it might be possible to perceive geographically, spatially – to catch an after-image in the retina even of exploded eyeballs left after the lightning flash of the event that shows the contours of its horizon. The weird global media event throws the space of its own possibility into relief, revealing it.

I would contrast this approach with two others, both of which are successful and revealing methods, but both of which appear to me to grasp only part of what this vectoral analysis of the event can discover. One approach is to take seriously the counter-narratives to the officially agreed-upon version that emerges belatedly out of an event. Jodi Dean: "Conspiracy theory is everyday politics."[12] The sources of such counter-narratives, more often than not, are in weird global media events that broke open accepted narratives and had to be stitched back into them after some prevarication. The Kennedy assassination and 9/11 are classic examples of this. While valuable, this approach tends to lose sight of the *evental* quality of media space, its turbulence and unpredictability. While Dean's critical theory does not subscribe to the credulity of the conspiracy theorists, it is inclined to make the leap from event to narrative, without looking closely at the horizon of the event and the structure of the vectoral relations visible in that instant.

Another approach is Jane Bennett's "thing theory".[13] Struck by the seemingly random flotsam she finds one day on top of a drainage grate, Bennett makes the stunning observation that the over-developed world is actually not a materialist culture. If it were, it would not keep generating what Philip K. Dick called "kipple," or the random physical detritus we can find piling up everywhere, in what Rem Koolhas calls "junkspace." Bennett calls then for a politics of things. One of her examples is the blackout that struck much of the North American northeast in 2003. But in laying stress on the agency of things in such an event, she loses sight of the space-time of the event that threads them together. We end up again with an empiricism that can only proceed by complicating any and every claim about an event with the evidence of yet more things and their stubborn complexity.

On the one hand, Dean draws us toward the complexity of narratives; on the other hand, Bennett draws us to the stubborn agency of multiple things. What slips from view in both perspectives is the spatio-temporal envelope within which an event unfolds and becomes known. In both Dean and Bennett, knowledge appears after the event, as if it were not part of the event, and proceeds as if the space and time of knowledge were somehow anterior to that of events.

The vectoral analysis I advocate here is rather one which knows itself to also be caught up in a space and time which is mediated, which has its own patterns of eventfulness, as it were, just of a much slower and more local kind. An old saying has it that news is the first draft of history. Rather, one might say that the first temporality of knowledge is that of news and its struggle with confounding events, while theory is a slower, more owlish time-frame, whose task is not to reify some subjective or objective field out of events but rather to grasp the space-time that makes events possible.

Let's consider events of three particular types. A first type of event is sudden economic turbulence. The global stock-market crash of 1987 was of this type, as was the collapse of the market in mortgage-backed securities in 2008, or the eurozone panic of 2011. Events of this type reveal as their horizon the vectoral logic of "financialization." Alex Callinicos: "financialization means the greater autonomy of the financial sector, the proliferation of financial institutions and instruments, and the integration of a broad range of economic actors into financial markets."[14] The credit economy reaches further and further into everyday life, becoming the means for any and every transaction. Meanwhile everyday debt, such as in real estate, can be aggregated, "securitized," resold, its risks hedged against or insured. A whole economy expands which accumulates, trades, and insures these new classes of commodity. While an economy that makes and sells actual things still exists, the vector vastly accelerates this parallel economy of simulated things.

Official narratives struggle with such events because their central premise is a kind of theology of the market. Actual markets are taken to be more or less perfect copies of the platonic idea of the market. This platonic market is all knowing and all seeing. It perfectly prices everything and hence everything is allocated as a resource with perfect efficiency. Crises can only be the result of the imperfect form of actual markets, for the platonic form of the market knows no flaws. That economic theory has known since Kenneth Arrow that even theoretically perfect markets can arrive at sub-optimal allocations of resources is neither here nor there.[15]

Third nature becomes a landscape, an environment, visible only interstitially, when it produces weird events. It is a realm with a peculiar geography all its own, and even its own weather system, which obeys strange laws that are only partly understood. Knowledge of its actual workings is hindered by certain beliefs about it which – whether intentionally or not – mask its actual tendencies. The platonic myth of the market is one such belief; the liberal notion of the public sphere may well be another. Its actual history pokes out through the fabric of these myths whenever the event befalls it, revealing not only some of its contours, but even something of the power struggle over the command and control of third nature itself.

A political economy of crises plays an important role in crafting counter-narratives. To the extent that political economy is a real social science, it might even predict them.[16] The role of a vectoral analysis is a bit different. With this kind of weird global media event, it might be looking toward the horizon of the event for a snapshot of the increasing intensity of the penetration of the vectoral mesh of financial transactions into all aspects of everyday life, on one side, and the aggregation of those particular instances of financialization at greater and greater scales into a third nature, which then creates a whole panoply of new kinds of property out of those particulars which become the stock in trade of a whole new kind of economy. Financialization means the appearance of a new class of things, things which exist only as abstractions, as instruments, but which can be traded as if they were the title to actual things. Our aim might be to begin a **thin description** of the aesthetic economy within which such things can exist and have effects.

The mortgage securities crisis of 2008 revealed the horizon of this financialization to be a rocky terrain. Banks no longer hold mortgages; they bundle and sell them. If the bank doesn't hold the mortgage itself, then what interest does it have in the likelihood of a default? And what if the bank does not even bundle the mortgages itself but contracts with a third party to do it? What if, knowing that there are risks in such securities, both buyer and seller resorted to another third party to rate its quality? What if that third party were paid for this service by the seller? What if the buyer tried to hedge its risk in buying these assets by insuring them with another financial firm that relied on the same ratings agencies? What if the insuring firm also hedged, or on-sold, a bundle of such assets, etc? What if the bank selling mortgage securities as a service to its clients also traded on its own account and bet against the quality of such assets? Fun and games are sure to ensue. Particularly given that markets may not be all that inherently perfectible, and even if they were, not much perfection is likely to result if what the market trades in are things of this peculiar, non-existent nature.

The horizon that repeated financial crises reveals is one in which third nature, far from correcting the faults of second nature, only makes them worse; and then adds new kinds of chaotic and turbulent behavior of its own making. This in turn will generate narratives about the need to reform the said financial world, and much perplexity as to why it seems resistant to such a notion. This will generate counter-narratives about the evils of "Wall Street," which in Dean's terms come close to a popular critical sensibility, however crude and paranoid. A sign on Occupy Wall Street in 2011 sums up this sensibility nicely: SHIT IS FUCKED UP AND BULLSHIT.

Weird global media events of the financial type might reveal a pattern of development of the vector, and the struggle over the narrative resolution of the weirdness of the event might reveal – if only in negative, as the dark matter of the vectoral universe – the current qualities of at least part of its ruling class. What if the ruling class of our time were not exactly capitalist any more, but more properly vectoralist? What if a fraction of that ruling class acquired its political–economic power through the ownership and control of vectors along which financial information flows, and with it the flows of that information, not to mention stocks of these weird para-things, these instruments of a purely digital private property, with somewhat attenuated relations back to referents in other natures, other worlds?

Let's bracket this question of the vectoralist ruling class for a moment, and consider two other kinds of events besides financial ones, and the horizon they might reveal. The second type of event might be imagined as the strategic surprise: 9/11 fits this category, but so too does an otherwise very different kind of event, the "Arab spring" of 2011, which led to the apparently successful overthrow of the Egyptian and Tunisian regimes. Events of the this type reveal the extent to which strategy becomes vec-toral. Both state and non-state actors have recourse to forms of power in which the vector connects the very local to the very global without intervening layers. A pilotless drone aircraft can be deployed in Afghanistan or Iraq from American bases in these regions, but piloted from a secure facility in Nevada. A social movement can mobilize crowds loosely cemented to it via social media, while the state's secret police use the same social media to spy on them and circulate disinformation. The proliferation of vectoral space multiplies the number of possible lines of force. This was the lesson of 9/11. Such events reveal the contours of a *strategy-space*.

There is a third type of event, however, and it might illuminate a quite different kind of horizon. It all started with a two-year-old taken to a Sydney hospital in a coma, who suffered from seizures and spasms. After checking a urine sample, Dr Kevin Carpenter of Westmead Hospital identified the cause of the toddler's condition as GHB, or Gamma Hydroxybutyric Acid. While GHB is a naturally occurring substance, which sometimes accumulates in the body because of certain medical conditions, it is also synthesized for use as a party drug. Dr Carpenter suspected that the child had taken drugs.

The child vomited up colored beads while under the effects of the drug. Dr Carpenter tested these in a mass spectrometer. This revealed the presence of a chemical compound he did not recognize. It turned out to be an industrial chemical used to keep water-soluble glues from getting sticky. When ingested, this chemical breaks down into GHB. Its use is strictly controlled in many countries. The distributor of the toy beads knew nothing of this, and referred Carpenter to the manufacturer, who in turn refused to answer questions from anybody. Once Carpenter had confirmed the cause and alerted the authorities, a worldwide recall commenced, along with a worldwide media panic.[17]

While hardly on the same scale, this is a weird global media event in a minor key, which reveals certain qualities of the vector. A child admitted to a hospital can trigger all kinds of protocols designed to detect vectors, not just of disease but of intentional harm. (The one place "biopolitics" is still a valid concept in the overdeveloped world would appear to be the biological and psychological integrity of children as a population.) Fortunately, Dr Carpenter was thorough, and suspicions about the parents and drugs quickly abated.

The mass spectrometer provided evidence of manufacturing malpractice that the arm's-length relation of the distributor with the manufacturer along the supply chain would otherwise conceal. A global media event of some modest scale ensued, which had panicky parents and caregivers scooping up craft beads kits and consigning them to the dustbin. This third type of event might be considered a crisis of logistics. Something breaks down in the vectoral chain by which things are managed, revealing the contours of a *commodity-space*.

In Gary Shteyngart's novel *Super Sad True Love Story*, end-of-an-era New York offers only two kinds of persona for anyone who counts: you can work in Credit or in Media. Failing that, there's always Retail. Meanwhile private armies quietly take over from the police and the army.[18] In the novel, men work in Credit; women in Retail. Media is more or less split between them. Anyone outside of these occupations becomes invisible in social space.

That might not be a bad comic map of what labor in the overdeveloped world, or at least in its glittering capitals, has come to.

Between them Media and Credit are how the labors of third nature are experienced. The labors of second nature are reduced to Retail, as things to do with actual production are sequestered in invisible cracks in the fabric of the city, or at the end of lengthy supply chains, stretching into a vast elsewhere. Meanwhile what used to be "nature," a domain external to the human labor on which it depends, becomes present within the space of the vectoral only as a space of strategic calculation and management.

In Shteyngart's novel, the glamorous worlds of Credit and Media elude his characters. The nameless forces of a privatized military control their fates, even as they "message" each other endlessly about the various merits of this or that piece of brand-name lingerie offered up by the all-enveloping world of online shopping and the boutiques that line the tourist-filled avenues of New York City. In short, commodity-space dominates their perception, even as an underlying strategy-space soon reveals itself in the course of events. Meanwhile the glamorous worlds of Media and Credit are both all-pervasive and perennially out of reach.

The United States has been through a period under President Clinton in which the interests of those in control of vectors of commodity-space dominated; and then through a period under President W. Bush in which the interests of strategy-space dominated. Both phases are developments of the same vectoral forces. In both cases, power resides more and more in control of the vector. The conflict between these two developments is less important than the fact that they stem from the same history – the emergence and enrichment of a third nature, through which not just nature but second nature appear as standing reserves, as objects cut from the scene. To the vector, the spoils.

President Obama represented no real break with the tendencies of his predecessors. The powers of the strategic vector were stretched to the limit by simultaneous wars in Iraq and Afghanistan, and not without consequences. This allowed the Russians to put pressure on Georgia. A rather stretched America was unable to offer much assistance to its new ally. Obama tried to wind down American involvement in Iraq and to find ways to limit its commitment of forces to Afghanistan. When civil war broke out in Libya he used American vectoral power to seek opportunistic advances there. The deployment of the strategic vector remained much the same, even if its rhetorical cover changed.

In the United States, the ruling class may no longer even be described as exclusively capitalist. It is becoming vectoralist. The power of the **vectoralist class** resides in the command of three things. First: the vector itself, which means on the one hand, the infrastructure of communication across space, but also that other dimension of the vector, communication across time. The archival storage and retrieval of information is itself a vector. Both dimensions are essentially about addressability. The historical development of the vector is among other things the refinement of addressable space. When I can instantly call up information in Newcastle, Australia, about events in New York, or histories of the Middle East, that is a whole series of kinds of addressability at work.

Second: the power of the vectoralist class also resides in the ownership of various chunks of the information communicated across space and time. This is also split along diverging lines. What is owned may be qualitative, in the form of intellectual property. Or it may be essentially quantitative, in the form of a financial instrument. Neither of these aspects of vectoral power means much without the capacity to mobilize it, either across space or time. On the other hand, owning the means of communicating information across space and time is not particularly valuable unless that communication has become the locus of power. Hence the vectoral class is invested, in every sense of the word, in this dual aspect of the vector as power: in movement between addresses, and also information packaged as discrete things that can be identified, valued, traded, and stored.

Third: vectoral power also takes the form of flows of information, or in the timeliness of information. Just as the logistics of supplying food in commodity-space involves both dry goods and fresh produce, so too third nature involves both durable and perishable information. Fresh information can become harder and harder to come by. News Corporation found itself involved in a whole series of scandals in 2011 when it was alleged that its journalists and editors were implicated in "phone hacking." By tapping the cellphones of people in the news, they obtained tips for stories before anyone else had them.[19] While this event might say something about the ethical standards of Rupert Murdoch's empire, it might also say something about the difficulties of building a business on the speed of information flows.

The power of the vectoral class rests on these three components: on the vector itself as infrastructure; on stocks of information; and, third, on the flows of information that populate it. The vectoral class itself combines these three powers in three different ways to produce power over three different kinds of terrain, and as a result different kinds of class interest. These interests are then coordinated – or not – by emerging kinds of state formation.

The first kind of vectoral power seeks control over the terrain of third nature itself. By securing the "high ground" of the information vector, it controls the space of possibilities for exercising power not only over second nature but over nature itself. Vectoral power as power over third nature takes two forms, and we could even call them Credit and Media. They are respectively control over quantitative and qualitative signaling.

A second kind of vectoral power deploys a sophisticated logistics to control the articulation and movement of things in space. Or, in short, it aims to control second nature as a commodity-space. This also has qualitative and quantitative aspects. A firm like Walmart specializes in quantitative logistics. It succeeds by squeezing costs out of the supply chain. On the other hand, there are firms that, while no doubt attentive to this, are more dependent on managing the poetic aura of brands. They manage the economizing of desire rather than the desire for economizing.

A third kind of vectoral power manages "nature." This nature has to be understood not as a pre-existing domain, but as that which comes to be perceived retrospectively as the hinterland to the processes of extraction and labor by which it is known and instrumentalized. To a man with a hammer, everything looks like a nail. To a pilotless drone, everything looks like a potential target. To a company with the technology to extract natural gas through "fracking," any piece of land looks like a potential gas deposit, even if it is in a watershed. Here again there are two aspects: on the one hand, nature appears as a geopolitics. The terrain has qualitative features that make it more or less easy to defend or seize territory. On the other hand, the terrain is the skin under which lie resources, quantifiable assets, ranging from oil and gas to rare earths or potable water.

Both of these aspects of nature appear now as constraints on third nature as a terrain of infinite geometric variability. Quite particular kinds of vectoral power try to manage the gap between nature's stubborn determinacy and third nature's pliability. This requires the investment of huge amounts of resources, whether in pipelines or drones. Either way the deployment of these assets is increasingly subordinated to vectoral powers of command and control. The existence of future resources becomes a mathematical probability. The future of strategy, for good or ill, is subject to the "revolution in military affairs."[20]

As I write this, I watch ships come and go from Newcastle Harbor, while a jet fighter from nearby Williamstown airbase roars overhead. Its power is quite useless against the "threat" that consumes the news feeds – tiny boats carrying impoverished or brutalized people to Australia's vast and sparsely populated shores. Oceans are still vast enough for multitudes to make their perilous way across them.

The military–industrial complex of the cold war era has been replaced, not by a juridical empire of global law and trade, but by a new formation, a **military–entertainment complex**.[21] Two aspects of this empire, its commodity-space and strategy-space, overlap and contradict one another. Both are driven by the same imperative – the vectoralization of the world. The vector is what produces the world as such, as a space of property and strategy, a plane upon which things are identified, evaluated, commanded. This new complex is partly anchored in the United States, but is not identical to it. It is, if anything, what is tearing the United States apart. The stress of this complex upon the fabric of American democracy and society is what prevents it from becoming, if you will, a "normal" state.

The military–entertainment complex forces Europe into a Union that can both manage and contain its own vectoralization. It also creates for itself the perfect double, the perfect enemy.[22] Al-Quaeda was a perfect and necessary enemy, in that it stood for opposition to all factions of vectoral power simultaneously. It attacked its most potent symbols: the Pentagon and the World Trade Center. It exploited the hunger of the news feeds against themselves.

These are precarious times, eventful times – not least for the forces that would oppose both the military–entertainment complex and its violent adversaries. Before 9/11, it seemed to some as if power of the vectoral class took a juridical form, to be confronted by a movement that addressed its highest councils of global coordination, such as the World Trade Organization. After 9/11, some argued that one confronts the old American imperial regime, ever willing to shed blood for oil. Neither diagnosis was quite correct. The becoming-vectoral of power was never just a matter of the globalization of trade and its consequences. Nor is it the case that there is a simple continuum between the imperial military adventures of the past and the emerging strategy-space.

Third nature often appears in the guise of a technical solution to what are otherwise political–economic problems. The contradictions of second nature were meant to be resolved by the intensification of third nature. The contradictions of third nature are supposed to be resolved by pushing third nature even further, or perhaps by layering further natures, one over the other, each compensating for the other. Financialization's eccentricities will be resolved by computerized trading at the speed of light. Security will be guaranteed by automating face-recognition, or by pilotless drones on autopilot, programmed to attack based on their own autonomous algorithms without recourse to a human controller.[23] What the last generation of Apple product failed to fix will be overcome with the next release, coming to a store near you soon.

But one has to ask in all seriousness, in the lightning flash of the event, whether this is the horizon that is revealed, or whether it is something altogether more comical. Matt Taibbi:

> What has taken place over the last generation is a highly complicated merger of crime and policy, of stealing and government. Far from taking care of the rest of us, the financial leaders of America and their political servants have seemingly reached the cynical conclusion that our society is not worth saving and have taken on a new mission that involves not creating wealth for all, but simply absconding with whatever wealth remains in our hollowed out economy. They don't feed us, we feed them.[24]

One cannot confront a vectoral power by renouncing the use of the vector. It is getting harder for multitudes to flee. When they manage it the method is usually molecular and dispersed. In any case the mobility of the multitudes always presupposes a vector along which to organize its flight. There is nothing outside the vector. Rather, it is a question of using the vector otherwise. It is a question of using the vector as a trajectory for the creation of an open plane upon which difference is possible on its own terms, rather than as an equivalence based in calculations of strategy or property. The space of the event need not be equivalent to the space of the disaster. It is not necessarily a question of confronting the military–entertainment complex, so much as of escaping it. It is not a question of resisting an imminent apocalypse in the name of nostalgia for a pre-vectoral past, so much as of constructing a present that escapes the logic of a destructive history.

Media artist Ricardo Dominguez found himself at the center of a media storm for the Transborder Immigrant Tool, an app for cellphones which could enable people attempting to cross the US–Mexico border to find sources of water.[25] He headed a team at the University of California San Diego that built the app, which also included poems to make new arrivals feel welcome. It is a brilliant example of the vectoral deployed in the interests of the multitude, and for its molecular trickle across a dangerous geo-strategic barrier. As far as "phone hacking" is concerned, this surely is a more vital example than that practiced by News Corporation. The vector, imagined outside the space of property, outside of the interests of the vectoral class, opens up other potentials to those revealed by the weird global media event. The perspective on third nature and its spaces of potentials revealed by the event can also be the subject of an experimental practice. There is more than one way to discover the contours of the vectoral unconscious.

8

Securing Security

Berlin, Germany

How one forgets! What was the creed for which the Allies supposedly fought in World War II? Who remembers the Four Freedoms? They were these: (1) Freedom of religion; (2) Freedom of speech; (3) Freedom from want; and (4) Freedom from fear. Only now, in what was formerly the United States, perhaps the demand could be for four new freedoms: (1) Freedom from religion; (2) Freedom from speeches; (3) Freedom from desire; and (4) Freedom from security. Of these four demands, at present I will take up only the last. What is the basis of security? What secures security? Its absence. Insecurity secures the necessity for security. The threat to security is – oddly enough – security itself. We have nothing to secure but security itself.

States act in the name of security – but what could be more Orwellian? The security state is an engine of violence. What secures the state is the production of insecurity. Preferably of a kind that is manageable. Insecurity getting out of hand every now and then is not the worst thing. For the state, it's good for business. As the American GIs used to inscribe on their Zippo lighters: "death is our business, and business is good."[1]

What is really threatening to the security state is the prospect of peace. From this point of view, the implosion of the Soviet bloc was a disaster. People really started to think about dismantling the security apparatus in the United States. There was talk of a "peace dividend." Thankfully, insecurity returned to the scene and all is well for the stock holders of the **military–entertainment complex**. Threats appear to abound, and their existence creates the appearance of necessity for the military apparatus, and the necessity of appearances for the entertainment apparatus.

The military–entertainment complex is not quite the same as the former military–industrial complex. Its infrastructure is not so much mechanical as digital. Where did this military–entertainment complex come from? The military–industrial complex produced ever faster, ever more complex machines for human warfare and welfare; so fast and so complex that they called into being whole new problems in surveillance and intelligence, planning and command. The military–industrial complex struggled to secure for itself a second nature. It transformed nature into second nature, into a world that could act as the object of an instrument, a "standing reserve." But this act of transforming the world piecemeal into objects creates a supplementary problem – the problem of the relationships of these instruments to each other.

Work on these problems calls into being, initially as a supplement, the digital as a technological effect. Computing meets communication and simulation. But eventually, these technologies no longer supplement the world of the machine; they control every aspect of it. Control becomes a matter not just of the management of bodies and their wants, but a more subtle business of extracting the required salience from components of the human, wired in increasingly segmented ways into components of the digital. The mobilizing force is not biopower but what Bernard Stiegler calls "psychopower."[2] Thus, not a military–industrial but a military–entertainment complex, not the world made over as a second nature but the world made over as a third nature.

The digital embraces not just logistics and command, but also fantasy and poetics. The work of the military–entertainment complex is two-sided. It has its rational, logistical side; but it also has its romantic, imaginative side. The latter invents reasons for the former to exist. Insecurities cannot simply be taken as given. That's no way to build a growth industry! They have to be fabricated out of whole cloth. Conrad Becker: "With hindsight, whole empires could turn out to be the product of cultural engineering."[3]

The rise of the military–entertainment complex is the mark of a society in decline. The United States is no longer a sovereign state. It has been cannibalized by its own ruling class. They are stripping its social fabric bare. They have allowed its once mighty industrial complex to crumble, and not as "creative destruction" – more like destructive destruction.[4] There's nothing left but to loot the state, abolish taxes on wealth, and move all essential components of the production process elsewhere. It's what Virilio, in a rare quasi-Marxist moment, called "endo-colonization," where the state treats its own population as a colonial one, rather than a population in some occupied territory elsewhere.[5]

From now on, what was once the United States lives on whatever rents it can extract from an unwilling world. It has only two exports: security and desire. First, the military–entertainment complex constructs a purely negative imaginary of what one might not want: security from nature's natural tendency to not give us what we want. Security appears at least to stabilize a bubble in space and time in which to exist, if merely to exist. Second, the other export industry of the United States is the presenting, in fungible form, of the promise of an elsewhere. Having with the one hand secured the bubble, with the other the military–entertainment complex punctures that bubble itself with its offerings of what can be desired, which are always fragments of an elsewhere.

Residents of the Hollywood Hills of Los Angeles are irate about the influx of tourists, traipsing up their winding streets, blocking traffic, leaving their cigarette butts everywhere. What brings them up these far from picturesque streets? The chance to see the famous HOLLYWOOD sign. What steers their steps through this unmarked maze? Their handheld GPS.[6] The most photographed sign in America: they like to have their pictures taken under it. The GPS provides a vector into a sign that can only be a vector out to nowhere. It's not like having your picture taken at the Taj Mahal or even the Empire State Building. While such attractions are signs they are surely also more than signs. The HOLLYWOOD sign is just a sign, a funny-shaped, blank white screen for desires, upon which it is possible to project oneself, thanks to the marvels of GPS.

The blank HOLLYWOOD sign is like a lawyer's contract. The military–entertainment complex has declared not only all present desires but all future ones to be its private property. Your culture does not belong to you. You will have to rent back your own unconscious. Unable to compete with others in an open market, the United States finds itself reliant on force and the threat of force to find new ways to expand. Iraq may be in part about oil, but it is also about the contracts to rebuild everything destroyed by the last decade of sanctions and war.[7]

In short, the military–entertainment complex has entered into a vicious cycle. It imagines threats so that violence may be unleashed against them, thereby producing the cause after the fact. Which came first: security or insecurity? Which came first: the chicken or the egg? McLuhan: "from the egg's point of view, a chicken is just a way to get more eggs."[8] We might similarly say that from security's point of view, insecurity is just a way to produce more security. It is just a way-station in the self-repro-duction of security.

Yes, I know: the planes that crashed into the World Trade Center were real. And so was Osama Bin Laden. But who called him into being, and why? Perhaps it was the Pakistani secret police, perhaps it was the CIA, perhaps it was Saudi Wahhabis. He was once an agent (however marginal) for the subversion of Soviet control of Afghanistan. Who imagined that this man was a threat to American interests, and why?

Debord: "The goal of the integrated spectacle is to turn revo-lutionaries into secret agents and secret agents into revolutionar-ies."[9] This prophetic statement tells us a lot about what transpired around the year 1989, not least in East Germany. It may even apply to events in the Ukraine in 2004.[10] It perfectly describes Allawi, Chalabi, and various other sockpuppets that populated the chat show formerly known as CNN during the salad days of the American occupation of Iraq. The integrated spectacle, or what I would call the military–entertainment complex, is a pro-ducer of a continuous, non-dialectical relation between security and insecurity. They are essentially the same concept. Security produces sameness out of itself.

There is a complication. What security really fears are the people it claims to secure. It fears their desire for peace. Security has to produce insecurity without to secure its own interior. David Harvey: "The evil enemy without became the prime force through which to exorcise or tame the devils lurking within."[11] Hence the charade of Iraqi parliamentary politics during the American occu-pation. On second thoughts we might update and amend Debord:

the goal of the military–entertainment complex is to turn mercenaries into patriots and patriots into mercenaries.

The devil lurking within the United States is, if anything, a
people completely indifferent to the security state that rules over
them. After the end of the cold war, people began to question its
necessity. That this questioning was best channeled by the right,
by Newt Gingrich's Contract on America and its Tea Party suc-
cessors, is an index of how compromised the Democratic Party
was by the military–entertainment complex and the manufacture
of insecurity for security's sake.

The Owl of Minerva flies at dusk: we talk now of "homeland
security," precisely because it is disappearing in the most basic
political–economic sense. It's not so much that what was once an
American's job is now in India or China, but that it could be. The
power of the vectoralist class is a power of logistics, of imagining
and ordering a world of information, a third nature, which orders
a world of things, a second nature, which orders what was once
a natural world – somewhere. In the age of telesthesia, the homeland of desires is always escaping from the envelope that would
secure it in place. Each tourist who comes to be photographed
under the HOLLYWOOD sign takes the picture of that sign away
with them. It belongs to them wherever they are.

What is the relation between the rise of the vectoralist class and
the transformation of the military–industrial complex into the
military–entertainment complex? It is both agent and beneficiary.
One notices, even while the United States is using an old-fashioned
army to occupy a country, that the so-called "revolution in military affairs" is proceeding apace. Every ruling class imagines military power in its own image. The vectoralist class is no exception.
It imagines warfare as third nature, as a video game of data management in realtime.

Afghanistan once ruled the fertile plains of Kashmir and Pesha-
war, but since it lost them it hasn't really had the means to support
itself. Only about 2 percent of the place is arable, and somewhat
more will support sheep.[12] Not that anyone really knows. It's not
somewhere about which there are reliable statistics. But it has been
a country at war or civil war for 30 years, wars that have killed
a million of its people. Not that things were all that great when
it was still ruled by kings. The king relied on the loyalty of the
great landowners, who squeezed the peasants and feuded with

each other, but also provided some minimum of order. Neither the landowners nor the king had any great interest in development, as this would have undermined their power. It was an economy based on a peasantry whose surplus was commandeered to support a pastoralist ruling class.

The king was deposed; the king's deposer was deposed. The communists took over in a coup. Then they too feuded with each other. They tried to impose a top-down reform of both village social life and property relations. Islam became a rallying point for resistance. The Americans and Pakistan took advantage of it to further destabilize a border state to the Soviet Union. The Soviets invaded it. The old pastoralist ruling class fled and their place was taken by resistance leaders, who became the new pastoralist class. With the Soviets in retreat, the rival factions could not cobble together a state. The Taliban, using soldiers recruited from refugee camps, at least brought some semblance of government to the Pashtun half of the country.

That they sheltered Osama Bin Laden became something of an embarrassment after 9/11, but they could hardly give him up. Nor could the Americans mount another invasion after their war in Iraq, so they fought another war in Afghanistan through proxies at first, but ended up colonizing the place. This might have been tolerated had they brought justice, food, development, or at least refrained from air strikes. That not being the case, the Afghans rose up against the Americans as they had against the Russians, not to mention the British, in what might be numbered the fifth Afghan war. What remains is a desperately poor economy of mostly peasants and shepherds, oppressed by a new pastoralist ruling class, no better than the old ones and probably worse. This ruling class props up a notional national government, which, as in the past, has no reason to want to change the situation all that much.

Why would the United States spend ridiculous amounts of time, lives, and money trying to keep a hold on this impoverished place? It has no oil or natural gas. But it is a convenient place through which to run pipelines from places that do. Hence the attempt to secure it, and the insecurity it has produced. Afghans shoot at Americans, so Americans call in air strikes, which might kill the "bad guys" along with everyone in the vicinity. It's a vectoral war, but one of surpassing crudeness. The Americans don't know where the enemy is or who the enemy is at any given moment, and in any case it has made enemies of most of the population.

This might at first seem unrelated to the release of the Kindle Fire by Amazon. As of 2011, Amazon was number 78 in the *Fortune* 500 roster of leading American companies. It grew from an online bookstore to an Internet retail giant, not to mention moving into webhosting and other vectoral services. Seeing the writing on the wall, as it were, for its book sales, Amazon came up with an eReader which integrated seamlessly into its online retail store. In 2011 it released the Kindle Fire, which challenged Apple's iPad as a gateway device (or gateway drug) to the audio-visual products its website sold. One feature of the Fire browser with which it shipped was that Amazon's "cloud" would do some of the computing for you before displaying your chosen websites on your Kindle. One of the curious side benefits of this is that Amazon would then reap a rich harvest of data about pretty much everything you were doing on the Internet.

Amazon took a leaf from Google's (e)book, and saw the virtues in offering, if not a free service, then at least a cheap device in exchange for potentially acquiring datasets with which to fuel not just its marketing but its whole corporate logistics. Companies like Google and Amazon could potentially track your movements, your purchases, your social networks, your communications, and come up with a quite sophisticated picture of you as a bundle of actions and desires.

This, in a word, is security in the overdeveloped world. The vectoral class has secured your data. This is usually discussed under the rubric of "privacy," as if that ship hadn't sailed. These companies are generally careful about securing the data they have about you (and not least from you). They don't want to lose access to that data. Nor do they particularly want to share it with other companies, even if they are clients. It's not really about the private in relation to the public, as neither domain can really be said to exist in the traditional way. It is about securing information within the space of the company with which to grow the company. It is about intelligence.

Intelligence is what Amazon and Afghanistan have in common. What is different is the refinement and subtlety of that information and the kind of vectoral power that can be built on top of it. In Afghanistan, intelligence means knowing the coordinates of a nest of snipers who just shot and killed an American serviceman, and ordering in an air strike to strafe them within minutes. In the overdeveloped world, it's considerably more subtle. Your interest in purchasing bondage porn novels is a piece of data that can be used to predict that you might be interested in bondage leather gear, and these can then be "recommended" to you. Or perhaps it will come to tracking, not just purchases, but which websites you frequent, and so the bondage novel you bought might have been recommended based on your viewing habits, or by keywords in your email.

It is not that vectoral businesses have any interest in invading your privacy and telling the world you have a thing for bondage. The only privacy being invaded is your privacy from yourself, your temporal privacy. You might not want to be reminded, when setting up your laptop to make a business presentation, of certain things in your recent search history. It might seem far removed from shooting Afghan peasants, and in many ways it is, but in one way it's not. These are two sides to vectoral power in its intensive and extensive forms. These are two degrees of resolution of the **transopticon.**

And so: we confront a rising form of power, based on a new class formation, which nevertheless is a decadent one. How is one to confront it? Or perhaps better, escape it. Giorgio Agamben: "In the final analysis the state can recognize any claim for identity . . . But what the state cannot tolerate in any way is that singularities form a community without claiming an identity, that human beings co-belong without a representable condition of belonging."[13] That perhaps might describe a strategy for playing the game of everyday life, in the age of third nature, under the reign of the military–entertainment complex, animated by the power of the vectoralist class, under cover of the ideology of "security."

A man in a mask holds up a sign that says THE BEGINNING IS NEAR. He wears what would be instantly recognizable, at least to a movie-going public, as a Guy Fawkes mask, from the movie *V for Vendetta*, based on a popular comic. These masks are popular for a certain strain of anonymous occupation of public spaces, a pop technique for what Agamben describes as not claiming an identity – even if the producers of the movie collect a few cents royalty on every mass-produced mask. They are a sort of blank persona, a community without identity, but one which gestures to the same pop references.

To speak of a multitude, or even of classes, is to highlight the subjective element within the social formation, at the expense of that element which is inhuman, or non-human, and within which the human is embedded. It is to avoid the systematic character of the development of third nature, which produces, among other things, the conditions of possibility for a new kind of ruling class, and the conditions of possibility for new kinds of multitude. The peculiar properties of the third nature need some kind of attention, which calls for some kind of method.

Here are three methods. The first, which I tried out in the early chapters, is a psychogeography of the vector, created by wandering along the antipodal lines of third nature. The second, to which I then turned, was the weird global media event, which reveals the contours of third nature in the lightning flash of its occurrence. Now I want to propose a third method, that of identifying new kinds of persona, or **interface**. These appear at first glance to be kinds of "person," but these faces are not entirely human. They don't have the qualities of interiority of the characters in a good novel. What is of interest is not their "inside" but their relation to an outside. Hence they are not faces but interfaces.

Through what forms of life can particular aspects of the everyday be experienced and made meaningful to those who inhabit them? How, in particular, can the non-human aspects of the everyday be grasped subjectively? The interfaces of particular interest, then, are not those which deal with the subjective self-understanding of the subject in relation to others from which it differs or with which it claims an identity. Rather, we might look to some other interfaces, which are ways of presenting the subject's implication with objects.

One such interface might be a way of returning us to the question of security in another light, namely, the interface of the **gamer**. There might be four ways in which to construct a persona in relation to third nature, as both abstract terrain and as intimate, everyday experience. Of the other three, more later. The interface of the gamer might be the one in which the world as perceived as one of the calculation of risk and assessment of resources, in short of securing an identity against threats, might most consistently express itself.

Before turning to interface, and in particular the gamer interface, perhaps a word or two on the question of game and play. Critical theory may have its roots in, for example, Lukács' understanding of literature, and may have extended itself in the hands of Adorno and Lefebvre toward cinema and everyday life, but it has had less to say about games. Both Adorno and Lefebvre have interesting things to say in the margin about play and games, but in neither case are these forms central to their argument. The transformation of games from residual to possibly even dominant cultural forms calls for a reappraisal of the concepts of play and game.

9

Game and Play in Everyday Life

Gijón, Spain

"Has Your Life Become a Game of Chance?" This is a headline I found once in *Time* magazine. The story begins: "The people in Washington have turned your life into a series of spins of the wheel that begin with day care and end with retirement . . . Washington has structured the game just as any gambling house would, so there are few winners but a lot more losers."[1] This is just the first in a long series I could assemble of instances in which we talk about life as if it had become a game. These days, the game is everywhere and nowhere, overflowing the special times and places that once defined it as a game.

Take for instance the sustained popularity of "reality TV" shows, where reality is presented as if it were a game. On *Average Joe*, regular guys compete against each other, and then against "hunks," for the affections of a cheerleader. On *The Apprentice*, entrepreneurs and B-school types compete to be Donald Trump's minion. As Breton and Cohen write: "By manufacturing game-worlds into which they slot their non-actor casts, creating pressurized and untested environments, where people are manipulated in cruel and extreme ways and begin to display the confusion and loss of perspective of the incarcerated, these productions use their power without adequate or sufficiently transparent checks and safeguards."[2] That sounds like a description of everyday life.

Warfare seems more and more like a game. In his memoir of the first Gulf War, General Schwarzkopf tells the story about running simulations of the war before it began, using, as it turns out, the same commercial simulation software as the Iraqis. The simulations continued after Operation Desert Shield commenced. Schwarzkopf recounts having the communiqués labels "actual" and "simulation" so that he and his staff could tell them apart.[3]

Of course, theory seems more and more of a game. Just as athletes have their signature moves, so too does Slavoj Žižek. His opening move for playing the theory game is to flip conventional wisdom over and read it backwards. Here's an example:

> It is . . . not the fantasy of a purely aseptic war run as a video game behind computer screens that protects us from the reality of the face-to-face killing of another person; on the contrary, it is this fantasy of a face-to-face encounter with an enemy killed bloodily that we construct in order to escape the Real of the depersonalized war turned into an anonymous technological operation.[4]

I think he has something there, but the Žižekian move can just as easily be applied to what theorists do. It is not the fantasy of theory as just a language game that protects it from doing real work on real stuff; it is the fantasy of real work and real stuff that protects us from the Real that scholarship is just a language game. And so: everything appears as if it were a game – everyday life, working life, warfare, knowledge, perhaps even love. And when we fail at any of these relentless, zero-sum competitions, we can flee to Vegas, and put our trust in another kind of game, where luck rather than competition rules.

These experiences seem disturbingly like Georges Perec's dystopian novel *W*.[5] This book is a memoir of Perec's childhood, hiding from the Nazis, within which he also reconstructs his childhood fantasy of a seemingly utopian island called W, which is organized around a complete devotion to an Olympic spirit of sporting competition. As Perec's account of W unfolds, we discover more and more of a dark side to its Olympian ideals. W's athletes compete not to win but to live. W seems less and less to describe the logic of games, but more of the camps, both of which in Perec's book end up being the same thing. If one is worth nothing more than one's rank against a competitor, one is eventually worth nothing. The competitive life is a living death.

The critical literature on games is not very extensive, and indeed, Perec's novel is better than some. On the theory front, there are four classics worth mentioning. Two of them are Johan Huizinga's *Homo Ludens*, and Roger Caillois' *Man, Play and Games*, both rather eccentric books. The third and fourth, even stranger, I will come back to later. From Huizinga we might take the idea that play is the primary category. While games formalize and regulate play, they may also reduce it to repetition. Games may be play in its decadent form.

From Caillois we may take the idea that there are different types of games. He offers a four-part classification: *agon, alea, mimesis,* and *ilinx,* or: games of competition, of luck, of make-believe, and of vertigo. Writing in the context of postwar reconstruction, Caillois has a strong preference for *agon* and *alea,* and sees *mimesis* and *ilinx* as dangerous forms of the play because they lack strong rules and limits. For Caillois, the roots of fascism are in play without limits. In our time, a world made up of games of *agon* and *alea* seems actually to have been realized, but in a somewhat uneven fashion. For the emerging ruling class, the game is *agon,* a competition. For the rest of us, it is *alea,* as the *Time* article suggests. We play a game we cannot master, never quite knowing the rules.

This critical preference of Caillois for the strongly rule-bound game over the free and open play was reversed in the sixties. In the United States, the New Games movement produced games of minimal rules aimed at creating cooperative play. *Earthball* would be a perfect example. Bernard DeKoven came up with the idea of the well-played game. Even competitive games only work if the players cooperate on playing well. DeKoven: "Playing well has to be the general state."[6]

In Europe, a more sustained critique emerged out of a rereading of Huizinga, Georges Bataille, Marx, and the historic avant-gardes of Dada and Surrealism. For Guy Debord, leader of the Situationists, the revolutionary task was to make the entire space of the city a space for play, overthrowing the alienating division between work and "leisure." For his sometime ally Constant, the goal was the construction of whole new urban structures for facilitating play, a project he called *New Babylon*. Both were influenced by the reading of Huizinga and Caillois to be found in the work of Henri Lefebvre, who took everyday life to be a domain within which groups sallied forth and challenged each other. For Lefeb-vre, the challenge was to modern life what the gift was to the ancients.[7]

Now is a good time to revisit this critical tradition, which makes play a central category in the critique of the military–entertainment complex, which calls it to account for its corruption of everyday life with the game. Against Caillois, we might argue that the problem is not too few rule-bound games, but too many of them. There is no longer any escape or retreat from an all-inclusive **game space**. Against the sixties play radicals, we might argue that play doesn't exist in its pure form. The being of the game and the becoming of play produce each other. In other words we might generalize Derrida's argument in "Structure, Sign and Play."[8]

If the emphasis has to fall somewhere, however, it is best to treat play as the primary category, and game as the supplement. Brian Massumi's *Parables of the Virtual* is useful here. The game is not the condition of existence of play, but vice versa. If play is pure difference, the game marks and sorts play into differences that differentiate according to the same principle. Massumi's example is soccer. The play itself is a flux that ripples through the field, and cannot be neatly distributed into objects and subjects. But the play always comes to rest in a digital result. The ball is in or out, the player offside or not, the team scores or doesn't. The game is a space in which becoming is reduced to being, flux to neat divisions between subjects and objects.[9] One plays not only at an interface, but as an interface.

This is an elusive point, but a key one. It helps us understand why games are the form culture assumes in the digital age. We live in an era when a new ruling class is emerging, one that requires a new form of private property, no longer tracts of land or facto-ries and inventories, but what the Raqs Media Collective calls "rainforests of ideas."[10] As Steven Shaviro writes, "Digitization goes hand in hand with privatization. It's our version of what Marx called primitive accumulation."[11]

The emergence of the intensive vector of the digital, but in particular the digital constrained within the bounds of property and strategy, is what lies behind the proliferation of the game, or more particularly of the game as *agon* and *alea*. As Jackson Lears argues in his book *Something for Nothing*, there has always been a tension in American culture between *agon* and *alea*, between predestination and the luck of the gods, between Protestant and animist. What we see in our time is that *agon* and *alea* move, in Raymond Williams's terms, from being residual to dominant cultural forms.[12]

This is because we are at the point where the homology between property, strategy, and the digital becomes the basis for the whole organization of life. That every aspect of being should be bounded, discrete, and finite is the order of the day. The chess board or the tennis court are the models for a digital world only now coming into being as a third nature, a general and abstract space, a universal game space.

The lines aren't drawn in powdered chalk on the freshly cut lawn; they are drawn invisibly by global positioning satellites. For what is GPS if not the very surface of the planet itself as a total chess board, every inch rendered discrete, finite, and bounded. The surface of the earth is no longer a topography, a space of writing, of maps and titles. It is a topology, the space of the *logos* itself, if of a somewhat limited and particular kind.[13]

The whole surface of the globe becomes a game space, or rather, two overlaid and overlapping game spaces, of commodity-space and strategy-space, of desire and security. There is a strategy-space and a commodity-space. We are living through an era in which the strategy-space dominates. The invasion of Iraq might stand as an emblem of it. But under the Clinton administration, to which some look back with nostalgia, what we may have seen is really just the predominance of the commodity-space, otherwise known as the "level playing field" of the free market economy.

It caused something of a sensation when the United States army started using an online computer game as a recruiting tool. You can download the first-person shooter *America's Army* free from the Internet. What is less noticed is how games allegorize the ideological kernel of game space as a way of life into other areas of the everyday. It is not "violence" that is intrinsic to games, but the logic of the digital, of difference restricted to the discrete and finite.

Defenders of games sometimes point to non-violent games like *The Sims* as evidence that game culture cannot be reduced to the question of violence. But maybe what is of more interest is what *America's Army* and *The Sims* have in common – the collapsing

of the whole of life into the digital, and the extension of the principles of the digital to the whole of life.

Spoiler alert! Orson Scott Card's sci-fi novel *Ender's Game* is a
favorite with military simulation types, and no wonder.[14] It's a
novel about training children to fight some alien enemy, and the
story of one child in particular, brutalized by boot camp, then set
to playing endless simulated wars on computer games against the
aliens. Only it turns out it was no simulation: what the child thinks
was the training exercise was the war. And it is the war. The *form*
of the digital game, irrespective of content, is now the form of
everyday life itself.

Now I don't want to suggest that all games are a bad thing.
Rather, I want to return to Huizinga's line of inquiry, as to whether
a given game culture is an enabler of play in its protean, creative
sense, or if it is a decadent form that merely induces play to repetition. This is where the question of property comes back into focus.
Marx once said that the people make history, but not with the
means of their own choosing. Now one might say: the people
create play, but not in the games of their own choosing.

Games, when they become decadent, trap play and repeat it as
endless variations of the same. Or, one might say, a decadent game
extends the digital to the point that it excludes any other kind of
difference. Writing in the 1950s, Situationists thought that play
offered some kind of critical leverage against the social factory,
against the extension of the commodity form to the whole of
everyday life. They invented practices of play, in and against the
city, as a step toward the imagining of a new city, built for less
mediocre games.

What they had not foreseen was that play of this kind could be
captured and made a functional component of commodification.
Rather than being a process that invents new forms, play is now
captured and made functional for the same forms, over and over:
the forms of commodity-space and strategy-space. The analog of
play calls into being the digital of the game. But the question is
whether the digital then suppresses or enables difference.

The space within which the Situationists discovered new possibilities of play was an **addressable** space, the space of the
city. Children of the war years, they knew all about aerial surveillance and its consequences.[15] And yet they discovered play
not only within but against an addressable space. The wager of

twenty-first-century avant-gardes is that the addressable spaces of the intensive and extensive vector can also be spaces of play, both in and against the digital.

Henry Jenkins famously celebrates play within the space of what he calls "convergence culture."[16] Culture industry artifacts, whether fantasy novels, TV series, games, or comics, become the raw material for the creation of new stories, or of communities, in which the consumer becomes the producer. But is this not just the **vulture industry** at work? Parallel to the outsourcing of producing the hardware to China is the "insourcing" of the production of "content" to the leisure hours of their own consumers. This is play in the space of the vector, but not against it. A little different is the path that stretches from the Electronic Disturbance Theater and Etoy to 4Chan, Anonymous, LulzSec, Wikileaks, and other more or less anonymous or pseudonymous groups who, like the Situationists, play in and against addressable space.[17]

Caillois was right to warn against the dangers of the fantasy of pure play, and the pure play of fantasy. Play does not know when to stop – as anyone who has been around small children has surely discovered. His privileging of *alea* and *agon* against *mimesis* and *ilinx* seems particularly aimed at Georges Bataille, who even in the postwar period was still hankering after rituals that could abolish the self and touch the absent presence of the absolute.[18] But, on the other hand, Caillois did not foresee the opposite danger: that the bounds and limits of the game would come to coexist, via a digital technicity, with a regime of property, and that this game space would become a totality.

The online version of *The Sims* was not popular, at least in part because newbie players were treated as "marks" by "griefers" who scammed them the minute they entered the game. The con, who cheats in real-life games, is a persona who advances along the lines of the vector. The "mark" is named after Ben Marks, who invented the "Big Store" con, using fake store fronts in frontier railway towns. Graham Parker: "The stores thrived in the heyday of the American railroads and had a symbiotic relationship with the burgeoning infrastructure as it sped across America . . . Marks was the first criminal to advance the mobile parasitic logic of the railroad grafter to match the ambitions of the host."[19]

The difference between game space as it is coming to being in reality and the ideology of the game is that in the ideology game space is a "level playing field" where the fittest survive; in actual game space, the big players have the umpire in their pocket. Exploitation today is a matter of meeting our opponents as if on a level playing field, but where they can change the rules to suit themselves. This is the meaning of "deregulation" – that the state is no longer even notionally the umpire.

This became particularly clear after the 2008 financial crisis. Most of the banks were bailed out on a largely no-questions-asked basis, while ordinary mortgage holders received only token assistance. If you bet a few hundred thousand on your house and lost, you were just a mark who lost. If you bet a few hundred million on mortgage-backed securities, your bad bet was covered.

David Graeber points out that, historically, debt crises are solved at the expense of debt holders, so that economic activity can resume again.[20] But this was not the case in Europe or the United States after 2008. The bond holders ruled. The two productive factions of the vectoral class, the strategic and the logistic, were held hostage by a third, which uses the power of the vector to secure control of flows not only of money in all of its forms, but flows of information about values.

Imagine you are playing a video game. There are things to avoid in this game, and things to find. Some things lower your score and some raise it. Only problem is, your opponent knows where they are and what their value is before you do. Worse, your opponent is your source of information about some of those values, and might not always tell you straight. The decadence of the overdeveloped world is this gaming of the game. It is as if the ball boys and umpires all had bets on the match and acted in their own interests, not the interests of the game. Leonard Cohen called it: "Everybody knows the dice are loaded. We all roll with our fingers crossed."

Two politics of the game suggest themselves. First, a reformist one, in which the state resumes its role as netural umpire of the game. One accepts the enclosure of the commons in strategy-space and commodity-space, but insists that the major players play the game by the same rules as everyone else. One should not be able to attack other countries unprovoked unless the UN allows it. The financial wing of the vectoral class ought not to game the game in its own interests and at the expense of creative investment. In this vision, play is still subordinated to the game. History becomes a matter of the ever-expanding and ever-deepening of a game space that is called upon to coincide with its own ideology.

But there might be another vision, in which the digital is freed from its identity within property, and the capacity to create game spaces becomes a new commons. Play, freed from a tyrannical and falsely universal game space, might then revert to the role Huizinga always thought it should have, as the engine of difference, oscillating between antipodes, the means of production of difference itself.

The Occupy Wall Street events of 2011 might be thought of as just such a "play," not to mention, on a much vaster scale, the occupation of Tahrir Square in Egypt that preceded them. These were occupations not just of concrete places but of abstract ones as well, situations in which a commons appeared, at least for a while. Of course, it is all about the endgame in such circumstances. What counts are the moves after such openings, and in these and many other cases, game space trumped open play in the end. But still, one can't but keep trying. The "great game" isn't Afghanistan any more, although that is part of it.[21] The great game is the game against those who would game game space itself, and put an end to that play which invents new rules.

So far I have been looking at game space "from above" as it were, like aerial surveillance. But what does it feel like to roll with your fingers crossed? A terrific example of the phenomenology of play is a book by David Sudnow called *Pilgrim in the Microworld*.[22] It is the third of our classic texts. A former ethnomethodologist, Sudnow found himself for obscure reasons outside the profession of sociology, making a living as a piano teacher. He even had his own distinctive method for this. *Pilgrim in the Microworld* is as detailed and nuanced an ethnography of the experience of play, and of one's relation to play in a *digital* world, as one could hope for, but it stays close to experiential frame. This offers a point of departure for taking the point of view of the gamer seriously, but working out from it, grasping the whole landscape of the military–entertainment complex from the point of view of one of the key personas that it has called into being.

Sudnow chronicles, step by step, how he became a **gamer**. It's the story of how he internalizes the goals of the game itself, how he trains his senses, and tunes his motor skills into his senses, and his senses into the feedback loop of the game. None of which is a conscious action. Like learning the piano, it's a kind of athletics, a shaping of the nerves and muscles, of carving neural pathways to speed the interaction of human with inhuman circuits. It's about a training in cycles of effort and reward, where these cycles become predictable loops. The gamer lives for quantifiable rewards. The persona, or rather the **interface**, of the gamer is the carapace which makes this training appear meaningful to the awareness of the body so trained.

The fourth classic book about games, alongside Sudnow, Caillois and Huizinga, is surely Bernard Suits's *The Grasshopper: Games, Life and Utopia*.[23] Writers on games often refer to its robust definition of the category of game, but neglect two other things about it, of which the least strange is that it ends with a description of utopia. It addresses that gamer awareness and asks about a larger reward for play than a score within a game.

Somewhat more startling is that this utopia is described by the fabled grasshopper of the title. Or, rather, by the acolytes of the grasshopper. The grasshopper preferred to play rather than to store up food for the winter, and died. His students are ants, who attempt to reconstruct his Socratic dialogues like so many insect Platos. Already, in Suits, there is a sense that the good life is at some remove. In the overdeveloped world, it seems that if one were to rewrite this work it would have to be the other way around – it is the ants that die, and we are all grasshoppers. Play is all we consume; even as play consumes us.

But perhaps even this striking work is now from another time. Galloway and Thacker: "networks involve a shift in scale, one in which the central concern is no longer the action of individuated agents or nodes in a network. Instead what matters more and more is the very distribution and dispersal of action throughout the network."[24] What is called for are personas which, unlike the ant and the grasshopper, don't return back to the integrity of a whole body on the one hand with a technology on the other. Rather, personas are specific, local, non-phenomenological.

Critical theory has learned to embrace a range of personas. It came to terms with its own petit bourgeois origins once it did not identify itself automatically with the party of the working class. It broke out of an anodyne humanism to understand a variety not only of class personas, but those of gender, race, sexuality. But why stop there? Why not embrace also those personas thrown up late in modernity? Why not embrace those that are not personas relating subjects to each other, but subjects and objects – **interfaces**?

Two interfaces come to mind as particularly interesting: the **gamer** and the **hacker**. Both are products of the military–entertainment complex. Both engage centrally with questions of play. The hacker still has remnants of the romantic idea of free, creative play, play that invokes its own rules. The gamer as an interface has the virtue of stepping away from such an idea of an interface as self-acknowledged legislator. The gamer plays within the game, as given. The gamer is an **antipodal** figure, playing against the game from within.

Gamer and hacker are the interfaces advocated by Caillois and Huizinga, respectively. Each has something to say to the other. The game as end in itself can become decadent, the gamer narrowly focused, perhaps tempted to cheat – to game the game. The hacker, on the other hand, has a tendency to ramble, to head off into the wilderness, to become unbounded from the constraints that shape play's anti-productivity in a paradoxically productive direction.

This would be to move in the contrary direction, to the now established field of game studies, which takes its cue from the work of Ian Bogost, under the banner of "proceduralism."[25] Bogost rightly insists that games are defined by their unique formal properties. Whatever values a game communicates are embedded in the design of the procedures for playing it. This has the effect, however, of privileging the game *designer* as the author of the rule-set and the procedures it generates. Bogost takes a step forward in identifying the formal qualities of the game, but a step backwards toward reviving the persona of its author. Needless to say, game designers are attracted to the procedural point of view, even if it aligns them with other servants of vectoral power as architects of game space rather than collaborators in that praxis that would try to game the system – or hack it. We shall see soon enough who has history on their side.

10

The Gift Shop at the End
of History

Philadelphia, Pennsylvania

The linguistic turn, the reign of the signifier, the art of simulation, the semiotics of everyday life, the society of the spectacle: the **postmodern** seems to come down to a wild proliferation of signs. Perhaps this is just a misdiagnosis. Perhaps it's just a matter of taking one's news feed to be representative of the zeitgeist. Terry Eagleton: "cultural theory's inflation of the role of language [is] an error native to intellectuals, as melancholia is endemic among clowns."[1]

So what was the postmodern? By the early twenty-first century the very term was something that even undergrads had learned was passé, like that bad haircut you had at a certain naive stage in your life. But it is precisely this abject, forlorn quality of the postmodern that now needs an analysis. To foreshadow a little: perhaps it was, with the best of intentions, if not the best of results, an attempt to resolve two vexing questions. The first is: what can we make of history? The second is: what has history made of us? As to what history is, and who we are – both these questions hinge on some other questions.

The postmodern proliferation of the sign is not so much a symptom as a syndrome. It is itself a cluster of heterogeneous signs which all have a family resemblance to each other, yet which cannot be reduced to a unity or dismissed as a random collection of differences. Some, but not all, may have a common "organic" cause, but this common cause has yet to receive a correct diagnosis.

It has something to do with a mutation in the commodity form. The intellectual's obsession with the significance of signification might point to a mutation of the commodity from thing to image. But is this just a further extension of capital, its formal subsumption of the social, its colonization of nature and the unconscious? Or is it rather a mutation in the commodity form itself? Maybe this is not "late capitalism" but early something else.

There is no shortage of postmodern takes on the modern, which proceed by reducing it to an array of surfaces, which are then treated as having formal equality, thus dethroning the formerly central or canonic personas. It's the death of God become viral malady. All well and good, except that this postmodern style tends to linger all too lovingly over its heap of broken images, and rarely even attempts to produce the concept that might account for this production of surfaces, including the mere surface that criticism itself has become.

What the times call for might not be a postmodern take on the modern but a modern take on the postmodern, which restores to it some coherence as the figure for a global and historical moment of transformation. In this other reading, the old powers are not simply dispersed to make way for a new dispensation, but that new cultural order is in turn subjected to a critical scrutiny. Perhaps it's time again for some destructive persona, to gaily sweep away the received ideas of the times.[2] We have already met one such persona, or rather **interface** – the gamer – but perhaps there are others.

The modern is only a figure, a rather peculiar type of sign. Jameson: "a way of possessing the future more immediately within the present itself."[3] Any return to it can only be tactical, a way of displacing the fragmentation of temporality urged by that other figure, the postmodern. The tactical return of the modern might have one and only one task to perform, which is to overcome both itself and its epigones. The great virtue of the modern is that it decays and disappears through mere temporal succession. Debord: "But theories are made only to die in the war of time."[4]

The *sine qua non* of a sophisticated, postmodern theory is to have nothing to do with any vulgar talk of base and superstructure. Which would seem to be enough reason on its own to insist on a return to this allegedly most retrograde figure – in this case a spatial rather than a temporal one. It's not hard to fathom the displeasure intellectuals and artists must have felt in a figure that renders their own significance marginal, floating in the superstructures, waiting for history. Just as theologians did not want to believe that everything revolves around the sun and not the earth, intellectuals do not like being told that history is driven not by them, but by the transformation of the relations of production through the development of the means of production. If an essential belief for any intellectual is that the sun shines out of one's own ass, one can imagine the shock of encountering the heliocentric view of the universe.

It is by letting go of the centrality of one's own narrative and studying the transformation of the economic relations of modern society that one finds, paradoxically enough, a renewed intellectual vocation. Perhaps it is not late capitalism that ails us, but a whole new stage, emerging out of the contradictions of the last. Perhaps we were merely waiting for new personas to emerge. And they are not unrelated to ourselves, even if in an age of the vector we no longer get to impersonate the proletariat as "the identical subject-object of the historical process."[5]

The modern, as a unitary conception of history, has been subjected more to a process of destruction than of deconstruction. The various flavors of thought that replace it settle on far more modest ambitions, as if it were enough to supplement the ruins of the modern with nothing more than a gift shop. And yet, almost in spite of itself, contemporary thinking about culture in historical time returns again and again to the big picture, but without the intellectual tools for saying much about it critically. The postmodern may have pulled the categories of history and totality apart, but what has filled the void is a lingering resentment of *globalization*.

Henry Flynt: "To defend modern art is precisely what a hopeless mediocrity would consider courageous."[6] We are not quite going to defend that then. However, these speculations will take a long detour through questions of class and history to return to a way of thinking through another sequence: what becomes of the avant-garde? The sequence from the Futurists to the Dadaists to the Surrealists to the Situationists reveals attempts to work in and against the aesthetic, to overcome it and supersede it. They run aground on the impossibilities attendant to "intellectual" practice: the poverty of its personas, its contingent relation to class.[7] The postmodern quickly consigned all that to the past. But perhaps the avant-gardes live on, just not where one expects them.

Thought and art find themselves occupying institutional niches in the university and the museum without adequate ways of creating distances from the relentless pressures of the institutional imperative. What were once critical or at least alternative currents find themselves recruited as mere updates on the modern form of bourgeois culture. While the avant-gardes of the modern era may in the end have been little more than a "loyal opposition" within bourgeois culture, at least they were an opposition, and at least they drove it forward to new and more adequate forms, concordant with their historical moment. This necessary tension may no longer exist. What was once critical theory becomes **hypocritical theory**.

It seems timely to inquire as to how the current situation came to pass. Out of the remains of modern narratives of history and totality perhaps one can at least cobble together something more ambitious than a gift shop in the ruins. This would reverse the usual method. Rather than pull apart the modern from the vantage point of a sense of the contemporary that remains unthought, one could think the contemporary with the toolbox of theoretical and rhetorical styles the modern bequeaths to us.

Another reversal may also be of service, one that is "spatial" rather than temporal, and using – or misusing – the resources of the postcolonial rather than the postmodern. The postmodern moment in the overdeveloped world presents itself as one of exhaustion. The grand narratives – code word for Marxism – are over. History is no longer a unitary movement centered on the overdeveloped world, therefore there is no unitary history. To each their own history. Let a thousand fragments bloom.

There is a certain hubris still lurking in this formulation. If history no longer centers on the overdeveloped world, then it simply must have ceased to exist. The task now is to relieve ourselves of the burden of thinking critically by accepting the formal equality of the doings and sayings emanating from any place at this time. The "contemporary" is then a purely formal concept. It appears as a liberal gesture, making the periphery the equal of the old centers, when in actuality it masks the insignificance of the old centers. Among the old peripheries arise new centers, coordinates through which world history now passes.

What if history still existed, but was elsewhere? What if the overdeveloped states were merely an historical cul-de-sac, and what really mattered was driven by the decisions of the tens of millions of industrial workers of China, busily making a second nature for us all? Or what if history had a whole new kind of spatiality? One that, more than ever, constructed circuits that cut across a divided world, without, for all that, uniting it or rendering all things equal? These questions call for a return of critical thought about the transformations of space and time that is quite contrary to the institutional instincts of the academy and the art world.

Within the institution the pressure is always to segment the world into chunks that can be managed as if they were the property of this or that specialist. The overturning of the modern "grand narrative" – Marxism – made the institutional world safe again for business as usual, for the specialists. The struggle over inclusion in this traditional field-coverage model is a real one and not to be slighted. It matters whether the arts of Asia, Africa, or the other Americas are included as fragments of world picture within the technology of the institution. But whether this is a critical project any more is clearly in doubt. Perhaps it provides the resources for a return to historical thinking, but it is not in itself that alternative. Hence the lingering prefixes – postmodern, postcolonial – and the hesitation to name the emerging world (dis)order.

The institutional world of the arts and humanities offers few alternatives to the rhetoric of the end of history. The triumph of the liberal capitalist model and the universal bourgeois culture that attends it is not exactly embraced in this world, but has hardly been refuted. The implicit policy has become: "if you can't beat 'em, join 'em." By pressing universal bourgeois culture to live up to its global pretensions, difference claims its crumbs from the table, and offers itself up as a token of legitimation.

There is at least one major alternative synthetic view of this timid new world, which views it as a grand struggle that pits empire against the multitude. Hardt and Negri correctly identify the postmodern as a syndrome, and quickly move on to a diagnosis of the new historical formation. But they do so at rather a

high price. Neither the materiality of the new modes of communication that make this new historical formation possible, nor the
new class formations that arise out of it and drive it toward new
points of conflict, appear clearly in this renewed narrative of
history.

Negri: "the revolution is running extremely, extraordinarily
late."[8] In many ways this seems to be the same revolution that
Negri and his comrades were waiting for in Italy in the 1970s,
only transposed onto a global terrain. Where the non-arrival of
the revolution was met by Lyotard with disillusionment, and was
dismissed as a fantasm by the relentless inward turn of critical
thought by Baudrillard, Negri opts instead to raise the stakes and
bet again. The optimism of this gesture is preferable to the shrug
of indifference of Lyotard or Baudrillard and sometimes even of
Deleuze.[9]

It is tempting in such circumstances to abandon the historical
materialist framework altogether and try to think the historical
moment in other terms, but the difficulty lies in the inevitable collapse into the fragmented thinking of disciplinary specialty.
Marxism is in decline. The promotion of revolutionary agitation
became the revolutionary agitation for promotion. But it retains
the charm of at least notional adherence to a world historical
project.

Perhaps one could go shopping for other brand names, other
styles. Bruno Latour offers a striking example of how to think
outside historical materialist categories while retaining a commitment to a larger project, in this case one that is ecological. The
modern, in his reading, is a dual constitution, of subjects ruled by
political discourse, and of objects ruled by a scientific discourse.[10]
These two constitutions are at once formally separate and sur-
reptitiously intertwined in strange hybrids and chimeras. The pro-
hibition on stem-cell research enacted by President George W.
Bush might then stand as an example of the contradictions and
tensions between these two constitutions.

This timely line of thought extracts itself from the follies
of European radicalism to think soberly about big-picture problems. The irony is that it could be used to enrich rather than
overturn an historical materialist account of the world. One's
Marxological instincts might be peaked particularly by this
word "constitution," and one might want to sniff out in Latour's

intellectual history of the dual constitution exactly what social forces might give rise to it.

The separation Latour finds between the political and the technical constitution might be a special case of the separation Guy Debord finds as the constitutive principle of what he named the society of the spectacle. Whatever the flaws and follies of Debord's thought, he at least had the impertinence to propose an historical mode of thinking that embraced, negated, and overcame the prevailing currents of his time. One could do worse than take up the conflict where he left off and ask how one might in turn embrace, negate, and overcome his own now ruined edifice.

The movement required at the moment may be to take two steps back to take three steps forward. The step back is from Negri to Debord, the step forward might involve taking the category of spectacle seriously, and asking how it poses a transformative question to historical materialist thought, of a kind that Negri and Hardt miss. The transformative power of communication is posed in Debord's theory and his practice, even if the question of how it transforms class power and the productive process is inadequately answered.[11] It's a question of getting out of the conceptual ghetto of the postmodern aesthetic, not to trade it for another, that of a retro "politics," but to ground the aesthetic turn in an **aesthetic economy**.

One of the famous Situationist slogans advocates "leaving the twentieth century." At the moment it might suffice to leave the 1960s. The return to Debord might be a way of extracting hypocritical theory from the sixties, or rather from a certain concept of the sixties. Let's not forget that the sixties were also the time of the Cultural Revolution in China and the massacre of the Indonesian Communist Party and the rise of Suharto. None of these is a version of the sixties about which one could now feel any romanticism. Not the least of the charm of Debord is his rejection of the spectacle on both the East and West sides of the Iron Curtain, and his strong distrust of postcolonial strongmen.

The costumes and language of revolt, as Marx says, occur first as tragedy, then return as farce. But if one wants to make a connection between the revolts in the overdeveloped world of the sixties and the series of events that cluster around the year 1989, perhaps it's the other way around: first as farce, then as tragedy. The year 1989 might mark not only the popular transformation of the frontline states of the Soviet empire, particularly Poland, Hungary, Czechoslovakia, and East Germany. It might also mark a parallel transformation of the frontline states of the American empire: Taiwan, South Korea, the Philippines, and Indonesia. To this one could add the failed popular uprising in Beijing, the end of apartheid in South Africa, and the transition to democracy in some key parts of the Americas.

That would be the good news. The two halves of the spectacle are torn apart at the edges, leading to the integrated spectacle. Debord: "It has integrated itself into reality to the same extent as it was describing it, and it has reconstructed it as it was describing it."[12] The tragedy might be that the ending of the state of cold war emergency cracks open a space for a whole new kind of spatiality. The breaking open of authoritarian state envelopes opens them up to the vectoral flow of information that paves the way for a whole new stage of the commodity economy. These popular democratic revolutions threw out all of the existing political economic models – including capitalism. Odd as it may seem, capitalism succeeds at the end of the cold war by superseding itself. But then there has already been a transition within the commodity economy from the agricultural phase to a manufacturing and capital phase "proper." So why not another? It's a matter of understanding the dynamics of historical sequences.

A class arises – the working class – able to question the necessity of private property. A party arises, within the worker's movement, claiming to answer to working-class desires – the communists. As Marx writes, "in all these movements they bring to the front, as the leading question in each, the property question, no matter what its degree of development at the time." This was the answer communists proposed to the property question: "centralise all instruments of production in the hands of the state."[13] Making property a state monopoly only produced a new ruling class, and a new and more brutal class struggle. But is that our final answer? Perhaps the course of the class struggle is not yet over. Perhaps there is another class that can open the property question in a new way – and, in keeping the question open, end once and for all the monopoly of the ruling classes on the ends of history.

There is a class dynamic driving each stage of the development of this post-post world in which we now find ourselves. The ruling class of our time is driving this world to the brink of disaster, but it also opens up the world to the resources for overcoming its own destructive tendencies. In the three successive phases of commodification, quite different ruling classes arise, usurping different forms of private property. Each ruling class in turn drives the world toward ever more abstract ends.

First arises a pastoralist class. They disperse the great mass of peasants who traditionally worked the land under the thumb of feudal lords. The pastoralists supplant the feudal lords, releasing the productivity of nature that they claim as their private property. It is this privatization of property – a legal hack – that creates the conditions for every other hack by which the land is made to yield a surplus. A vectoral world rises on the shoulders of the agricultural hack.

As new forms of abstraction make it possible to produce a surplus from the land with fewer and fewer farmers, pastoralists turn them off their land, depriving them of their living. Dispossessed farmers seek work and new homes in cities. Here capital puts them to work in its factories. Farmers become workers. Capital as property gives rise to a class of capitalists who own the means of production, and a class of workers dispossessed of it – and by it. Whether as workers or farmers, the direct producers find themselves dispossessed not only of their land, but of the greater part of the surplus they produce, which accumulates to the pastoralists in the form of rent as the return on land, and to capitalists in the form of profit as the return on capital.

Dispossessed farmers become workers, only to be dispossessed again. Having lost their agriculture, they lose in turn their culture. Capital produces in its factories not just the necessities of existence, but a way of life that it expects its workers to consume. Commodified life dispossesses the worker of the information traditionally passed on outside the realm of private property as culture, as the gift of one generation to the next, and replaces it with information in commodified form.

Information, like land or capital, becomes a form of property monopolized by a class, a **vectoralist class**, so named because it controls the vectors along which information is abstracted, just as capitalists control the material means with which goods are produced, and pastoralists the land with which food is produced. This information, once the collective property of the productive classes

– the working and farming classes considered together – becomes the property of yet another appropriating class.

As peasants become farmers through the appropriation of their land, they still retain some autonomy over the disposition of their working time. Workers, even though they do not own capital, and must work according to its clock and its merciless time, could at least struggle to reduce the working day and release free time from labor. Information circulated within working-class culture as a public property belonging to all. But when information in turn becomes a form of private property, workers are dispossessed of it, and must buy their own culture back from its owners, the vectoralist class. The farmer becomes a worker, and the worker a slave. The whole world becomes subject to the extraction of a surplus from the producing classes that is controlled by the ruling classes, who use it merely to reproduce and expand this spiral of exploitation. Time itself becomes a commodified experience.

The producing classes – farmers, workers, hackers – struggle against the expropriating classes – pastoralists, capitalists, vectoralists – but these successive ruling classes struggle also amongst themselves. Capitalists try to break the pastoral monopoly on land and subordinate the produce of the land to industrial production. Vectoralists try to break capital's monopoly on the production process, and subordinate the production of goods to the circulation of information. Each successive ruling class rules in a more **abstract** way. The vectoral class rules through control of abstraction itself: "The privileged realm of electronic space controls the physical logistics of manufacture, since the release of raw materials and manufactured goods requires electronic consent and direction."[14]

That the vectoralist class has replaced capital as the dominant exploiting class can be seen in the form that the leading corporations take. These firms divest themselves of their productive capacity, as this is no longer a source of power. They rely on a competing mass of capitalist contractors for the manufacture of their products. Their power lies in monopolizing intellectual property – patents, copyrights, and trademarks – and the means of reproducing their value, the vectors of communication. The privatization of information becomes the dominant, rather than a subsidiary, aspect of commodified life. "There is a certain logic to this progression: first, a select group of manufacturers transcend their connection to earthbound products, then, with marketing elevated as the pinnacle of their business, they attempt to alter marketing's social status as a commercial interruption and replace it with seamless integration."[15] With the rise of the vectoral class, the vectoral world is complete.

As private property advances from land to capital to information, property itself becomes more abstract. Capital as property frees land from its spatial fixity. Information as property frees capital from its fixity in a particular object. This abstraction of property makes property itself something amenable to accelerated innovation – and conflict. Class conflict fragments, but creeps into any and every relation that becomes a relation of property. The property question, the basis of class, becomes the question asked everywhere, of everything. If "class" appears absent to the apologists of our time, it is not because it has become just another in a series of antagonisms and articulations, but, on the contrary, because it has become the structuring principle of the vectoral plane which organizes the play of identities as differences.

The **hacker class**, producer of new abstractions, becomes more important to each successive ruling class, as each depends more and more on information as a resource. Land cannot be reproduced at will. Good land lends itself to scarcity, and the abstraction of private property is almost enough on its own to protect the rents of the pastoral class. Capital's profits rest on more easily reproducible means of production, its factories and inventories. The capitalist firm sometimes needs the hacker to refine and advance the tools and techniques of productions to stay abreast of the competition. Information is the most easily reproducible object ever captured in the abstraction of property. Nothing protects the vectoralist business from its competitors other than its capacity to qualitatively transform the information it possesses and extract new value from it. The services of the hacker class become indispensable to an economy that is itself more and more dispensable – an economy of property and scarcity.

As the means of production become more abstract, so too does the property form. Property has to expand to contain more and more complex forms of difference, and reduce it to equivalence. To render land equivalent, it is enough to draw up its boundaries, and create a means of assigning it as an object to a subject. Complexities will arise, naturally, from this unnatural imposition on the surface of the world, although the principle is a simple abstraction. But for something to be represented as intellectual property, it is not enough for it to be in a different location. It must be qualitatively different. That difference, which makes a copyright or a patent possible, is the work of the hacker class. The hacker class makes what Bateson calls "the difference that makes the difference."[16] This is the difference that drives the abstraction of the world, but that also drives the accumulation of class power in the hands of the vectoral class.

The hacker class arises out of the transformation of information into property, in the form of intellectual property, including patents, trademarks, copyright, and the moral right of authors. These legal hacks make of the hack a property-producing process, and thus a class-producing process. The hack produces the class force capable of asking – and answering – the property question, the hacker class. The hacker class is the class with the capacity to create not only new kinds of object and subject in the world, not only new kinds of property form in which they may be represented, but new kinds of relation, with new properties, which question the property form itself. The hacker class realizes itself as a class when it hacks the abstraction of property and overcomes the limitations of existing forms of property.

The hacker class may be flattered by the attention lavished upon it by capitalists compared to pastoralists, and vectoralists compared to capitalists. Hackers tend to ally at each turn with the more abstract form of property and commodity relation. But hackers soon feel the restrictive grip of each ruling class, as it secures its dominance over its predecessor and rival, and can renege on the dispensations it extended to hackers as a class. The vectoralist class, in particular, will go out of its way to court and co-opt the productivity of hackers, but only because of its attenuated dependence on new abstraction as the engine of competition among vectoral interests themselves. When the vectoralists act in concert as a class it is to subject hacking to the prerogatives of its class power.

The vectoral world is dynamic, struggling to put new abstractions to work, producing new freedoms from necessity. The direction this struggle takes is not given in the course of things, but is determined by the struggle between classes. All classes enter into relations of conflict, collusion, and compromise. Their relations are not necessarily dialectical. Classes may form alliances of mutual interest against other classes, or may arrive at a "historic compromise," for a time. Yet, despite pauses and setbacks, the class struggle drives history into abstraction and abstraction into history.

Sometimes capital forms an alliance with the pastoralists, and the two classes effectively merge their interests under the leadership of the capitalist interest. Sometimes capital forms an alliance with workers against the pastoralist class, an alliance quickly broken once the dissolution of the pastoralist class is achieved. These struggles leave their traces in the historical form of the state, which maintains the domination of the ruling-class interest and at the same time adjudicates among the representatives of competing classes.

History is full of surprises. Sometimes – for a change – the workers form an alliance with the farmers to socialize private property and put it in the hands of the state, while liquidating the pastoralist and capitalist classes. In this case, the state then becomes a collective pastoralist and capitalist class, and wields class power over a commodity economy organized on a bureaucratic rather than competitive basis.

The vectoralist class emerges out of competitive, rather than bureaucratic, states. Competitive conditions drive the search for productive abstraction more effectively. The development of abstract forms of intellectual property creates the relative autonomy in which the hacker class can produce abstractions, although this productivity is constrained within the commodity form.

One thing unites pastoralists, capitalists, and vectoralists – the sanctity of the property form on which class power depends. Each depends on forms of abstraction that they may buy and own but do not produce. Each comes to depend on the hacker class, which finds new ways of making nature productive, which discovers new patterns in the data thrown off by nature and second nature, which produces new abstractions through which nature may be made to yield more of a second nature – perhaps even a **third nature**.

The hacker class, being numerically small and not owning the means of production, finds itself caught between a politics of the masses from below and a politics of the rulers from above. It must bargain as best it can, or do what it does best – hack out a new politics, beyond this opposition. In the long run, the interests of the hacker class are in accord with those who would benefit most from the advance of abstraction, namely, those productive classes dispossessed of the means of production – farmers and workers. In the effort to realize this possibility the hacker class hacks politics itself, creating a new polity, turning mass politics into a politics of multiplicity, in which all the productive classes can express their virtuality.

The hacker interest cannot easily form alliances with forms of mass politics that subordinate minority differences to unity in action. Mass politics always run the danger of suppressing the creative, abstracting force of the interaction of differences. The hacker interest is not in mass representation, but in a more abstract politics that expresses the productivity of differences. Hackers, who produce many classes of knowledge out of many classes of experience, have the potential also to produce a new knowledge of class formation and action when working together with the collective experience of all the productive classes.

A class is not the same as its representation. In politics one must beware of representations held out to be classes, which represent only a fraction of a class and do not express its multiple interests. Classes do not have vanguards that may speak for them. Classes express themselves equally in all of their multiple interests and actions. The hacker class is not what it is; the hacker class is what it is not – but can become.

Through the development of abstraction, freedom may yet be wrested from necessity. The vectoralist class, like its predecessors, seeks to shackle abstraction to the production of scarcity and margin, not abundance and liberty. The formation of the hacker class as a class comes at just this moment when freedom from necessity and from class domination appears on the horizon as a possibility. Negri: "What is this world of political, ideological and productive crisis, this world of sublimation and uncontrollable circulation? What is it, then, if not an epoch-making leap beyond everything humanity has hitherto experienced? . . . It constitutes simultaneously the ruin and the new potential of all meaning."[17] All that it takes is the hacking of the hacker class as a class, a class capable of hacking property itself, which is the fetter upon all productive means and on the productivity of meaning.

The struggle among classes has hitherto determined the disposition of the surplus, the regime of scarcity and the form in which production grows. But now the stakes are far higher. Survival and liberty are both on the horizon at once. The ruling classes turn not just the producing classes into an instrumental resource, but nature itself, to the point where class exploitation and the exploitation of nature become the same unsustainable objectification. The potential of a class-divided world to produce its own overcoming arrives not a moment too soon.

Once upon a time, class politics involved the mobilization of masses, or at least of a significant body which could effectively represent those masses: the union and the party, for example. One of the effects of the vectoral is to make possible quite new kinds of exploit in the name of the exploited, without the resort to such administrative and in the end bureaucratic structures. The hacker class is not interested much in parties or even in popular fronts. It prefers to act using the strategies specific to its interface: "The exploit creates a shift in the ontology of a network."[18]

Two instances of the avant-garde of such a strategy might be WikiLeaks and Anonymous. The former has a frontman – Julian Assange – and the inevitable splits and dissentions. Anonymous has mostly been true to its name. Both mobilize the ability of small groups of discreetly connected people to seize hold of often very, very large amounts of sensitive information and leak it to the public. Both exploit the distinctive quirks of network architecture to route or secure information or to disrupt circuits. Both deploy, when necessary, networks of loosely connected actors whose adhesion may only be temporary and who may not know much, or anything, about who they are working with. Their slogan, were there to be one, might well be "information wants to be free but is everywhere in chains."

And so, as the thread emerges, in the avant-garde as in any other domain where hackers hack the new out of the old, the leading forces are those that ask "the property question" – from the Futurists to Dada to the Surrealists to the Situationists, to (pick your precursors) nettime.org, tactical media, etoy.CORPORATION, Critical Art Ensemble, The Yes Men, aaarg.org, 4chan, and so on. Where the property question is asked – and novel forms proposed, there are the forces for social change.

And, just as clearly, we have the defining features of the art of the eternal bourgeois, which draws on exactly the same avant-garde sequence, but strips from it its questioning of the property form in the realm of the aesthetic. Neo-bourgeois art legitimates the new ruling class just like the old one, by producing a realm of quasi-sacred, scarce things – even if these things are no longer art objects but installations. The difference is that these newer things lack the "objective" qualities of bourgeois art, its lush surfaces, its residues of the painterly hand. Art is reduced to a taut relation between property and pure information. The question of value becomes indifferent to material support.

The rigorous pursuit of abstraction was indeed a revolutionary project – but one that merely aided and abetted the installation of a new ruling class. It is the proof, in the realm of aesthetics, of a system of value indifferent to any material support. What the vectoral class achieves in the realm of general economy, neo-bourgeois art achieves in the restricted realm of aesthetic economy.

While it may seem, as Fredric Jameson once remarked, that money is the last surviving absolute, there is yet one other – the category of property itself. The ideological function of art is to invest information with value as property in the absence of any material attribute. If the avant-garde was the loyal opposition within bourgeois culture, upon its election into the institutional apparatus of art, it became what it beheld. But one must be wary of the ideology of the death of the avant-gardes. The project of the realization and suppression of art in the world perhaps just takes new forms, even if the official project is now the realization and suppression of the world in art.

The ideology of the "contemporary" perpetuates the ideology of the modern without the latter's claim to an historical vision of progress. Realizing that support for the concept of the modern as progress offers bourgeois culture as a hostage to historical fortune, the art world obliges with a new idea, the contemporary, as the ever-renewable mask for a new cultural constellation – the eternal bourgeois.

We meet the persona of the eternal bourgeois in Buñuel's films or Barthes' mythologies, but as a troubled interface, still vulnerable to attack in the name of historical obsolescence. The eternal bourgeois emerges fully only with the foreclosure of the temporal horizon. The eternal bourgeois may be legitimated by God or by

Nature, in the language of theology or genetics, in a conservative or "liberal" guise.

But what is most troubling for the eternal bourgeois is the renewal of class struggle, either in its traditional forms in the underdeveloped world, or in new forms in the overdeveloped world. And with this new wrinkle: that the abstraction of the property form, from land to capital to information, has indeed reached the point where a world beyond necessity emerges. The proliferation of information confounds both property and propriety. Information wants to be free, but is everywhere in chains. Progress is possible, plagiarism implies it. As to just what it implies, not for critical theory but for *critical practice*, for whatever takes the place of the old-modern problem of the "intellectual," that is another story.

11

From Intellectual Persona to Hacker Interface

New York, New York

We later civilizations . . . we too now know we are mortal. We had long heard tell of whole worlds that had vanished, of empires sunk without a trace, gone down with all their men and all their machines into the unexplorable depths of the centuries.

Paul Valéry

As Valéry suggests, it's all a question of how one thinks of time.[1] The modern is not so much a period in aesthetics as an aesthetic of the period. To invoke the modern is to invoke a temporality of the passage by which things vanish from an inchoate present, to trace the line of the past. The modern was, after all, just a figure, an inescapable image of time. Jameson: "one cannot not periodize."[2] The modern was a very particular kind of sign, a tempo, a time signature. Likewise, the postmodern – it was just the necessary other, the adjacent signifier. It was what the modern was not. And yet it had this one significance: the modern no longer attained its meaning in relation to a predecessor, the ancient, but a successor – the postmodern. It's a shift in time-keeping. The drummer moves the accent from the preceding to the anteceding beat.

The desperate attempt to ascribe a positive content to categories defined by a mere temporal negation is the sure sign of ideology at work. Lukács: "Modern critical philosophy springs from the reified structure of consciousness."[3] In thinking itself modern, the modern temperament turns time itself into a thing, bounded by what precedes it. Postmodern critical philosophy does not escape this reifying gravity; it merely updates it.

The modern was the great temptation for artists and intellectuals. It creates a positive identity by purely negative force. The modernist is the one who determines what is not modern. What is not modern calcifies out of the flow of culture as a thing of the past. Hope is invested in the empty place marked for that which has not yet been beaten into temporal shape as an artifact of the old order.

Eventually, this negative process of marking time consumes itself. The beat catches up with itself, and finds within itself a meta-beat, a move of such consummate elegance that intellectuals will make a good living for quite a time by merely repeating it. The postmodern opens as a new negative horizon, as the modern itself ossifies into a thing of the past.

Time and again, intellectuals will try to assign meaning to the modern and the postmodern. Whatever one is, the other isn't. Lists proliferate. A small industry emerges. Compare and contrast. A myriad of things emerges as potential candidates under the respective headings of modern and postmodern, each defined by what it is not, as each props the other up. A slew of forgettable books ensues.

The unanswered question – ironically enough given the temporal fetish of the modern gesture – is "why now?" Why the shift in accent from what precedes to what antecedes the modern? Maybe it's something to do with consumer culture, with simulation, with the breaching of the bounds between high and low culture. The answers are tentative, and never very satisfactory, and in any case can always be somebody else's problem. The specialists in culture deflect the question off to political economy, while the specialists in the latter return the favor.

The question is not to identify the thing intellectuals determined was postmodern. The question is to determine the altered provenance of these intellectuals themselves. In talking about culture as if it could be nominated as a domain of objects, some from the now, some from the then, intellectuals are really only describing their own mirror image. The question of "why now?" is best approached not from the point of view of the cultural object, but of the cultural subject. What passage took place that shifted the accent from something (or rather someone) to come, to someone that came – and went? The periodizing, temporalizing machine, always moving on, always open toward a future yet to come, consumed its own agents, closing the space within which they felt free to nominate a past as past.

Capitalism, ironically enough, might be an infernal engine of transformation – "all that is solid melts into air" and all that – but it has itself been reified as if it were merely a trans-historical thing. It always is and always was and always will always be. This is not just the mantra of its apologists, it is wanly accepted even by its supposed critics. The best they can manage now is a simulated form of "resistance." Simon Critchley: "Is resistance itself the most felicitous response to late capitalism? Is it not too reactive in the Nietzschean sense? Should we not, rather than opposing late capitalism reactively, seek to think through some kind of active affirmation of its enormous creative and destructive energy?"[4] But perhaps that very move requires a thinking beyond this mode of periodizing, beyond late capitalism, toward something altogether different and still rather "early."

What if the commodity economy had already had two quite distinct historical phases, of which "capitalism" was only one? Might this not clarify the terms in which we could see the current moment as a passage to a third? This might be a quite different way of reimagining the temporalizing gesture. Rather than merely qualify an ahistorical fiction of capital eternal as "late capitalism" or "cognitive capitalism" or whatever, perhaps there's a way of thinking the commodity economy as historical in the strong sense. It has stages, and these succeed one another, logically if not strictly temporally. And it could in some sense come to an end.

Here is a story about the commodity economy. First comes the transformation of land into private property. All the local, negotiated rights are extinguished. A peasantry still in command of the immediate means of production is transformed into a class of tenant farmers. A feudal ruling class holding traditional privileges is transformed into a pastoralist class with outright ownership of land, which extracts rents from its tenant farmers. This is the first "modern" class relation.

This transformation of land dispossesses a great mass of peasants, who find themselves in the towns and cities. There they are transformed into workers by a rising capitalist class, which claims the tools and resources of manufacturing as its private property.

The worker is now obliged to sell labor power to this capitalist class, who profits from the difference between the cost of this labor and the price it receives for the finished articles of the manufacturing process. This is the second "modern" class relation.

The "intellectual" (or the "artist") occupies a strangely antipodal space in both these transformations. To be an intellectual is neither here nor there. One is neither farmer nor pastoralist; neither worker nor capitalist. One may advocate in the name of town or country, but that is really just to prefer one scene of class conflict to another. But generally, to the extent that an intellectual is modern, is an agent of modernity, speaks in its name, invokes its ideological trappings, all this means is naming as past all that belongs to the feudal world preceding both these transformative struggles.

The modern artist and the modern artist's interpreter, the modern intellectual, sit uneasily not only between capitalist and worker, but between the industrial economy of capitalist and worker and the agricultural economy of pastoralist and farmer. This precarious position is only maintained by the insistent nominating as other of something outside of both great historical struggles – the archaic, the traditional, the pre-modern. As Gayatri Spivak shows, even philosophy needed its unreasoning other, elsewhere, via which to orient itself.[5]

Granted, the objects that crystallize out in this domain may be recruited as critical weapons against this or that aspect of the modern experience. The modern intellectual may embrace the modern or react against it. Either way the structural relation is much the same. It's a question of retaining a precarious position outside of two parallel class struggles, of keeping open the domain of the aesthetic, for example, or the "public sphere."

This antipodal, inessential position of the artist and intellectual is the key reason for the proliferation of big commitments – to communism, to fascism; to anti-communism, to anti-fascism. Not to mention the revival of "communism" again.[6] Or – it amounts to much the same thing – to art for art's sake, or to the subordination of art to constructivist ideas of aestheticized production. If there was an overriding commitment, it was to modernity itself, perhaps not least out of a nagging sense that the categories of the intellectual and the artist were themselves the biggest anachronisms.

What if capitalism were not the last word in the progressive abstraction of the commodity form? What if there were a stage beyond? The commodity economy begins with the transformation of land into private property, sundering the motley feudal ties, and producing two antagonistic classes, farmer and pastoralist, with the latter extracting a surplus out of the former in the form of rent. The second phase produces even more abstract private property forms that can encompass complex means of production, but that yet again produce two antagonistic classes, worker and capitalist, with the latter extracting a surplus from the former in the form of profit.

The third phase produces a still more abstract private property form, which turns the old negotiated rights of copyright, patent, and trademark into "intellectual property." This privatization of information produces a new class struggle, between what one might call the hacker class, producers of information, and a vectoralist class, which owns the vectors along which information moves and the means of realizing its value. This is the new "postmodern" class relation.

With the emergence of so-called intellectual property as a private property right, intellectuals of all kinds lose their liminal status and are incorporated into the central productive processes of the commodity economy. They are no longer the servants or self-appointed leaders of other classes, but a class in their own right – the hacker class. While the intellectual division of labor accelerates, producing arcane distinctions among kinds of intellectual labor, this labor is nevertheless for the first time rendered equivalent by the abstraction of intellectual property. Marx could write of money, the general equivalent, that it makes X amount of coats worth Y amount of wheat, but with the extension of the private property form to information, X amount of my copyrights are worth Y amount of your patents. It's all the same to the market, no matter what arcane distinctions scientists may hold between themselves and musicians, or writers, or programmers. The hardening of patent and copyright into absolute private property rights "modernizes" the relation of the intellectual to the commodity economy.

One attempt to provide modernity with a positive content was the ideology of the information society or the postindustrial society. As Richard Barbrook shows, these quintessentially modernizing discourses attempted to abolish antagonism from the social terrain by simply declaring it obsolete.[7] They offered a rising ruling class a way to interpret its own history via a Marxism without tears. But it is quite another thing to argue that the class relation, far from disappearing, mutates into a new form. Moreover, the emergence of a new terrain of class struggle between hackers and vectoralists does not render obsolete those previous forms of class relation. On the contrary, at the start of the twenty-first century, the great struggles remain that of the transformation of peasants into farmers through the expropriation of their land, and the transformation of the landless surplus peasantry into industrial workers. It is just that these intense class struggles are happening elsewhere, far from the overdeveloped world.

The form of these struggles is however marked by the imposition of new antagonisms. The great workhouses of the underdeveloped world labor to make goods stamped with trademarks and copyrights that are owned by others, using industrial processes patented elsewhere. The struggle over land is also the struggle over the ownership of the genetic material of the seed stock. Vandana Shiva:

> today, companies, commercial laboratories, universities, researchers and more particularly governments – all seem to be in a "high stakes scavenger hunt" to collect "patents" which can be sold for billions of dollars. As a result, the end of the twentieth century saw patents being granted for indigenous knowledge and plants and also for microorganisms, genes, animals, and even human cells and proteins.[8]

Thus the postmodern collides with the postcolonial, not to mention the posthuman.[9]

If one cannot not periodize, one might at least periodize in a way that reveals the present as a site of struggle, in both continuity and difference from the struggles of the past. The postmodern as a periodizing gesture consigned to the dustbin of history class struggle, the totality of the commodity economy, the historical evolution of the forces of production – and much else that returns with a vengeance early in the twenty-first century. The postmodern was critical theory's way of leaving the twentieth century by becoming merely **hypocritical theory**. From now on, it declared, power is elsewhere, or everywhere, or just too complicated.

Postmodern talk betrayed a constant anxiety about its own timeliness. The irony is that this very timeliness defeats the critical irritant of the asynchronous that is critical theory's weapon of last resort. Debord: "When 'to be absolutely modern' has become a special law decreed by some tyrant, what the honest slave fears more than anything is that he might be suspected of being behind the times."[10]

Perhaps it is time to revive a distinction Gramsci made between the organic intellectual, connected to the emerging points of conflict, and the traditional intellectual, who sinks like sediment to the backwaters of the social order, cast off by the temporal energies of the commodity economy.[11] Seen in this light, it is not an accident that artists and intellectuals working in the traditional mode could only declare what was dead in the modern. They were merely revealing, in this gesture, their own obsolescence. The new appeared elsewhere, under other names, nominated by organic intellectuals who emerged spontaneously at a new interface of struggle.

Those intellectual labor processes most thoroughly touched by the coming of the digital are the ones which threw up the new contradictions, and generated the new intellectual movement which filled the vacuum left in the wake of the postmodern turn. The digital terrain, at one and the same time, opens toward a brave new world in which scarcity is a thing of the past, and yet which is under relentless pressure from a new "business model" in which the commodity economy would perpetuate itself through control over information rather than land or capital. Adilkno: "On leaving the twentieth century, the world has acquired a sixth continent that encompasses and dwarfs the previous five."[12]

With the coming of the digital, information escapes from scarcity. It is finally possible to imagine a realm of the free play of production beyond the realm of work. This possibility is glimpsed early on by programmers – those leading organic intellectuals of the new stage of the commodity economy. Richard Stallman: "Hacking means exploring the limits of what is possible, in a spirit of playful cleverness."[13]

But hacking quickly finds its limit when it comes up against the rise of the vectoralist class, which seizes upon the abstraction of information as the basis of a new kind of private property – intellectual property – built on but distinct from traditional forms of patent and copyright. Information becomes the new zone of conflict. Kroker and Weinstein: "politics is about absolute control over intellectual property by means of war-like strategies of communication, control, and command."[14]

The formerly liminal character of intellectual labor dissolves on contact with the privatization of information. All forms of intellectual labor are rendered equivalent, and a new class emerges – the hacker class. Whether it is programming language or the English language, whether one works with the diatonic scale or the periodic table, one is a hacker. What makes one a hacker is the equivalence thrust upon one and all by the necessity to sell one's hacker-power to a class that owns the means of realizing its value – the vectoralist class.

The ideology of "intellectual property" is nothing but the blurring of the line between producers of new information – the hacker class – and those who come, in the long run, to be its owners: the vectoralist class. As Courtney Love says, it's the media industries who are the pirates.[15] To which one might add the drug companies, agribusiness, indeed all of the *Fortune 500*, to the extent that these are shedding manufacturing capacity, outsourcing and offshoring supply, and attempting to control the whole production cycle through the management and policing of its portfolios of brands, patents, and copyrights.

The postmodern was merely the symptom of the decay of traditional intellectual formations, not least the decline from critical theory to **hypocritical theory**, as theory was swallowed by the academy just as the academy was swallowed by that even bigger fish – the commodity economy, as "imagineered" for the twenty-first century by the vectoralist class. And while this might just repeat the modernizing gesture, it might do so in a new way: the postmodern can now be assigned the status of a thing of the past, along with all the other ancient relics. The new terrain that opens up, however, has the tantalizing prospect of offering a renewal not only of the great categories of class, history, production, and dare I say even totality, but also of the utopian promise of a world beyond scarcity, after the commodity form.

The promise of a realm beyond scarcity might be restricted to the one thing that escapes necessity – information – the peculiar ontological properties of which are as yet poorly understood. Understanding information is now a practical rather than theoretical matter. The mission of the hacker class as a class might be to hack into existence practices by which information can be extracted from the commodity form and returned to the realm of the gift. The realm of the gift might no longer be a realm of particulars, where each gift relation imposes a particular and limited obligation. Rather, the gift may, in the era of file-sharing and peer-to-peer networks, become as abstract as the commodity form. The obligation it imposes may be borne more lightly, but might extend beyond the immediate other toward the infinite.

If the commodity economy is a philosophy made concrete, the emergent forms of an abstract gift economy – in which information may be freely hacked, in which difference escapes from scarcity – might point to a wholly new concretizing of a quite other philosophy. Far from being consigned to the dustbin by the postmodern gesture, the double project of the critical and the utopian – the negative and the positive beat respectively – might only now be finding its conditions of renewal. "In this tiresome age, when even the air melts into airwaves, where all that is profane is packaged as if it were profundity, the possibility yet emerges to hack into mere appearances and make off with them. There are other worlds and they are this one."[16]

12

Disco Marxism vs Techno Marxism

Detroit, Michigan

Jamie Kirschenbaum joined the image production department of Electronic Arts, a leading computer game firm, in 2003. In 2004 he filed a class action lawsuit against the company for failure to pay overtime. He claims Electronic Arts has him working 65 hours a week or more, sometimes coming in six or seven days. Crunching – as this kind of labor is labeled – used to happen around deadline time. Now it happens all the time, he claims. Every time is crunch time.

Crunches were once followed by periods of time off. EA wound back this down time, which was never formally codified, to a token two weeks per project. Kirschenbaum reports that his own promised "comp time" disappeared altogether. At this point, he said, "he would be glad to enjoy a Labor Day without laboring, or eat a Fourth of July spread at some place other than his cubicle, pleasures he has not enjoyed for two years."[1] All this for a lousy $60,000 a year. Sure, there are stock options, but it's not as if they are ever going to net you much. And sure, there's the free ice cream. There's even a laundry service. But basically these amenities are there to keep EA employees crunching.

Troy Stolle labors not for Electronic Arts, but in the kind of world it has created – the massively multiplayer game *Ultima Online*. In that world he is a blacksmith called Nils Hansen, as well as two other characters, an archer and a magician. He "purchased" property and put up a house for his characters. To pay for it, he has to work in the game as a blacksmith, making imaginary swords and chain mail to sell to other players. Over and over, he has to sit at his computer, click on the hillsides to mine ore, click on the forge to turn the ore into ingots, click again to turn the ingots into weapons, then click on the hills all over again. It's probably not all that different from what Jamie Kirschenbaum does, and the hours are also pretty long, except that Troy Stolle pays for the privilege.

Stolle does not own the means of making digital artifacts. He is not a major stockholder in Electronic Arts. So he has to labor within *Ultima Online* as a blacksmith to pay for the necessities of digital life. To pay for the necessities of actual life, including his *Ultima Online* subscription, Stolle works as a carpenter. As Julian Dibbell writes:

> Take a moment now to pause, step back, and consider just what was going on here: Every day, month after month, a man was coming home from a full day of bone-jarringly repetitive work with hammer and nails to put in a full night of finger-numbingly repetitive work with "hammer" and "anvil" – and paying $9.95 per month for the privilege. Ask Stolle to make sense of this, and he has a ready answer: "Well, it's not work if you enjoy it." Which, of course, begs the question: Why would anyone enjoy it?[2]

Here are two vignettes from the life and times of third nature in the overdeveloped world. If second nature is the collective production of a built environment that creates a partial freedom from necessity (Stolle, the carpenter), **third nature** is the collective production of a communication environment that tries to overcome the new necessities imposed by the class relations of second nature (Kirschenbaum, the animator). And yet third nature often seems to do nothing more than reproduce the characteristics of second nature in a more abstract and pervasive form. On the one hand, Kirschenbaum labors night and day so that Stolle might labor night and day, producing and reproducing a world in which third nature reproduces nothing but endless work and endless scarcity.

In *A Hacker Manifesto*, I tried to create a theory adequate to the labor and everyday life of this third nature, where every social process within second nature is doubled by **telesthesia** which does more than represent second nature, it controls it. Here is how *A Hacker Manifesto* starts: "A double spooks the world, the double of abstraction. The fortunes of states and armies, companies and communities depend on it." Generalized abstraction is the key property of third nature, its distinctive contribution to world history.

And yet third nature perpetuates, if in somewhat altered form, an old refrain:

> All classes fear this relentless abstraction of the world, on which their fortunes yet depend. All classes but one: the hacker class. We are the hackers of abstraction. We produce new concepts, new perceptions, new sensations, hacked out of raw data. Whatever code we hack, be it programming language, poetic language, math or music, curves or colorings, we are the abstracters of new worlds. Whether we come to represent ourselves as researchers or authors, artists or biologists, chemists or musicians, philosophers or pro-grammers, each of these subjectivities is but a fragment of a class still becoming, bit by bit, aware of itself as such.[3]

The language of *A Hacker Manifesto* is in some part recogniz-ably Marxist, although it may not always be clear which part. Marx is everywhere again, a canonic figure, particularly in the English-speaking world. But whenever he reappears now, it is usually as someone with an answer, a statement, rather than someone with a problem or a question. Derrida: "People would be ready to accept the return of Marx or the return to Marx on the condition that a silence is maintained about Marx's injunction not just to decipher but to act."[4] Here might be one of Marx's questions that is elided, the question of a practice. There may be others.

There are many "spirits of Marx," all heterogeneous to each other. There is a French Marx, a German Marx, an Italian Marx. He mutates and adapts to specific historical environments. The Marx whose spirit I want to channel I think of as an English Marx. This is the Marx who is a reader, for example, of David Ricardo.[5] It is the Marx, in short, whose project is a critique of political economy, and for whom property is a central category of thought, and a useful one, given its liminal status between the cultural-political and the techno-economic realms.

This is a Marx, also, for whom the tension between the techno-economic infrastructure and the cultural or political superstructures is a key question. And yet if one reads the leading **hypocritical theory** of the early twentieth century, one finds this tension has all but disappeared, and the Political assumes a kind of ontological primacy. It's a bizarre kind of bourgeois liberalism in reverse.

Perhaps the crucial moment in Marx is where he follows his persona of the worker as he leaves the sphere of circulation for that of production and becomes an **interface** within the world of production:

> This sphere that we are deserting, within whose boundaries the sale and purchase of labor-power goes on, is in fact a very Eden of the innate rights of man. There alone rule Freedom, Equality, Property and Bentham. Freedom, because both buyer and seller of a commodity, say of labor-power, are constrained only by their own free will . . . On leaving this sphere of simple circulation or of exchange of commodities, which furnishes the *Free-trader Vulgaris* with his views and ideas, and with the standard by which he judges a society based on capital and wages, we think we can perceive a change in the physiognomy of our dramatis personae. He, who before was the money-owner, now strides in front as capitalist; the possessor of labor-power follows as his laborer. The one with an air of importance, smirking, intent on business; the other, timid and holding back, like one who is bringing his own hide to market and has nothing to expect but – a hiding.[6]

Supposedly Political versions of critical theory have returned to the sphere of circulation, and seize upon only one of the ideas of this Eden – equality. Žižek: "what all of the French (or French oriented) theories of the Political, from Balibar through Rancière and Badiou to Laclau and Mouffe, aim at is . . . the reduction of the sphere of economy . . . to an 'ontic' sphere deprived of ontological dignity."[7] This might be the next problem in Marx that is commonly elided: the question of the relation of the economic and the political. It is not enough to suggest, rightly enough, that the political cannot be reduced to the economic. The reverse is true also.

Political or "French" Marxism, as Žižek calls it, may only amount to that French Marxism that anglophones read as an antidote to their home-grown cultural studies. From Raymond Williams to Stuart Hall and beyond is a tradition that invests

Culture with just as much seriousness and authority as is elsewhere invested in the Political. The difference is that while the Political lends itself to apparent rigor, Culture always comes with a certain ordinariness and subtlety. It calls for thick descriptions, nuance, a readerly practice. It is frustrating for those in search of conceptual clarity to get lost in the weeds of the everyday.

Political and Cultural retreats from Marx's passage into the sphere of production nevertheless have quite a bit in common. Both together might be considered as successive stages of what Simon Critchley cheekily calls Disco Marxism, which is "an approach that abandons the socio-economic dimensions by reducing all experience to modes of discourse, a gesture that politicizes Marxism at the price of leaving capitalism unquestioned."[8] Disco Marxism withdrew from the techno-economic into Culture, where it found a world of differences played out through discourse. But the discursive rendered differences functionally equivalent. This in turn sets the stage for the return of the Jacobin notion of "equality," a cutting away of differences which nevertheless stays within the discursive realm, no matter how "ontological" it may want to make the Political appear.

Class occasionally reappears as a term in Disco Marxism, but not in a way it can itself clarify. Critchley: "one might talk of a multiplication of class actors in society, of society being made up by an increasingly complex fabric of class identifications, rendered even more intricate by other sets of identifications, whether gender, ethnicity, sexual orientation or whatever."[9] I want to frame this slightly differently. Disco Marxism doesn't know how to think the possibility of different kinds of difference. At best, it talks about the articulation of differences, the formation of a counter-hegemonic bloc, but it does so on the assumption that discourse is the homogeneous terrain upon which such articulations happen.

Disco Marxism has less and less interesting things to say about class – and certainly nothing to say about the class location from which it is itself produced. If one takes one's eye off the techno-economic process, one quickly finds oneself dancing to a hypnotic but somewhat repetitive Disco beat, in which capitalism becomes a ubiquitous but somewhat featureless environment. Disco Marxists lapse into traditional petit bourgeois intellectual personae, having not thought through their own role in the production process.

It might not be the case that there is a "multiplication of class actors." The transformations in class relations might be relatively straightforward to map. It might be that with the emergence of **third nature**, the techno-economic now disperses the experience of class throughout the experience of what was once politics or culture. The insistence on an autonomous domain, of Culture or the Political, is actually made possible by the subsumption of both culture and politics more fully within third nature, as domains of strategy-space and commodity-space. Disco Marxism is a longing for something that has passed. Disco is dead; long live the New Flesh!

Outside of Disco Marxism one might look instead to a kind of Techno Marxism, in which the techno-economic figures strongly, but not as a pre-discursive realm to which the political can be reduced. I will briefly consider the writings of Michael Hardt and Antonio Negri (hereafter Negri) and also of Arthur Kroker and Michael Weinstein (hereafter Kroker), which draw on Italian and – surprisingly – Canadian flavors of Marx respectively, and which work outside the limits of the Disco beat. Between them they map out two ways to avoid the fetishizing of the old idols of the superstructure.

Negri argues for a new concept of labor, based on transformations in what constitutes its leading form, what he calls "immaterial labor": "Labor that creates immaterial products, such as knowledge, information, communication, a relationship or an emotional response."[10] While not disputing the relentless persistence of agricultural and manufacturing labor, Negri argues that immaterial labor is now "hegemonic in qualitative terms." This labor is flexible, mobile, often precarious. It respects no division between work and leisure. It absorbs what was once "women's work" – the maintenance of affective relationships – into wage labor.

Immaterial labor is highly social. Rather than being organized by capital, immaterial labor organizes itself. The products of immaterial labor, moreover, are social and common. It produces not so much products as relations. The property that results is also immaterial and highly social:

> [E]xploitation under the hegemony of immaterial labor is no longer primarily the expropriation of value measured by individual or collective labor time but rather the capture of value that is

produced by cooperative labor and that becomes increasingly common through its circulation in social networks. The central forms of productive cooperation are no longer created by the capitalist as part of the project to organize labor but rather emerge from the productive energies of labor itself.[11]

For Negri, the social character of immaterial labor comes into contradiction with its private property form, "immaterial property." "When communication is the basis of production, then privatization immediately hinders creativity and productivity."[12] Hence the complicated struggles over ownership of intellectual property, which try to assign to private individuals what is really produced in common.

Immaterial labor has outgrown the property form in which it finds itself. "Capitalist private property rights are based on the individual labor of the producer, but on the other hand capital continually introduces more collective and collaborative forms of production: the wealth produced collectively by the workers becomes the private property of the capitalist. This contradiction becomes increasingly extreme in the realm of immaterial labor and immaterial property."[13]

Negri does not, however, spend much time on the peculiar qualities of communication as a form of labor. The growth of immaterial labor reconstitutes labor in general, forming the basis of the famous concept of the multitude, which is more a political than an economic category, and more a matter of what labor may become than of what it is. Negri's is an optimistic approach to the new qualities of labor, but not from the point of view of communication a particularly precise one.

Somewhat less optimistic is the work of Arthur Kroker.[14] Where Negri has the whole spirit of Italian postwar working-class rebellion behind him, Kroker looks over the bleak and wintry Canadian border toward the United States: close enough to understand it intimately but with enough distance for memories of overdevelopment. Kroker's focus is more on the transformations of the ruling class, rather than of labor. Kroker writes despairingly of "the global consolidation of multinational corporations into branded electronic networks, not domiciled in a fixed geographical location, but representative only of a strategic node in the circulation of the digital circuit." This produces what he calls "Streamed capitalism . . . a dynamic vector populated by a global multitude of increasingly wired isolated individuals, driven forward by alternating currents of wealth and necessity."[15]

For Kroker, the mutation brought about by communication within the production process creates less a new class politics from below than a new form of domination from above:

> [T]he politics of virtuality bring into existence a new class: a class with no previous collective identity. A virtual class which, forcibly breaking with the mode of (industrial) production, quickly aligns itself as the class representative of the digital commodity form. The virtual class is global, liquid, networked, controlling, and fungible in its technical labor skills, a specialist class of the digital nervous system.[16]

Kroker is as vague about the property relations that produce the virtual class as Negri is about the multitude. He sees the virtual class as composed of the agents of digital finance, media, and technology, but sometimes lumps in web designers and other kinds of labor – even if in Negri's terms it is immaterial labor. Kroker has not properly posed the property question.

Both Negri and Kroker dispense with the classic Marxist analysis of production. No more use value, exchange value, and surplus value. For Kroker, "the new mode of production – digital production – ushers in a qualitatively new historical epoch typified by knowledge-power not labor power, virtual-value not exchange-value."[17] And yet both have a lingering suspicion that labor and class are indispensable categories.

Where Negri sees the new regime from the bottom up, Kroker sees it from the top down. He talks of "factored labor," not immaterial labor, of "our reduction to the inertia of the standing reserve."[18] What for Negri is the self-organization of labor through its newfound communicability is for Kroker a deepening of the subordination of the body to the logic of commodification. They see the same thing, perhaps, but from opposite points of view, and drawing opposing conclusions. Far from pointing toward a new liberatory politics of the multitude, Kroker concludes that "it may well be that the proletarianization of knowledge work is only about to begin."[19]

One might reflect here on the experiences of Troy Stolle and Jamie Kirschenbaum. On the one hand, the EA employee, deprived of the immediate means of production by the industrialization of post-Fordist digital labor, finds himself confronting the classic struggle around the length of the working day. On the other hand, for Stolle, even his formerly private time outside of labor takes the form of labor, a labor that he pays for, and that returns nothing but the value of recognition.

Both Negri and Kroker point in their own way to the growth of conflicts around intellectual property. Kroker: "Intellectual property . . . is the motor force of the digital commodity form."[20] Negri: "The rising biopolitical productivity of the multitude is being undercut and blocked by the process of private appropriation."[21] But I don't think either really grasps how extraordinary the extension of the private property form to the products of intellectual labor really is.

My thesis is not that labor has changed, or that the ruling class has changed, but that there is both a new productive class and a new exploiting class. Intellectual property is a third stage in the **abstraction** of private property. First came the enclosure of the land, and the rise of an agricultural commodity economy; second came the formation of capital and the rise of a manufacturing commodity economy. I think we are now well within the rise of a third stage of the abstraction of property. So-called intellectual property, which presents itself as in continuity with the history of patent, copyright, and trademark law, is really nothing of the sort. As Lawrence Lessig argues, it is a break with tradition. It is the project of turning these formerly negotiated rights into private property rights.[22]

This new stage of private property creates a new axis of class conflict. We should remember that there have already been two previous axes of class conflict, not just one. The terrain over which classes have struggled are nature, second nature, and third nature, respectively. Naturally, these stages overlap and ramify within each other. Their development is also very unevenly distributed. Each creates spatial experiences of antipodality distinct to it. That these stages succeed each other need not imply that each succeeding stage is a "higher" stage, and yet each is qualitatively different and – so far – irreversible.

First comes the conflict over the privatization of land. It turns peasants into farmers and feudal lords into what I would call a pastoralist class. Peasants and lords negotiated around local, traditional rights. What the lord expropriated was often in kind. But when farmers confront pastoralists, land has become the private property of the pastoralist class. Farmers are dispossessed of all traditional rights. They pay rent in cash rather than in kind.

The transformation of peasants into farmers and lords into pastoralists is still going on today. Class conflict over the privatization of land is still the dominant class struggle in much of Asia, Africa, and Latin America. But this class conflict finds itself intertwined with another, between capitalists and workers. So, if we unpack the somewhat ahistorical category of "capitalism," we find already two axes of class conflict, and four classes, forming alliances and negotiating with each other over the course of three centuries.

If there are two axes of class conflict, two kinds of ruling class, two kinds of labor – why not a third? I think Negri and Kroker are right to insist that something is changing, that the commodity form is mutating. Where I differ is in arguing not that labor has changed, or that there is a new kind of potentially dominating class, but rather that there is a whole new axis of class conflict, which pits a new kind of ruling class against a new kind of productive class.

The new ruling class I call the **vectoralist class** rather than the virtual class. Unlike Kroker, I don't want to offer up the concept of the virtual to the enemy. Like Negri, I want to preserve a more strongly optimistic, forward-looking critical theory. So this chapter concludes with the vectoralist class, so called because they control the vectors along which information circulates. They own the means of realizing the value of information – and information emerges as a concept precisely because it can be quantified, valued, and owned.[23] In the following chapter, I shall turn to some examples of the kinds of companies that might be considered exemplars of this new ruling class.

13

The Vectoral Class and Its Antipodes

Redmond, Washington

Each era in the development of the commodity economy has its emblematic business. Think of the dark satanic mills of laissez-faire capitalism, or the Fordist assembly line that replaced it. Each has its typical products, from the cheap cotton goods of the former to the T-model of the latter. What then might be the emblematic firms, products, or processes of commodity production in its vectoral stage?

Put the term "chinese factory" into your search engine and it yields pictures recognizably connected to earlier ones of the satanic mills or the assembly line, but with one small difference. The pictures often have the industrial-sublime aesthetic of images of Fordist factories – the repeated rows of machines and workers stretching into infinity. If anything the factories are a bit smaller than the blast furnaces and refineries one can also easily find in digital pictures with a bit of searching. The difference is that the Chinese workers are often elaborately clothed not only to keep hair from getting caught in machines, but to keep any detritus of the body from flaking off into the sometimes minute labors they are performing. While the factory itself remains vast and orderly, at least part of the object of labor becomes minute and delicate.

Consider for a moment not these images but the fact that one can so easily search for them. What makes that possible? Search for the term "server farm" and the results show a similar industrial sublime to the rows of Chinese factory workers, but now the difference is that in pictures of server farms there are rarely any humans visible at all. Just rows and rows of servers and cables, as if they worked all by themselves. As if they weren't themselves made in factories, by intricate meshings of flesh and machine. As if they weren't kept running by other hands and brains.

If you want pictures of how or where things are made, you have to search for them, even if you don't have to search very far. If you want pictures of the emblematic products and their logos that these factories make – those are probably visible right now, wherever you are. If you are reading this book, chances are you live in a world where the names of Google, Apple, Nokia, and their rivals and competitors swim by the eye on most days.

In an odd loop back to the vectors of the eighteenth century, Google filed a patent for server farms of the seas.[1] If the overdeveloped world needs fish farms, then why not nautical server "farms"? The idea seems to have a few benefits. One is getting the servers closer to customers, overcoming certain geopolitical limits that still remain to the trajectories of vectors. The floating farms also generate their own power from the motion of the sea. The brilliant brands of **third nature** would like us all to think they are different from the nature-destroying industries of the old industrial order, but this is hardly the case.

Considered as an emblem of the vectoral class, how does Google's business actually work? Google is the prime example of how the **vulture industry** supplants the culture industry. Google doesn't make all that much information that is either useful or entertaining. It just connects you to it. It takes a vast industrial infrastructure to do it – witness the server farms, floating or not – but it doesn't involve actually making the information you desire. Google's business is in that sense parasitic. It sells advertising, like the broadcast version of the culture industries. But it doesn't offer any entertainment to attract its flickers of neural presence. It really assumes we will entertain each other, while Google collects the rent.

This is very different from the strategy pursued by Apple. Famous for its beautifully designed computers, laptops, phones, and other devices, the problem for Apple is that the production of these sorts of machines – in China and elsewhere – has become something of a commodity business. It's hard to charge a premium for such devices when ones that are as good or almost as good can be bought "off-brand" for less. So Apple has to invest in its brand. Apple has to become meaningful in the "discourse" of the time.

Apple's other strategy is to make the devices portals to a marketplace. The device connects you seamlessly to a world of movies, tunes, books, and games, not to mention "apps" that do all sorts of handy things. It is not free, but it's convenient, and that is worth something. Meanwhile, Apple extracts a rent from all the third parties who want to sell stuff in their marketplace.

Both Google and Apple are *Fortune 500* companies. In 2011 Apple was ranked number 35 and Google was 92. The list is a mix of mostly familiar names, some of whom grew to massive size in a previous era – ExxonMobil (at number 2), General Motors (8) – and some of whom got big precisely at the transition toward third nature: Hewlett Packard (11), Verizon (16). Some are identified with bricks-and-mortar second-nature economy but got big at this through the power of the **vector**. Walmart (1) is a key example. The comparative advantage of Walmart, besides ruthless control of labor costs, was logistics. The company was built around control of the whole supply chain, from pulling a carrot out of the dirt or a T-shirt off a loom, all the way into the hands of the customer.

Some of the top companies owe their fortunes to control of strategy-space more than than commodity-space: Boeing (36), United Technologies (44), Lockheed Martin (52). These companies still make incredibly expensive things using the most sophisticated manufacturing technologies, but in order to make them, the whole process, from design to project management to the control of machine tools, is increasingly digital.

Some companies aren't obviously in the information business: Proctor & Gamble (26), Pfizer (31), and Merck (53) are mostly in the drug business. The drug business, like the chemical business, is only partly about making things. It is also about the manipulation of the chemical and biological worlds to produce compounds that can be patented, and that can be shown to have some therapeutic or industrial use. Some companies have survived through the whole development of the ruling class through three phases, from pastoralist to capitalist to vectoralist. Archer Daniels Midland (39) would be a classic example. Once it was in the food business, then it was in the processed food business, then it was in the genetically modified organism business.

Each of these companies is a fascinating story, even more amazing than the business press generally makes out. It's a see-saw saga of luck and talent, of competition and coercion, of business acumen and state subsidy, of intercorporate shenanigans and class conflict. Each company has particular interests tied to its perceived vulnerabilities. Sometimes these interests conflict with each other. Old-style culture industries such as News Corp (83) are hardly fans of the vulture-industry strategies of Google. News Corp is still interested in ways to rope off its "intellectual property" so that it can sell its own ads alongside it, rather than have Google "pirate" that content and sell the ads for its own benefit.

On the other hand, Google has had to move fast to keep up with the refinement of the vector as the devices become more portable and cellular telephony replaces landlines. Hence its investment in Android, which it intends to be to Apple's closed world of hardware and software what Windows by Microsoft (38) once was. Needless to say, Microsoft has its own ideas, and has an operating system for handhelds to rival Apple and Google, and tried to take on Google's search engine with one called Bing.

Companies also form shifting alliances and mount expensive campaigns against each other, using their vast portfolios of patents as pawns in the game. These are not unlike feudal titles, which the courts rather than the Court is obliged to adjudicate. A minor industry sprang up just around opportunistic legal challenges to the ownership of intellectual property. Given how arcane and expensive this can be, open-source licensing can in some situations be a viable business strategy, even a political strategy. It works to create a space between competing interests to grow a market for services, but it also works to create a *modus vivendi* with the hacker class.

The struggle between capital and labor produced its own compromise formations, of which the welfare state is the key instance. Labor forced capital to socialize part of the surplus. Much of this came under the heading of mutual interest. The rentier class of urban landlords might not like it, but social housing keeps down a key component of labor costs for everyone else. Education and healthcare likewise maintained the quality of labor at a time when capital was held captive to some extent within national boundaries.

The virtuous circle of Fordism could accept partial socialization of the surplus, so long as rising productivity of labor could support rising wages, which gave labor the purchasing power to clear the markets by buying back the larger portion of what it had itself made in the first place. All of which went swimmingly until the rate of improvement of productivity went into decline, leading among other things to the temporary return of the Political around 1968.[2]

The solution to the problem was, in a word, **telesthesia**. The vector becomes much more flexible, elaborate, refined in its flows of data. It is no longer necessary to cluster related parts of the production process physically near each other. The vector opens the way to a spatial disaggregation of production. It isn't the multitude that fled the scene. It was capital.

With capital no longer captive within the same spatial envelope of the nation-state as labor, the ruling class has less and less interest in its life-support systems. There is always another pool of labor, elsewhere. In the overdeveloped world, the welfare states slowly unravel. Meanwhile whole new manufacturing economies bloom, on an unprecedented scale, but elsewhere. In this sense, the great age of capitalism only just gets going as the twentieth century ends.

Capital still produces its familiar landscapes, only now in gigantic form: container ports, road and rail links, industrial parks, dormitory suburbs with their serried rows of tower blocks. Tributary towns manufacturing components cluster around transport links. Other transport links bring in raw materials. Follow back along these lines and there are the vast open-cut mines for coal or iron ore or bauxite. Far from going away in the **postmodern** age, all this is being built on a bigger scale than ever before. If you have ever seen an open-cut coal mine, like a city in negative, building down rather than up, it is hard to take seriously too much talk of the Political (or of Culture). Politics is to mining what a butterfly is to a dragline.

And yet this vast production of second nature, and the extraction of resources out of what was once nature that it entails, is in turn the object of a more fluid but pervasive third nature. That the vectoralist class has replaced the capitalist class as the dominant exploiting class can be seen in the form that the leading corporations take. These firms divest themselves of their productive capacity, as this is no longer a source of power. They rely on a competing mass of capitalist contractors for the manufacture of their products.

Their power lies in monopolizing intellectual property – patents, copyrights, and trademarks – and the means of reproducing their value: the vectors of communication. The privatization of information becomes the dominant, rather than a subsidiary, aspect of commodified life. Naomi Klein: "There is a certain logic to this progression: first, a select group of manufacturers transcend their connection to earthbound products, then, with marketing elevated as the pinnacle of their business, they attempt to alter marketing's social status as a commercial interruption and replace it with seamless integration."[3]

As private property advances from land to capital to information, property itself becomes more **abstract**. Capital as property frees land from its spatial fixity. Information as property frees capital from its fixity in a particular object. This abstraction of property makes property itself something amenable to accelerated innovation – and conflict. Class conflict fragments, but creeps into any and every relation that becomes a relation of property. The property question, the basis of class, becomes the question asked everywhere, of everything. If "class" appears absent to the apologists of our time, it is not because it has become just another in a series of antagonisms and articulations, but on the contrary because it has become the unacknowledged structuring principle of a third nature that organizes the play of identities as differences.

The hacker class arises out of the transformation of information into property, in the form of intellectual property, including patents, trademarks, copyright, publicity rights, and the moral right of authors. The vectoralist class goes out of its way to court the hacker class ideologically, to insist on the essential complementarity of the ownership of information and the production of new information.

This might lead some – such as Kroker – to blur the distinction between the hacker class and the vectoralist class. One can recognize the contours of this ideology in the fetishizing of the entrepreneur and of technology, where the whole question of labor is ignored, or sublimated into a discourse on "creativity," of work as play, play as work. As Kirschenbaum's case makes clear, hackers and vectoralists are far from sharing a common interest.

There is an essential difference between the hacker class and the vectoralist class. The hacker hacks, producing new knowledge, new culture, new science – but does not own the means of realizing the value of what it creates. The vectoralist class produces nothing new. Its function is to render everything equivalent, to commodify the new. It owns the means of realizing the value of the new. The hacker ends up selling his or her labor, one way or another, to the vectoralist class. Intellectual property, while it is presented as the defense of the rights of producers of the new, is in actuality about maintaining the rights not of producers but of owners of information.

The hacker class includes anyone who creates new information, in any media. It includes not only musicians, writers, and film-makers, but also chemists, biologists, philosophers – anyone who produces new information, including Marxist or post-Marxist theorists. The products of hackers' labor may be even more differentiated than the products of workers' labor or farmers' labor, but the commodity form renders them equivalent. X words from my book are worth Y tunes from your album are worth Z amount of the royalties on your patent. To the vectoralist class, all these things are merely part of a portfolio of intellectual property that these days often accounts for a substantial part of the "assets" of a company.

The hacker class makes new information; the vectoralist class turns it into private property. Information is a strange thing, as theologically subtle as the commodity was to Marx. It has a peculiar ontological property. Information is never immaterial. Information cannot *not* be embodied. It has no existence outside of the material. It is not an ideal or a ghost or a spirit. (Although it may give rise to these as mystifications.) And yet information's relation to the material is radically contingent. This contingency is only now starting to be fully realized. The coming of the digital is the realization, in every sense of the word, of the arbitrary relation between information and its materiality, of which the arbitrary relation of signifier to signified is but a special case.

Everyday life confirms this. I could make you a copy of this text, and the information in it, or rather the potential for information in it, which would then be on a CD in your possession. And yet it would still be "right here," on my hard drive. Now isn't that strange? My possession of information does not deprive you of it. Whatever information is, it escapes the bounds of any particular materiality. That is its unique ontological promise, now fully realizable in the digital. As much as it might alarm Polity Press, you may have downloaded this text for free as a PDF from the Internet.

Information has then at least one very strange property. It can escape scarcity. And it is this property that makes it very troubling for that other kind of property – private property – which is all about the maintenance of scarcity. Information is what economists call a "non-rivalrous good" – a term that is clearly an oxymoron. Information poses not only an intellectual challenge but an historical challenge to economic thought. The challenge is not only to think what else it could be, but to practice the production and reproduction of information otherwise.

The new ontological properties that information introduces into the world bring forth, as a reaction, new kinds of property relation in the legal sense – what we now call "intellectual property" – another oxymoron. As I would understand it, intellectual property grows out of, but is distinct from, patents, copyrights, and trademarks. Intellectual property is the tendency to turn socially negotiable rights into private property rights. The enormous ramping-up of intellectual property talk results from the contradiction between the newly realized potential of information to escape from scarcity and the commercial interests of those who want to stuff it back into the limits that scarcity and the commodity would impose.

The ontological property form of information is as socially produced as its legal property form. The question is how and why these two senses of "property" have come into conflict. The question is why, if "information wants to be free" in the ontological sense, it is "everywhere in chains," in the legal sense.[4] Coming from a certain mode of the Marxist tradition, I can't help but see the law as superstructural, as reactive, and most particularly as a terrain upon which class interests negotiate.[5] In particular, I am interested in law as a terrain where successive ruling-class interests manage the transition from one mode of production to another. This might sound rather "vulgar," but perhaps in this case it is the reality of the situation that is vulgar, not the theory.

Where the capitalist class found it useful for information to remain relatively free, in the interests of the expansion of production and consumption as a whole, the vectoralist class initially insisted on the enforcement of strict private property rights over information. One might gauge the relative strengths of these rival ruling classes by looking at the state of intellectual property law. One might gauge the preponderance of capitalist and vectoralist interest within a given firm by looking at its policies on the technical and legal enforcement of intellectual property law. One might gauge the place in the development process of a particular country by the way it responds to the demands from the overdeveloped world for the enforcement of international agreements on these "rights." In short: by extending the logic of class analysis, one can show how, far from being relegated to the dustbin of history, class is alive and well in our times, even if in forms we have hardly begun to name.

We can account for the obsession with enforcing intellectual property law in class terms. It is in the interests of an emerging ruling class. We can account then for the ideologies of information as property also. James Boyle suggests that there is a tension between the idea of maximizing the "efficiency" of the economy as a whole and producing "incentives" for information creators/owners.[6] To be "vulgar": the shift from the former to the latter is the shift from capitalist to vectoralist thinking about the place of information in the economy, from peripheral to central. But what is striking is that despite legal and ideological coercion, information still wants to be free. Its legal properties clash with its ontological properties. So, on the one hand, we see increasingly vigorous attempts to outlaw the free sharing of information; and, on the other, we see the persistence of file-sharing and piracy. How can we account for this tension?

This is the nexus where one might reinvent a kind of critical theory. A critical theory is one that thinks in terms not only of the actual but also of the virtual. The virtual could be thought of as the grounds of possibility. The virtual is what makes the possible possible. Where this critical theory might begin is by saying that perhaps what this tension over information signifies is that we have finally found the point where we can escape from material scarcity, and from all economies of scarcity. Perhaps we have found the one domain in which we could realize a certain "utopian" promise: "to each according to their needs; from each according to their abilities."

That is what I believe. And I don't think I am alone. There is, as Marcel Mauss observed a long time ago, a latent class instinct that all the products of science and culture really ought to belong to the people as something held in common, indeed as what is common. Mauss: "One likes to assert that they are the product of the collective mind as much as the individual mind. Everyone wishes them to fall into the public domain or join the general circulation of wealth as quickly as possible."[7] The public is not "pirating" anyone else's property. It just does not recognize the new enclosures of information within private property as legitimate.

File-sharing is a social movement in all but name. It rarely announces itself as a social movement, but then I don't think that is uncommon. Likewise, I think that the gift relation in culture and knowledge has been alive and well and resisting commodification for centuries. Only now it may finally have found an ally in the digital means for reproducing information, so that one's possession of it can be the possession of all. The technicity that makes possible the abstraction of information from its material substrate is not only calling into being something that can be captured by regimes of economic value or legal jurisdiction, but something that can escape them.

This brings us back to the hacker class. If there is a gift exchange that is alive and well among the people, will the producers of information as property side with that people, or with the vectoralist class? That is the question for our times. This is what is at stake in the struggle between the principle that "information wants to be free," and all that ideological talk about "incentives" versus "efficiencies" and other attempts to deny the radical ontological nature of information itself. The hacker class has a choice to make. Either it sides with the vectoralist class, or it realizes that intellectual property does not protect producers of information; it protects owners of information. And who – in the long run – comes to own information? Those who own the means of production, the means of realizing its value. The ideological move is to blur this distinction between producer and owner, when in reality the hacker, like the worker or the farmer, has to sell the product of her labor to those who own the means of realizing its value.

As those of us from the antipodes know: commodification has always been global. "Globalization" is nothing new – except perhaps to those in the overdeveloped world who have started to feel the effects of it only lately, with the breakdown of the Fordist or corporatist state and its attendant Keynesian class compromise between capital and labor. But I think that the rise of the vectoralist class gives us a handle on the form that the globalization of the commodity form took in the late twentieth century.

It is the vectoralist class that produces the means of establishing a global division of labor. It develops the vectoral production process, where information is separated from its material embodiment, thus allowing the materiality of production to be spatially separated from the information that governs its form. And so we end up with a new global division of labor, in which the old capitalist firms of the overdeveloped world mutate into vectoralist firms by shedding their productive capacity. Manufacturing becomes the specialty of the underdeveloped world; the overdeveloped world manages the brands, husbands the patents, and enforces the copyrights. Unequal exchange is no longer between a capitalist economy in the North and a pastoralist economy in the South; it is between a vectoralist economy in the North and a capitalist economy in the South. But the vectoral goes one better: it scrambles the once relatively homogeneous economic spaces within various nation-states. One can find the underdeveloped world now in Mississippi, and the overdeveloped world in Bangalore.

This process is complex and contradictory. The paradox of our times is that both the privatization of information, and the expansion of an informal commons, are happening at the same time. What might give us hope is the very fragility of the vectoralist position, which runs counter to the ontological properties of information itself, and can only protect its interests by a massive ramping up of the level of legal coercion. Where land lends itself to "natural monopoly" and the extraction of rents, this gets harder and harder as property becomes more and more abstract. And now we arrive at the very brittle monopolies of the vectoral economy. The very means of producing and reproducing information that it creates are the forces of its own undoing.

There is an alternative model to both the absolute commodification of information and its piracy. (Piracy, after all, is merely the reversal of Proudhon's dictum "property is theft" – it makes theft property.) The alternative is the gift economy. As John Frow has argued, rather than the gift being a pure, ideal, and harmonious state existing prior to the commodity, it is the commodity's necessary double.[8] But I think that the coming of the digital opens up a new possibility for the gift to distance itself from the commodity. What one can create, on the Internet, for example, is the abstract gift relation. If the traditional gift always involved a giver and a receiver who are known to each other, who obligate each other, the abstract gift involves no such particular obligation. When one gives information within the networks, the obligation one invokes is something common, not something particular. One invokes the gift as something abstract. This is the as yet unrealized potential of third nature.

This seems to me to point toward an ethics – a hacker ethics – and also a hacker politics. If critical theory is to resist becoming merely **hypocritical theory**, it has to engage with its own means of production and distribution. A hacker politics is one of participating in, and endeavoring to create, both technically and culturally, abstract gift relations, within which information can not only want to be free, but can become free.

14

From Disco Marxism to Praxis (Object Oriented)

Delhi, India

From the outside it looked like Occupy Wall Street. There were tents and a free library. There were signs that said things like END WAR ON WORKERS. The curious part was that the police seemed to be protecting the occupation, rather than protecting property owners from the occupation. That's because it wasn't part of the OCCUPY social movement spreading like wildfire around the country at the time, seizing public space and opening "general assemblies" to practice some kind of popular politics. It was a set for the long-running TV show *Law and Order*, which was doing an "occupation" themed episode.

A case could be made that *Law and Order* is one of the few segments of prime-time television that actually deals in any way with American politics. While news has become mostly infotainment, and current affairs has pretty much ceased to exist, *Law and Order* actually broaches sensitive and topical material. This was not how the people who descended upon the set and tried to take it over saw things, however. "We made it so they could not exploit us and that is awesome," as one actual occupier put it.[1] Perhaps the producers of *Law and Order*, that bastion of the old broadcast media form, did not anticipate how effective social networking could be as a way of quickly mobilizing people without the kind of advance logistics involved in running a film shoot. At least a hundred real occupiers descended quickly on the set, and tried to actually occupy the tents. The police tried to keep them out, then announced over a bullhorn that the permit for the shoot had been revoked.

The occupiers declared it a victory, but one has to wonder. There are worse ways for people to learn about Occupy Wall Street than *Law and Order*. If this was an act of resistance, then what exactly was being resisted? On the other hand, it does seem like an almost perfect allegory for the takeover of one form of **vector** by another. Anyone who has ever seen a film crew at work on a New York street knows how slow and cumbersome the process is, even though the result is usually polished and professional. But this is the age of the kudzu-like spread of rough-as-guts instant videos, shot with no planning, no permits, no actors, and no crew.

What if this allegory applied more broadly? What if it indicated the possibility, not just of the superseding of one kind of media by another, but one kind of economy by another? Ironically, the occupiers in this story depend on the latest in media technology to organize and publicize an event against a broadcast age dinosaur. Perhaps there's something to be said for pursuing the development of the vector to the limit. Simon Critchley:

> Should we not, as traveling theorists and jet-set professors, try to ride the surf of late capitalism in some sort of parasitic low-wage parody of the deterritorializing displacements of late capitalism, whose agents I sit next to on the aeroplane (he reads *Business Week*, I read Guy Debord), hoping that the enormously creative and destructive energy of late capitalism turns over into cyber-revolution?[2]

Well, yes. First, this kind of thinking is a vegetative fantasy, spun out of Deleuze and Guattari's collaborative work and spreading like crab grass around the Internet. It's a kind of mania. There may be something to be said for mania, however, if one conceives of it as the repressed other of the gloomy quietude of much post- or pseudo-leftist thought. A little burst of mania might be an overdue corrective. I for one am tired of always "resisting" everything.

"Philosophy begins in disappointment," notes Critchley.[3] One would traditionally say that it begins with wonder at what is. As a corrective, Critchley suggests that it begins with disappointment at what is not. Continental philosophy, born of disappointment, has itself become disappointing. It became a consolation even for the loss of the consolation of philosophy. Perhaps it's no bad thing then to step outside of it, toward other practices, and the **low theory** that emerges spontaneously out of them. This third path, other than wonder or disappointment, might begin with a joy for what might be, for the possible. Perhaps one has to have a little mania in order to have something to be disappointed about.

A mania for riding the surf of third nature need not be economistic. It may be about a more productive reading of the notorious "vulgar Marxist" diagram of a techno-economic base that determines its legal, political, and cultural superstructures. Actually, I suspect that the rejection of any version of economic determination is the new vulgarity. The "relative autonomy" of the political and cultural has become an absolute autonomy, fitting in all too neatly with the academic division of labor. Which is why I want to return to the project of thinking base and superstructure together, as the site of a problem rather than a dogma. Critchley: "What force does Marxism retain if we set to one side its materialist account of life, production, economy, praxis and history?"[4] Not much.

A mania for "cyber revolution" need not be a theodicy, but it might be about a phase-shift in history, a transformation of the plane upon which everyday, eventful life happens. I'm hardly the only one who has intuited this phase-shift. To call this "late capitalism" still presupposes that what's imminent is early-something-else. I just want to shift the emphasis from what is passing to what is emerging, and give it new names. Even if this is just a mania that happens when one reads Guy Debord at high altitudes.

Why Debord? He seems to me, to borrow a phrase, a sort of "untranscended horizon" of thought. His is the most vigorous version of what Critchley calls an "active nihilism," offering a complete overturning of commodity fetishism in terms of an ontology of human needs.[5] Not the least of his virtues is that he was never in the least tempted by Leninism, Stalinism, Trotskyism, or Maoism – all of which were revived in weird, spectral forms in the twenty-first century. As a "traveling theorist," he hitchhiked. He observed early that "one cannot go into exile in a unified world."[6] This is an intimation of what I would call **third nature.**

Debord offers in extreme form one of the three modes in which, according to Ernesto Laclau, the Marxist tradition splits. This first mode is "ontological," and stresses the reconciliation of society with itself once distorted representations are overcome. The second mode is "ethical." It weakens the ontological dimension and subsumes it under a regulative ethical idea. History becomes contingent; class as the agent of transformation disappears. One can see something of Derrida and Critchley in this mode. The third mode is perhaps "aesthetic," and can be traced to Sorel and Gramsci. As Laclau writes, "the anchoring of social representations in the ontological bedrock starts dissolving."[7] Laclau belongs to this mode – Disco Marxism.

But what if one were to rethink the ontological as not something outside of representation, to which it can be reduced, but rather to think an ontology of the image – an ontology of "information" and its expression? This might be one way to read Deleuze and Guattari's *Anti-Oedipus.* They do not attack representation in order to reduce it to an ontology that is "pre-deconstructive." Rather, it is an ontology of the production of signs. Perhaps, to vary Critchley's terms, theirs is a constructivist nihilism, which attempts to detach itself from the ruling values rather than overturn them, to make possible the construction of an ontology of human possibilities, via "concepts that arc aerolites rather than commercial products."[8] *Anti-Oedipus* takes the Nietzschean wager that "perhaps the flows are not yet deterritorialized enough, not decoded enough," that perhaps it is possible "to go further," and that "the truth is that we haven't seen anything yet."[9] In this mode, Marx's problem is not the end of history, or a theodicy of reconciling flesh and spirit, substance and sign. It is rather the problem of the phase-shift. When does history jump from one plane of possibility to another?

Perhaps it takes a moment of pure mania to entertain this possibility, but there it is. Maybe the phase-shift to third nature opens up a certain **abstraction,** a certain new relation between materiality and the information that spooks it. Maybe it's possible to construct something other than the commodity economy on the terrain of third nature. Maybe it's already happening.

The practice exists. It's all already being done. It's just a question of identifying the new forces for social change, of producing an analysis that shows what they have in common. This is the antidote to the disappointment some feel about how seemingly impervious the commodity economy is to any challenge. Critchley: "If someone found a way of overcoming capitalism, then some corporation would buy the copyright and the distribution rights."[10] I know the feeling – but I don't think it's inevitable, and the invocation of intellectual property here contains the "question" that precedes this "answer." The forces for social change, as Marx and Engels insist in the *Manifesto*, are those who ask the "property question."

A double spooks the world, the double of abstraction.[11] One might be reminded here not just of Marx's specter, but of Derrida's remarkable "hauntological" reading of Marx. For Derrida, Marx combines a hauntology of "spectral simulacrum" with an ontology that Derrida has the chutzpah to describe as "pre-deconstructive."[12] As Critchley says of Derrida's reading, "The specter is the apparition of the inapparent."[13] It is that which escapes the act of apprehension. This is the properly Derridean Marx, and one that could be set to work most productively. As Critchley remarks, "one might link the logic of spectrality to the logic of hegemony; that is, if one renounces – as one must – the communist eschatological 'a-theodicy' of the economic contradictions of capitalism inevitably culminating in revolution, then politics and political–cultural–ideological hegemonization are indispensable to the possibility of radical change."[14] Here Critchley gestures toward linking Derrida to Laclau's third Marxian mode.

But perhaps that's not the only tack one can take. Perhaps the first mode, the ontological, is not as exhausted as Laclau would have us believe. Perhaps the other question might be one of how the current techno-economic regime produces this spectral difference. And perhaps, rather than a one-sided abandoning of the base/super metaphor, one might put it to work also. One thing we can say about Disco Marxism is that it does not really move past the base/superstructure metaphor. It hides from it in the superstructures. Perhaps it's time to rethink the relation, via an **antipodal** concept – the concept of property.

The private property form is something that belongs strictly to neither the techno-economic base nor the political, legal, and cultural superstructures. It is the space of translation of one language – of price and profit, of wages and loss – into another, of cases and precedents, of statutes and the police. It is a border to watch if one wants to understand how new class relations can emerge. In one way, one follows the money; in the other, one follows the law.

What is happening to the private property form is the transformation of information into private property, which consolidates the legal standing of an emergent ruling class, on the one side, and provides the relations within which new forces of production can be harnessed, on the other. On the one side, a logic of hegemony, perhaps. On the other, a logic of production which proffers new class positions which may or may not negotiate and align in new ways.

The transformation of information into private property is a new codification of the "spectral" – of information. It generates a new producing class, the hacker class, producers of the new, of what is captured by intellectual property. They are the class who make the "difference which makes a difference."[15] It doesn't matter that culturally chemists may have nothing in common with musicians or programmers or philosophers. The property form of intellectual property renders what we all produce equivalent.

Intellectual property produces a new ruling class – the vectoralist class, which owns the means of realizing the value of what the hacker class produces. And sometimes not much more. According to *Business Week*, vectoralist firms not only outsource the extraction of raw materials and the production of the manufactured article, but are even outsourcing design, using the vectoral networks to drive down the value of the hacker's labor.

> Who will ultimately profit most from this outsourcing of innovation isn't clear. The early evidence suggests that today's Western titans can remain leaders by orchestrating global innovation networks . . . What is clear is that an army of in-house engineers no longer means a company can control its fate. Instead, the winners will be those most adept at marshalling creativity and skills . . . around the world.[16]

The vectoralist firm, in other words, may control copyrights, key patents, a recognizable brand, and the logistical means of managing the vectors along which information is transformed into materiality. It may dispense with pretty much all else. That might describe Viacom or Nike, Merck or Sony. It's happening across industry sectors, and its effects are felt in both the underdeveloped world and the overdeveloped world.

So far one might think this is a grim story, where commodification may change form but, if anything, proliferates. Even if one concedes that there are new classes forming around a new property form, the experience of class may become so dispersed and microscopic as to seem invisible. And yet: the transformation of information into property has one peculiarity to it. It lacks all necessity. Information, unlike land or capital, knows no scarcity. The property form has become so abstract that its ambition is to encompass the very thing that escapes it.

Now you may ask: why speak of information and not of discourse or language, or, for that matter, the spectral? This brings us back to the techno-economic. "Information" arises out of a double movement. First, the technics of the digital produce information as a concept at the same time as they liberate it from any particular embodiment in a given material form. Once information is digital, its relation to materiality becomes contingent, arbitrary. It has to take a material form, and yet it can always exceed any embodiment. Second, this production of information makes it available for commodification, but only to the extent that it can be reduced to its identity with an object and assigned as a possession to a subject. The legal "superstructure" here has to intervene directly to create the conditions for the commodity regime to extend itself into the digital domain.

Isn't information always embodied, contextual, relational? If we are trained as humanists or social scientists, we're likely to insist on this, as a kind of nervous tic. But what exactly is it that is embodied, contextual, relational? That's the spooky part – information per se. About which we know very little, even though it is now thoroughly contained within the legal form of property and commodity, authorship and ownership. And yet it keeps escaping. Fire up your laptop, find a broadband connection and suck down the latest festival of explosions and car chases from Hollywood. Rip your CDs and share them with your friends. Plagiarize a few term papers while you are at it.

This leaves us with one last question from Marx – the question of organization, of forms of association. It may not be a question of having to invent anything here. Perhaps hackers do not lack for modes of organization. Perhaps it's no longer just a question of "workers of the world unite!" Perhaps a hacker politics is more a question of "workings of the world untied."[17] The alternative to a hacker ethics, a hacker politics, is all too clear in the case of Troy Stolle: that we labor within a world in which information is reduced to scarcity, and we pay for the privilege of the recognition that comes from acquiring something that, in this world of absolute property, another cannot have.

Continental philosophy would like the Marxist legacy to be less heterogeneous than it actually is. Taking materialism seriously always leads one away from philosophy, even the practice of philosophy, toward practices that engage the world in other ways and find other confirmations of its existence, and the low theory that emerges out of such practices. But, for philosophy, it's easier to cut Marx off at the roots and make him a philosopher, to take him out of the world of **low theory** and restore him to High Theory. The attempts to do so for a long time severed the superstructure from the base, or subject side from the object side of matters. The result was Disco Marxism.

Things change with the rise of "object-oriented ontology" (hereafter OOO), which dispenses with the hermeneutic side of continental philosophy, in which the contemplative subject plays a constitutive role in the nomination of the true.[18] The challenge here is not so much to prize Marx loose from a philosophy, as to reinstall his legacy into one. At first glance, Marx ought to be more at home in an object-oriented world than flying high with the Disco Marxists.

I am not a philosopher. What I know about philosophy is very limited, particularly when it comes to phenomenology. My readings of OOO, I should also say, are quite pragmatic. I am interested in a particular politics of knowledge. Here I think there's a certain community of interest between OOO and something else, which I shall attempt to describe.

I am not a philosopher, but I am a Marxist. Marxism is not a philosophy. The extent that it has anything to do with philosophy has I think been rather overstated. Marx was a reader of Hegel but he was also a reader of Darwin and Ricardo, and his relation to them might be far more important. He has very little to do with Plato or St Paul. His doctorate, let's remember, was on the materialism of Democritus and Epicurus.[19]

It was hardly accidental that Engels tried to ground Marxism in the natural sciences. The labor process is a subset of a wider theory and practice of processes, natural processes. That Engels' nineteenth-century account of natural philosophy is refutable on the basis of more modern science might actually be a merit of *The Dialectics of Nature* rather than a fault.[20]

What we call Western Marxism was formed on the basis of a break forged by Lukács, Korsch, and Gramsci, or at least certain readings of them, which deflected Marxism away from the natural sciences and the question of the relations objects have with each other.[21] The Marx who was keenly interested in the chemistry of soil fertility finds little resonance in Lukács' *History and Class Consciousness*.

And so Jane Bennett can write that she pursues "a materialism in the tradition of Democritus-Epicurus-Spinoza-Diderot-Deleuze more than Hegel-Marx-Adorno."[22] She, like many others, seems to accept a certain Kantian version of Marxism as its dominant one, in which the partition between the real of human freedom and the realm of unknowable things has remained in place. And as if, as a consequence, one could not think back and forth along the antipodal line between base and superstructure.

If there's a key moment in the diverting of the Marxist tradition away from its Democritus-Epicurus origins, not to mention its connection to Darwin, it is the reception of Nikolai Bukharin's textbook on *Historical Materialism*. Lukács, Korsch, and Gramsci all object to it.[23] A key dissent is from Bukharin's focus on the social production of the means of subsistence as the key to the historical materialist world view. For Lukács, for example, this matter–labor interaction is entirely secondary to the labor–capital interaction. The primary dynamic is internal to the social realm, in other words. Bukharin, writing in the wake of the civil war, the failures of war communism, and the great famine, quite naturally has a more practical view of the relation between the history of necessity and the necessity of history.

Not the least virtue of Bukharin's book is that it contains a more or less correct account of the possibility of climate change happening as an unforeseen consequence of collective human labor's interactions with the natural world. This is not as astonishing as it seems. The physics was pretty well known in the early twentieth century. What was less common was Bukharin's openness to the question of totality as one that could be posed in concrete terms, as the interaction of objects that make up the open system that is the planet.

This side of Bukharin comes from the great teacher he had to disavow: Alexander Bogdanov. Bogdanov wrote about global warming even earlier.[24] If Bukharin is the most celebrated victim of Stalinism, Bogdanov is his dark precursor, a victim of Leninism, forced out of the party even before 1917. Hence Bukharin's official distance from him. But why, now, in the twenty-first century, should the brutalities of Lenin, Stalin, and the Orwellian forgetfulness of the liberal West stand in the way of a restitution of a vital tradition, not just of thought but of the practice of thought?

It seems particularly important at the moment to reconnect to this tradition. What I think we need is a certain practice of knowledge which is both conceptual and pragmatic, which takes its research agenda from a certain agenda external to it, but does not predetermine its own results. A pragmatism of questions, not of answers. A low theory, traveling the antipodal lines between the practices of the humanities and the sciences.

Like Tim Morton, I take so-called climate change to be the central fact governing such an agenda.[25] This agenda for knowledge is not a political or social agenda. It may actually be an agenda regarding what happens in the world of objects. It is a social or political agenda only to the extent that objects are social and political in and of themselves.

What seems useful in OOO in getting out of Disco Marxism is the move away from the vanity that is hermeneutics, considered not as one method among others but as the exclusive and sovereign one. Neither the contemplation of an object by a subject, nor for that matter the praxis of an object by a subject, can know the implication of that object within a world of other objects. Incidentally, Marx already thinks this. The first part is in the critique of Feuerbach, but second part, the limits of praxis, is in the theory of commodity fetishism. Social labor organized as wage labor is a praxis that seizes on only one aspect of objects.

Central to the Marxist tradition is this notion that praxis is social. On the subject side, it isn't performed by monads. But less noted is that it isn't one thing on the object side either. In the chapters on the labor process in *Capital*, we get a clear picture of the multiplicity of objects that interact in the transformation of nature into second nature. Marx's writings abound in instances of the unintended consequences of these multiple praxes. It's already in his account of the ecological consequences of wood-theft laws that on his own account are the basis of his whole intellectual project.

To a person with a hammer everything looks like a nail. To a continental philosopher with the idea of a hammer, any praxis looks like hammering a nail. But, for Marx, praxis isn't reducible to man-with-hammer. It is always-already a multiplicity of objects. As the great Marxist anthropologist Vere Gordon Childe shows, this is true even back to Paleolithic times. There was always-already a network of objects and part-objects to which the hammer belongs.

It's quite astonishing to read, in Childe's account of the Indus Valley civilizations, that they were like a bubble that formed on the surface of a stream.[26] He is talking about forms of life that lasted for thousands of years. But if your timeframe is half a million years, then a few thousand isn't much. A few hundred is nothing at all. Through a very patient sorting of archeological objects, Childe achieves an essential decentering of knowledge. Objects, in other words, can take their time.

There's an equivalent decentering in Bogdanov. Part of his origi-nality is that he tried to extend Darwin's concept of "selection" to the inorganic world. He uses Darwin to update the Epicurians. Why do objects persist? Why isn't the world of objects a pure chaos? What he ends up creating is a theory of the change and stability of objects that is completely scale-independent. He called it "tektology."[27]

Bogdanov built tektology out of a phenomenology, but it was that of Ernst Mach. It was a different solution to the problem of Kantian dualities. It's an Occam's razor move, eliminating the thing in itself as a vestigial concept. It was a time of retreat for the philosophy of science, for science itself was just getting too interesting and complicated. Mach and Bogdanov retreated to a minimal defensible position. I would like to suggest that there's something viable in this position, but I'm not a philosopher, and it's not my department. Nor was it Bogdanov's. He retreated to a minimal defensible position – over Lenin's vitriolic objections – to open a space for a new kind of politics of knowledge.

What is significant is not Bogdanov's "empiro-monism" so much as why Bogdanov was reading philosophy of science at all. It is precisely because social labor as praxis is limited in how it apprehends the world that a tectonics is called for. Tektology is a heuristic program for the self-education of labor. Tektology is a scale-free and field-independent theory of the dynamic equilibrium of any object. It is not a dogma, however. Its purpose is to guide experimental praxis in the domains of both science and art. It opens up one area, the particular relations to objects of particular labors, into the conceptual field of all possible relations of all objects. It was, in short, a hacker pedagogy. Bogdanov thought that the 1917 revolution, if it meant anything, would open the way for the synthesis of the praxis of labor with the praxis of invention.

Tektology failed as a politics of knowledge, and for a lot of reasons, some to do with its own limits and aporias, some to do with the rise of big science under Lenin, some to do with the disastrous politicizing of science by Stalin. These are topics for another time. What I want to highlight are a few limited things:

What kind of practice of knowledge do we really need now? Is it not something that might look a little like tektology? Something that enables collaboration across specialization with the goal of a knowledge of concrete problems which are nevertheless utterly irreducible to the field division of labor of university discourse? I mean, how do you mitigate climate change? Not with philosophy, not with physics, certainly not with politics. But perhaps there's a chance a kind of agenda-oriented praxis, something like tektology, might help.

Within the humanities, this might mean turning away from our solipsistic regard for merely human timeframes and scales. Within the science, it might mean a certain caution about the drive to render objects transparent within a verifiable theory. The practices rather than the theories, and the applied rather than the so-called pure sciences, might be what is most worthy of attention, and not least by humanists. This is the domain of the hacker.

One of the things I admire about Reza Negarestani's *Cyclonopedia* is the way it makes carbon imaginable as an agent, and even then it is but a by-product of the trauma of sunlight's stirrings of the earth.[28] But there's an element of romanticism at work in this area (and in a different way) in Bennett. That's why I'm advocating a certain constructivism – an asocial constructivism – latent in Marxism's neglected Epicurian and Darwinian side.

So: rather than OOO, or object-oriented ontology, I advocate P(OO), or praxis (object-oriented). A praxis which knows itself to be limited, but which constructs a praxis of praxis, aimed at a useful knowledge of the strange praxis objects entertain amongst themselves. And, to make it possible, a certain conversation. One which does not have a stake in the language-game of professional philosophy, but which raids it for the odd useful thing, for hammers and such.

P(OO) is, as its name implies, a messy business. It is not the neatly ordered hierarchy of knowledges, whether philosophical, scientific, or social-scientific, that Althusser tried to legislate. Rather, it might look far more like J. D. Bernal's contribution to the invasion of Normandy during World War II.[29] This was a knowledge that responded to events outside of itself rather than eternally explicating its own internal agenda.

Could a tank drive out of an amphibious vehicle and up onto a particular beach? What kinds of knowledge might answer this question? For Bernal it included: the engineering specs of the tank, sand samples from the beach collected by commando frogmen, postcards and snapshots of the beach collected from servicemen, the working knowledge of fishermen, the history of cartography (including a theory of the cartographic business), and a medieval romance describing the escape of the hero across a causeway no longer in evidence but possibly covered in sand.

This is not exactly science, but it isn't non-science. It's a hack. It's similar to what Ben Bratton calls geopolitical design.[30] It might be more like the way physicians work than the way either philosophers or scientists work. Perhaps it's no accident that Bogdanov trained as a physician. Perhaps the praxis of knowledge in the twenty-first century will be about physicians of non-human bodies. This is the praxis of knowledge that I'm calling P(OO). I expect we'll need more of it, and in something like wartime conditions, before the century is out.

The turn toward a certain kind of materiality in OOO is welcome, then. It breaks with the concerns with culture, language, politics, ethics, the subject, and so on that are characteristic of

Disco Marxism broadly conceived. And yet by making the object itself an object of contemplation rather than action, it turns away again from the problem of the politics of knowledge. No object exhausts itself in its encounter with another object. No praxis exhausts an object in its instrumental action upon an object. Perhaps the way forward is at least to put different practices in communication with each other. The practices of the humanities and the practices of the sciences, but extending also to the low theories of art and politics between them, at least open partially the domain of possibilities of the world. The hacker is, among other things, the **interface** between such practices.

But to speak of the hacker is to raise again the property question, and to turn away from a purely scholarly production of knowledge. Could the kind of knowledge needed to mitigate climate change actually be produced within the current aesthetic economy, where knowledge is subordinated to intellectual property? Where all that counts even in the domain of knowledge is measured within a **game space** of formal rules and moves?

15

Considerations on a Hacker Manifesto

Paris, France

Nicholas Negroponte is the public face of what the vectoral class would like the hacker class to be. He is an evangelist. Once upon a time the bourgeoisie sent missionaries out into the world equipped with Bibles. In its declining phase it sent technocrats armed with Milton Friedman to budding dictatorships. Negroponte has a better idea.

> Nicholas Negroponte plans to airdrop [One Laptop Per Child tablet computers] to remote villages to teach the children within them to read . . . The tablets won't be accompanied by any adults or teaching resources; Negroponte said that he was convinced that they were designed for children, and that he wanted to see if the tablets could be used to teach them to read without additional instruction.[1]

Fortunately, the tablet computers are designed to survive a 30-foot drop, although children's heads might not be designed to have the tablets dropped upon them.

Here, in the overdeveloped world, the bourgeoisie is dead. It neither rules nor governs. Power is in the hands of what I called the vectoralist class. Where the old ruling class controlled the means of production, the new ruling class has limited interest in the material conditions of production, in mines and blast furnaces and assembly lines. Its power rests not on the ownership of such things but in control of the logistics by which they are managed.

Vectoral power has two aspects, intensive and extensive. The intensive vector is the power of calculation. It is the power to model and simulate. It is the power to monitor and calculate. And it is also the power to play with information, to turn it into poetry and narrative. The extensive vector is the power to move information from one place to another. It is the power to move and combine anything and everything as a resource. Again, this power has not just a rational but also a poetic aspect.

Vectoral power can thus dispense with much of the machinery of the old capitalist ruling class. It is a matter of indifference who actually owns a furnace or an assembly line. The vectoral class contracts out such functions. The rise of manufacturing industry in China and of service industry in India is not the sign that these underdeveloped states are joining the capitalist developed world. Rather, they now confront an overdeveloped world ruled by vectoral power.

The vectoral class is united only in desiring a world free from the compromises with labor that its capitalist predecessor was obliged to make. For all its tragedies, the twentieth century was the century of socialism – but its victories were mostly confined to the West. In the West, labor fought capital to a draw. Capital was obliged to concede to a substantial socialization of the surplus. We got free education, healthcare, the vote, the (partial) emancipation of women. The tenets of the *Communist Manifesto* were indeed realized – in the West. This is the compromise that is now unraveling.

The vectoral class has less and less interest in the viability of national spaces of production and consumption. Fordism is dead.[2] What the vectoral class desires is a relationship with the world in which the world makes its body totally available in exchange for no commitments at all. Which is perhaps why the cultural form which best explains vectoral power is porn.[3]

And yet the vectoral class is not coherent in its strategies and interests. It has at least two factions. The vectoralist class as a whole we could describe as a **military–entertainment complex**. What distinguishes its two factions is that while one pursues entertainment as a military strategy, the other pursues military strategy as entertainment. Between them is what William Gibson, in his novel *Spook Country*, calls the cold civil war.[4]

What we see playing out in the spectacle of American politics in the early twenty-first century is the surface effect of this cold civil war. One faction is interested only in the strategics of resources. It thinks it acquired in Iraq the last untapped source of oil and natural gas and tried to build the logistical infrastructure to secure it. Far from being a failure, its Iraq adventure has proven a complete success. It never had any interest in Iraq as a "democracy." In many ways the more unstable it is the better. The bases being built are to secure the oil, not the people.

The other faction within the vectoralist class is increasingly worried about the costs of this strategy. Its interest is not in the strategics of nature but the logistics of second nature. Its business is the business of coordinating all aspects of life under the power of the brand, the patent, and the copyright. If capitalist power reduced being to having, then vectoralist power reduces having to appearing.[5] The actual qualities of things become secondary to the logistics and poetics that decorate the commodity.

This faction of the vectoralist class confronts quite different issues. The dematerialization of the commodity threatens to undermine the very principle of the scarcity of value. As soon as digital technology perfected the separation of information as content from material form, the way was open for a massive socialization of cultural material. To some extent this took the vectoral class by surprise. It did not quite occur to them that private property is not the "natural" form of culture.

We are witnessing a massive, nameless, faceless social movement, which takes the raw material of commodified culture and turns it back into common property. And the good news is that this movement has essentially won. After centuries of privatization, culture is ours again. This victory is partial and limited, of course, just as the victory of "socialism" in the West was limited. It only applies to culture, and not to many of the other aspects of vectoral power. But still, it is worth celebrating.

Politics now for the vectoralist class is the politics of attempting to recommodify some aspect of the value of culture, to make it scarce and rare again. Consider the politics of Apple's iPod, which attempted to make a fetish object of the device. Or Facebook, where the proposition is that we should all entertain each other and put up with advertising merely for this privilege. Far from being a step forward, such media are a decadent form of the "society of the spectacle." Not only are we passively to consume these images, we have to make them ourselves.

The model here is to reduce the paid labor force in the production of images as close as possible to zero, and pay them only in the currency of recognition. We have to pay for the privilege of producing our own spectacle. The power of the vectoral class retreats from the direct ownership of the cultural product but consolidates around the control of the vector. We get all the culture; they get all the revenue.

Parts of the vectoral class are heading in quite the opposite direction, to completely closed, proprietary worlds. Online gaming is usually like this. In a game like the popular *World of Warcraft* you pay for the privilege of laboring to acquire objects and status that are only artificially scarce.[6] And you never get to own them. They remain private property. *World of Warcraft* is the fantasy version of the power of the vectoral class perfected. You pay to rent everything, and they can deport you any time.

Caught between the social movement that tries to liberate information, and the faction of the vectoral class that seeks to control it, is the **hacker class**. Anyone who labors for someone else producing so-called "intellectual property" is a hacker. It's an ambivalent class. On the one hand, we depend on the vectoral class, who own the means of realizing the value of what we produce. On the other, we hardly profit from private property in information. If anything, it is a fetter on our own productivity.

I first proposed the idea of the hacker class in 2000, and in the intervening years have repeatedly been told that even if it exists it can never become conscious of itself as a class. But, frankly, I think the recent politics of information bears out the thesis. The hacker class does not march down the boulevard behind red banners on May Day. But it is fully capable of organizing around Net neutrality, creative commons, open publishing in science, challenging stupid and harmful patents, and so on. The contemporary equivalent of the "trade union consciousness" of the old labor movement has well and truly arrived.

Andrew Ross notes that some dismiss the projects of the hacker class as that of a "thwarted technocratic elite whose libertarian world view butts up against the established proprietary interests."[7] There is some truth to that. However, if one were to look with too cold an eye at the practices of organized labor in the United States, one might come up with an equally cynical take. There's always a gap between what a class is in practice and what it could make of itself.

It's a question of pushing the often local- or issue-based approach to hacker class consciousness into an entire world view, or rather, world views. The challenge is to think the whole social totality from our point of view. To imagine worlds in which our own interests and the interests of the people are aligned. The way to do this, I think, is to push beyond the compromise formations of things like Creative Commons. What would it mean, not to "liberalize" intellectual property but to conceive of the world without it altogether? What would it mean to really think and practice the politics of information as something that is not scarce and has no owners?

It's important, I think, to cultivate a studied indifference to the co-option of our movement by compromise formations, which offer limited liberties but leave the ownership and control of the vector in the hands of the vectoralist class. No good tactic goes unrecuperated, not least those of the most extreme of avant-gardes, the Situationists. Christine Harold: "Perhaps this is because, like all good brands, situationism [*sic*] is easily appropriated towards new ends."[8] Yet sometimes what look like bankrupt tactics prove themselves again later, and what look like serious, "professional," and mature developments of a movement can end up collapsing under their own weight. There is still a role for an avant-garde that has left the stale forms of art and politics behind, and that confronts the emerging forms of power of our time with the possibility that they, too, will pass.

It was a sign of the times, of the strength of the free culture movement, that when the musicians of Radiohead were released from their contract with EMI in 2007, they offered their new album *In Rainbows* via the Internet for fans to purchase at the price of their own choosing. You could even choose to pay zero pounds and zero pence, and still have it. There's a certain understanding of the gift implied in this. The gift always creates obligations in the receiver. If I sell you something, I am obliged to you. I must provide the goods and services to which we agreed. If I give you something, you are obliged to me, or at least under a weak and very general obligation to return the gift, somewhere, to someone. Radiohead understood this. The gift of the new album created publicity, goodwill, future concert ticket sales, and even the gift of money. Many fans really want to pay for their music, but to pay as a gift, because they want to honor an obligation, not because they are being forced to pay or risk legal sanctions for alleged theft or piracy.

But the limit to making a gift of culture to everyone is that doing so adds value to the **vector** through which it is distributed, and that is not free. The more forward-thinking strategy of the vectoral class is to retreat to this stronghold but to insist on it. This is why I suggest that free culture be considered a tactic rather than an end in itself. I think the hacker practice is to keep asking questions about property rather than just settle on one model.

An example might be what I call copygift.[9] Besides copyright there is copyleft, but both copyright and copyleft take the property form for granted. Copyleft is the dialectical negation of intellectual property. It turns it against itself. But perhaps there are other, non-dialectical strategies, not for opposing intellectual property but for escaping it. What if – rather than giving one's culture to everyone in the abstract but no one in particular – one made it always a particular gift to particular people? This would be more like the model of a chain letter, for example. Long before the Occupy Wall Street movement, "occupation" literature circulated, and in the curious form of PDFs. They were designed to be transmitted, if not hand to hand, then email to email, to not be too readily searchable and retrievable by just anybody.

Of course, vectoral power is already here. They call it "viral marketing." The game is to imagine other uses to which such a strategy can be put. And to go beyond, to invent new kinds of relations. Who knows what a relation can be? We haven't seen anything yet.

Lastly, I just want to caution against one of the common modes of self-understanding that we have, I think, accepted a little too willingly, without thinking it through. I am speaking of the romance of the pirate.[10] We are not pirates; we are hackers. And the distinction is this. The pirate is someone who takes another's property. Pirates take what does not belong to them. There is a romantic side to the pirate, but it is the romance of transgression. A transgression which, of course, mostly confirms the very notion of property in the act of coveting the property which belongs to another.

Call it what you like. If not hacking, then something else. But not piracy. The pirate takes another's property. The hacker makes something new out of property that belongs to everyone in the first place. Information wants to be free but is everywhere in chains. The figure of the pirate draws attention to the chains. The figure of the hacker insists that information is in its very being something that is free, that always escapes the property form. It is where we are and remain social beings. It is where, far from being on the run or in retreat, the game has only just begun.

Not that the persona of the pirate is without its uses. In 2011, the Pirate Party won seats in Berlin's municipal elections, on a platform that combined support for a guaranteed minimum income with the legalization of drug use and sophisticated positions on information rights.[11] However, the future of progressive politics in the overdeveloped world may lie in a range of experiments combining the interests of labor and the interests of the hacker class broadly defined. That is, if politics can be said to exist outside of the use of the vector for marketing purposes. In the following two essays, I want to turn first to what became of politics in the United States as third nature developed, and lastly to one of the key **interfaces** of its postpolitical landscape.

16

After Politics: To the Vector, the Spoils

New York, New York

Politics is always a matter of both images and vectors. For there to be politics, somebody needs to persuade someone else that a certain power is legitimate, that a certain course of action is in their interests, that a certain policy is just, or that a certain leader is worthy. But persuasion is not enough. Political actors and their actions require coordination. People need to be brought together to act in concert. Politics, in short, is always mediated in this double sense: image and vector. And so the question arises as to what effect changes in vectoral form – the rise of the Internet, for example – might have on the possibilities for political action. Some imagine the Internet changes everything, in politics as in everything else. Some, like Michael Walzer, are more skeptical.[1] Teasing out what does and doesn't change in politics when the media form changes turns out to be a subtle thing.

One way to understand the impact of the Internet is to compare it to the relation of previous vectoral regimes with politics. Modern politics takes place within three successive regimes. The first regime is the postal service and print. The second regime is telephony and broadcast (radio, then television). The third regime is the cellphone and the Internet. This is, of course, rather crude. Media and communication cannot be so neatly periodized. New media do not replace but rather displace old media. One could enter many other caveats. Nevertheless, certain tendencies are at work.

The vectoral can be broken down into two aspects: media and communication. Take the successive coordinating communication forms: post, telephone, cellphone. The speed increases, as does the "bandwidth." More can be conveyed faster. But between the telephone and the cellphone is a significant break. Communication is no longer between fixed points but mobile points. Those points are no longer households but individuals. It no longer makes any sense to list a "home" phone and an "office" phone. The cellphone is both – and neither. It breaks down the distinction between public and private space. After cyberspace comes – let's call it – cellspace.[2]

Let's have a look now at media form rather than communication form. Here there is a different story. Between the print form and the broadcast form there is massive consolidation and centralization of senders, and a corresponding expansion of receivers, to cover pretty much the whole of the United States. This starts to break down, not with the Internet but with an intermediate form – cable television. Cable starts a segmentation of audiences that the Internet only accelerates. In this respect, it is a partial return to the kind of media form of the pre-broadcast era.

The distinction between media (newspaper, television) and communication (post, telephone) becomes less clear in the era of the Internet and the cellphone. Both have the flexible point-to-point routing of the post, but can also support the one-to-many communications characteristic of mass print or broadcast media. The means of motivating and of mobilizing are no longer quite so separate.

All else being equal, the spoils of political office will be in the hands of those best able to exploit the distinctive envelope of possibilities of a given media regime. This has always been the case. There is no politics prior to media or outside of communication. All that changes are the available strategies. It's true enough that these days it is hard to get elected if you don't look good on TV. In a previous era, it would have been impossible to get elected without looking good riding a horse. If looking good on TV were all there was to it, then John Edwards would have become the 42nd President of the United States.

Using the available media and communication forms to best effect is a mark of political genius. Franklin Roosevelt did not resort to the fireside chat via radio very often, but when he did he showed a real understanding of the fact that radio was a domestic and household form.[3] Where most politicians still used radio as if shouting to a crowded hall, FDR knew that to be on radio was to be a guest in people's homes. Reagan extended this sensibility to television. It sounds obvious, but try watching videos of Ted Kennedy shouting at you from the screen as if addressing a union hall, and try to resist the temptation to turn down the volume.

Howard Dean's campaign for the 2004 Democratic Presidential primary ran aground when a video circulated of him on stage letting rip with a seemingly psychopathic roar. Seen on the small screen, in close-up, he did look rather nutty. It was hard not to wince or chortle. But Dean was appearing before a large and noisy crowd at a public gathering. His gestures would not have seemed so crazy to people in that audience. The problem was in negotiating between the two terrains, the physically present and the mediated one.

Ronald Reagan had a personal genius for the television medium, honed through his years as pitchman for *Fortune* 500 giant General Electric.[4] His public appearances were carefully calibrated to work also as mediated images. From Roosevelt, he took the model of the fireside chat and perfected it for the television era, appearing as a gracious guest in the living room rather than a shouting demagogue.

The Reagan era Republican Party possessed a quite different advantage in computerized direct-mail campaigning. It used the old media of the post to good effect by gathering detailed data on the habits of households and tailoring direct-mail campaigns accordingly. Got a subscription to *Guns and Ammo*? Here's a message from your friends at the NRA. It was the beginning of a sophisticated use of the database, borrowed from other forms of direct marketing.

It's possible that the relative success of the Democrats in 2008 was enabled at least in part by a canny use of the Internet and the cellphone. The Dems' Internet strategy dates to the Howard Dean campaign and its use of meetup.org to bring Democrats together socially, as a modest secular alternative to the ability of the Republicans to mobilize via the conservative churches.[5] It is also well known that the 2008 Obama presidential campaign took care to harvest cellphone numbers at rallies, so that the cellphone could be used as a broadcast platform. While the Republican robocalls languished unheard on obsolete landline answering machines, Democratic text messages prompted voters, wherever they happened to be on the day, to the polls.

Long before the electoral tide turned against the Republicans in 2008, the media tide turned. This would require a more subtle analysis – one that went beyond media form alone, to consider form in relation to rhetorical strategy. With Republican domination of talk radio and the ubiquity of Fox News, Democratic counter-media had to take a different tack. At the level of media form, the rise of the blogosphere is worth a mention. Of course there is a right-wing as well as a left-wing blogosphere. But where the right-wing blogs cannibalized existing media attention, the left-wing blogs filled a real vacuum, and in a way that Al Gore's *Current* cable network and *Air America* failed to do.

The key rhetorical move has to do with affect.[6] Put simply, the right has a monopoly on angry derision. One can't compete with shockjock Rush Limbaugh and *Faux News* sockpuppets like Bill O'Reilly on that terrain. Ironic distance never quite worked as counter-affect, despite the best efforts of TV comedian Jon Stewart. Nor did parody, although one might plausibly date the endgame for the Bush junta to Stephen Colbert's scorcher of a roast at the 2006 White House Correspondent's Dinner. As Simon Critchley has pointed out, the rhetorical genius of the Obama campaign was to co-opt faith and color it with the affect of hope rather than anger.[7] But for this strategy to work required a harnessing of new and old media that, while it has precedents in Dean's failed primary bid, was relatively new.

Part of it was a judicious filtering and enabling of more or less spontaneous propaganda efforts. The Shepard Fairey HOPE poster and will.i.am's "Yes we can" song and video are key examples. While not exactly "roots" media – both are by media professionals – they are not top-down productions blasted into people's awareness with strategic ad buys. Rather, they circulated laterally, via email, blogs, YouTube. Of the thousands of media productions, amateur and professional, official and unofficial, these were the ones that selected themselves at least in part via popular Internet filtering as iconic markers of the campaign.[8]

But good media are worthless without the means of communication to mobilize voters. This is where the cellphone and the Internet come into play. The Obama campaign was able to mobilize secular people with secular means (if with spiritual affect). The cellphone, in particular, is worth examining in this context. The Internet is still something of a household or organization-bound device. It is as useful to the religious right as to anyone else. It is perhaps even more useful in households that are patriarchal in structure. But the cellphone is different. It is ideal for mobilizing young voters, or those whose identities are not defined by the authority of Church or household "fathers."

Like many other industries, politics has replaced labor with capital where it is cheaper to do so. Digital era campaigning does away with the need for some of the local knowledge once carefully guarded by local political machines. The votes that carried Obama into the White House came from the exurbs, the edge cities, where the network of social organization is not dense and the megachurch looms as the only solution to this social deficit.[9] You can blast these places with broadcast ads, but what probably had the most effect was the door-to-door get-out-the-vote effort, the logistics of which are best handled by the Internet and cellphone.

All this is expensive. Hence the significance of Howard Dean's emphasis on the Internet as a fund-raising tool. It is still easier to raise money in big chunks from wealthy donors, but anything that reduces the cost of raising money in small amounts from a wide base is to be welcomed. It changes, if only slightly, the class composition of influence within the party. The Internet is the political weapon of choice of the educated, white-collar working class, not to mention the hacker class.

Every vector creates a space of possibilities for political action. Political actors discover these affordances by trial and error. The effects are often subtle and complicated. The media's discourse about itself favors stories in which new media forms are always revolutionary, which prompts counter-narratives which conclude that there is nothing new under the sun. The real story is always more interesting.

After the election of President Obama in 2008, the rules of the game changed somewhat, and corporations found themselves free to spend unlimited sums of money without even necessarily declaring themselves. The courts took the view that since corporations are "people" too, they should not be limited in the amount of money they spend to speak their minds. "Freedom of speech" collapses back into market freedom.

Stephen Colbert highlighted how the new rules worked by forming his own "Superpac" to fund comic political ads, seemingly just for the hell of it. Political campaigning started to look more obviously like what it has long been anyway: a branch of marketing. Richard Nixon allegedly said that one campaigns in poetry and governs in prose. These days one campaigns in tweets and governs in status updates. Fox News turned the most televisual talent in the Republican Party into viewer-bait, amassing a giant cable audience to sell to its advertisers.[10] Politics becomes a genre of the **aesthetic economy,** and one imbued with the interests of the class that rules it.

Hence one of the new Four Freedoms might be not freedom of speech, but freedom from speeches. Not that freedom of speech is a bad thing, but the complicated liberal discourse on the nuances of the term seems entirely bypassed by "conservative" jurists, for whom law has no meaning other than as the rules of the road for the circulation of capital at maximum velocity. The celebrated oratory of President Obama turned out to be just so many empty words. The speechifying that will be most heard is that which is most eloquently paid for.

Does politics still exist? Or does it go the way of all those other practices and artifacts of second nature? Open your laptop or turn on your computer and you will see a "desktop" with maybe some "files" on it, maybe a "trash can" down in the corner. Maybe your browser opens on a "face book" and maybe you will read "books" on it or watch a "film." Yet none of these things actually exists. They are just dead skins for new creations, ways of making the vectoral seem familiar. Perhaps politics is another such dead skin. To the vector, the spoils.

17

The Little Sisters Are Watching You

New York, New York

One by one the eyes of the Big Brothers are closed and coins placed over them. While a third generation of Kim family dictators is groomed to take over the family business of ruling North Korea, enough portraits of Saddam Hussein and Colonel Gaddafi went to the pyre to increase global warming. Now there's a more subtle and effective image of omnipotence, more consonant with the minutia of present-day consumption. The little sisters are watching you, staring out at you from billboards, magazines, screens large and small.

Behind the production of her image is not some quirky dictator and his nervous minions, but a small army of agents, stylists, hairdressers, photographers, and of course models.[1] Whole industries exist to find and groom actual bodies that might embody this abstract **interface** who is one of the central modes of the contemporary imaginal world.[2] She has a privileged place within the world that **telesthesia** reveals. She won't send the secret police to kick in your door in the middle of the night, but she might send you to the mall to get new shoes – and quite possibly in your sleep.

Let's call her **The Girl**. She hasn't much to do with actual women, although women might or might not feel obliged to mark their distance from her. The Girl is not even necessarily female or even all that young. Sometimes men's bodies or older bodies populate the images that constitute her. She isn't always white. She isn't always human. Sometimes she is a robot or a cartoon or a flower. The norms around which she gravitates are geometrical.

The Girl is a curious kind of interface. One can inhabit the interface of the Gamer or the Hacker, but The Girl is more elusive. She is rather like the interface of the child with whom our tour of the panorama of telesthesia began. She enables certain flows of image and story access to some parts of your awareness, rather than allowing your awareness to access certain parts of the knowable world. Perhaps, like the image of the child, the image of The Girl is a sort of non-persona. She makes the inhuman look like something approachable.

In 2005, the Svedka vodka company started using a "fembot" as its public face. Designed by Stan Winston, who worked on *Aliens, Avatar,* and the *Terminator* movies, the fembot is an apparently female robot who stares out of billboards under punning slogans, such as R U BOT OR NOT? An ad on the side of buses has her reclining, with the slogan: THE ULTIMATE PARTY MACHINE.

As is often the case, the advertising here is not being in any sense false. It is quite candid about the fact that The Girl is not only not a woman, but is not even human: MAKE YOUR NEXT TROPHY WIFE 100% TITANIUM. The publicists for Svedka assure us it's all meant in a playful spirit: ALL THE GOOD ONES ARE MARRIED *AND* GAY. Play would hardly exempt them from the charge of promoting a certain misogyny – even if what is more striking is the campaign's frank acknowledgment that the desires The Girl massages are hardly even human.

The Girl is the marker of the success and failure of feminism. Like most social movements, feminism's gains come at the price of a certain incorporation into the very order it opposes. The women's liberation movement begat, as an unintended consequence, "girl power." As the anonymous writers of *Tiqqun* have it: "The supposed liberation of women has not consisted in their emancipation from the domestic sphere, but rather the extension of that sphere over the whole of society."[3]

Life in the overdeveloped world is not a social factory, but a social boudoir. It even extends itself into the workplace, which now harbors rituals of tact and gestures of discretion that would be worthy of a Proust, but which will have to settle for being chronicled by the screenwriters of *Sex and the City*. Labor became affective labor. Politics became family drama. Art became interior decoration. The struggle over the remaking of the form of social life became kitchen renovation.

For actual women, and perhaps not just for women, The Girl is an interface that can't be occupied, but with which one has to negotiate, somehow. The movie of *The Devil Wears Prada* addresses this by splitting the problem between four characters, who manage the distance between body and interface in different ways. When Anne Hathaway joins the staff of a *Vogue*-ish magazine, she finds herself the third of a series of satellites. One will become her gay confidant (Stanley Tucci), and one her female rival (Emily Blunt). The three of them orbit the devil herself – the editor (Meryl Streep).

Blunt tries too hard to be The Girl – many not-bad jokes here about how she starves herself. Tucci as the gay confidant is "always the bridesmaid never the bride" to The Girl. Hathaway has to resolve the confusion of whether to be The Girl, or to wield The Girl, which is the secret of Meryl the devil. In the end she quits to go work for a magazine more like *The Nation*. Her flirtation with being, or doing, The Girl is over. It's a wannabe Bildungsroman about the difference between being and interface.

The images of The Girl are the currency through which a modification in the world of images is managed and felt. The omnipresence of The Girl only shows that the myth of the intimacy of woman with nature has found a new home, that of second nature, which is now apparently a domestic world of finishes and veneers. Jean Baudrillard: "This is called information and it has wormed its way into everything, like a phobic, maniacal leitmotiv, which affects sexual relations as well as kitchen implements."[4] The domestic world of second nature is impregnated with significance. The Girl presides over the communicability of surfaces.

The Girl's utopia is domestic, but the domicile of the domestic is imagined as the whole world. The Girl will save that world by being photographed offering food to needy children somewhere, or being photographed with a product some tiny percentage of the proceeds from which will send someone else over there to feed them. She never appears as a mother. The Girl does not have children of her own, but her interface forms a pact with other interfaces, including on occasion the child.

Pictures show "supermodel" Tasha de Vasconcelos "visiting the clinic in Malawi that she helped set up." She is of course pictured holding a black child. Or: "Supermodel vows to stay naked till USAID funds reach starving children."[5] (A supermodel, incidentally, is just a model who became famous for her impersonations of The Girl.) Going "naked" would be the appropriate kind of strike for someone paid to put on The Girl as appearances. The Girl can be nude but never naked.

The affective tone of The Girl ranges from friendly to sexy, from pliable to indomitable. Her look can be inviting or a fuck-off stare. Her face is never a "Jane face" (google it) but often pictures the moment before or after. She is not always available, but she might be available to be available. Just as there is a range of affect so too there is a range of decor: she can be on the street, in an office, in the boudoir, or even on the moon. The Girl makes every scene an interior, as if any place in the world could be made her private domain by her presence.

Her power to create this domain is beauty. She is sequestered in her own beauty. A certain moralizing tone in contemporary discourse holds somewhat paradoxically that beauty is only skin deep and what matters is really inner beauty. But, as with the Greeks, the world of The Girl regards beauty as having both spiritual and philosophical import. Debord: "what is good appears; what appears is good."[6] The good that appears – beauty – is outside of time. Experience, aging, procreation, memory – in short, history – is not to appear. Time is marked out by the structural permutations of the fashion cycle. Fashion has nothing to hide but its recent past.

The Girl is quite naturally not just about beauty but also about sex. Or, rather, she is about a "sexiness" detached from any particular sex act. Ever since Manet's *Olympia*, The Girl has had an embarrassing relation to the specifics of sex, not to mention the specifics of money.[7] She is not supposed to be locatable in any particular intercourse of either kind. It's why in a world apparently so laissez-faire about its desires, porn is with few exceptions a domain cordoned off from the world of "legitimate" models and actresses. The exceptions, such as porn-star-turned-actor Sasha Gray, confirm the rule on closer analysis.[8]

The Girl is about seduction more than sex. She appears to be practicing seduction without any specific person in mind. She makes seduction a constant. She appears as the bearer of an apparently esoteric knowledge of what it is to be wanted. Baudrillard: "The irony proper to the constitution of [The Girl] as an ideal or sex object: in her closed perfection, she puts an end to sex play and refers man, the lord and master of the sexual reality, to his transparency as an *imaginary* subject."[9] This might be the untapped potential of The Girl, her **antipodal** relation to the whole dichotomy of the gendered imaginary.

But it is not the use to which she is put. Baudrillard: "In advertising it is not so much a matter of adding sex to washing machines (which is absurd) as conferring on objects the imaginary, female quality of being available at will, of never being retractile or aleatory."[10] The Girl seduces on behalf of a brand or a product, or sometimes even a cause. Somebody was paid to embody or invoke her and assume the aura of seduction on behalf of shampoo or champagne. And yet there is a certain nobility about The Girl which is not supposed to be questioned. She stands, as embodiment of beauty, on the one side for venal seduction, but on the other for romantic love.

Love is the last unquestionable ideology. Laura Kipnis: "Consider that the most powerful organized religions produce the occasional heretic; every ideology has its apostates; even sacred cows find their butchers. Except for love."[11] After the death of God comes the death of the Oedipal father-figures who are His stand-ins, including Big Brother. No third term mediates on behalf of the symbolic order any more between the self and what appears to it. Yet romantic love lives on. Pop songs still speak endlessly of it, declaring their loves to "you, you." The "you" addressed in pop songs is The Girl, who does not replace the father and his stand-ins, looking down from above. She is, in several senses, "a bit on the side," between but not above the subject and the object.

There's a certain tension in this interface. The Girl has to embody, at one and the same time, a romantic love become banal and self-involved, and a beauty become seamless and sheer. The domesticity of sharing toothpaste and the domesticity of beauty in Photoshopped splendour tend to cancel each other out. As *Tiqqun* might say: her love, like her ass, is an abstraction. Love and beauty are extracts, mined and circulated for purposes not intrinsic to themselves.

The Girl is only partly there as the object of desire, as stand-in for the commodity. *Tiqqun*: "The Girl is the dominant social relationship, the central form of the desire of desire, within the spectacle."[12] As Kojeve parses Hegel: I don't desire the other as a thing. I desire the other's desire. Or to translate that into pop: I want you to want me, I need you to need me. The Girl is a commodity that appears to desire its acquirer. Or, rather, she might desire us. The suspension is key. The universal and eternal seduction projected by The Girl might or might not alight specifically on us. She is available to be available, but she isn't cheap: "Because I'm worth it!"

Incidentally, the slippage in slogans used by L'Oréal, from BECAUSE I'M WORTH IT to BECAUSE YOU'RE WORTH IT to BECAUSE WE'RE WORTH IT, might indicate a certain ambiguity as to who is worth what. Where and how is value created in this chain of production, seduction, and consumption? Pierre Klossowski once proposed the idea of "living currency."[13] What if one thought of the medium of exchange of an economy not as cold hard cash but as warm fuzzy emotions?

Bodily presence might already be a commodity, quite apart from any commodity it produces. Think of the shop assistant or waitress, standing around, bored, waiting for customers. If it is an expensive store or bar, she will of course be beautiful. She will have to "model." In a sense, she will embody The Girl *in vivo*. Is she not already a commodity, even before any customers walk in wanting frocks or cocktails? These bodies – waitress and drinker alike – both produce and are produced by an economy of sensations. They inhabit a world in which desires, emotions, fantasies are exchangeable – if only for store credit.

Klossowski draws an interesting distinction between fantasy and simulacrum. Fantasy is implicated in the real. It is not purely private and can involve others. And yet it is not exchangeable. It is fantasy in the sense that the Surrealists thought could be the raw material for a political imagination. Simulacra, on the other hand, are exchangeable. They are what the velvet goldmine of the Surrealists really turned out to be: the raw ore of commodified desire.

Simulacra in Klossowski's sense are not the general equivalent that is represented by money, but currency of another species: specific equivalents, represented as often as not by bodies, in particular by the body doubles of The Girl. In Klossowski's economy, and perhaps in our own, fantasy and simulacrum are reversible, as are object and subject, and use value and exchange value. A simulacrum can have use value. It's the affective charge of The Girl that is the use value consumed in the purchase and wearing of a shoe. *Tiqqun*: "The Girl's ass represents the last bastion of the illusion of use value."[14]

The one constant is the push-and-pull of desire, the one remaining gold standard. The Girl is the central embodiment of the golden standard of affect. Large-scale industrial production of The Girl is a hedge against the depreciation of affect in the overdeveloped world. Not only is the symbolic order in decline, the imaginary machinery that replaces it requires constant (sal)lubrication. The Girl returns to the sullied world of commodities their lost honor. Like gold, The Girl radiates a certain rarity and uselessness. And, like gold, finding the raw awe out of which she is refined takes an industry of prospectors.

THE PERSONAL IS POLITICAL: by this slogan, the women's movement sought to extend the image of the political into the domestic realm, to open it up to a certain critique and action. THE POLITICAL IS PERSONAL: this is what The Girl proposes by way of a response. The social, communal, or political imaginal world is compressed into the personal, domestic domain. Interestingly, it is this domestic domain at least partially imagined after feminism. But it is not a politics. It is not the effect of what Castoriadis calls the imaginary institution of society, but rather of a simulated economy of desire.[15] Little sister is watching you. Or being watched by you, or encouraging you to join her in admiring something, maybe a bag – or a watch. The domestic becomes the horizon of how life can be conceived.

The Four Freedoms that might form the basis of imagining a politics in the overdeveloped world are: (1) freedom from religion; (2) freedom from speeches; (3) freedom from desire; and (4) freedom from security. Of these, the third might seem the most puzzling. Surely the liberation *of* desire was one of the great themes of the twentieth century? Surely freedom from religion *is* the freedom to desire? Wait! Not so fast! There's a slippage here. It's true enough that freedom from religion was a partial achievement of modernity. What the psychoanalysts call the "demise of symbolic efficiency" really did take place.[16] God is dead, and with

Him the law of the Father. The virulence with which religion returns in the overdeveloped world is a rearguard action. The megachurches sprouting on the fringes of suburbia are (tax-exempt) centers of entertainment as much as anything else.

God is undead. He is the living dead who passes out of the center of everyday life to stalk instead the fringes of its every night. But this partial disenchantment of the world leads not to the installation of rational enlightenment, but the installation of **game space**, where the meaning of a value is its measure. And where that fails, new interfaces jostle the ghost-white Father aside and take His place in the front ranks of our spectacular Olympus. One of his least expected rivals is The Girl. She has few memorable biblical precedents, but her distant ancestors almost kept Odysseus from returning home.

The Girl is denominated not as the currency of faith but of desire. She presides over the exchange of money, not for things, but for the penumbra that surrounds things. She guarantees not the thing but its aura. What is little noticed about Walter Benjamin's evocation of the aura is that it is about provenance.[17] The aura of the artwork derives from the chain of title that guarantees its authenticity. In the absence of such a chain of title, The Girl appears as the living currency that denominates a kind of alternative aura that can be drawn around even the most mass-produced of commodities. It might be just a thing, made from raw materials, shipped to China, run up in some giant factory, and shipped by container over the seas, but it has been in the presence of The Girl.

Freedom from desire does not mean that, like the Taliban, one should ban the image of The Girl or shut down the vector. Or even that one should settle for the old petit bourgeois claim to be above all these things, to shun fashion and read only good books. To abjure fashion is a move within its game, and literature has been obsessed with the problem of The Girl for some time (on which see *Madame Bovary*). Rather, it's about asking Benjamin's question concerning the provenance of both the form and content of **telesthesia**.

As Benjamin was already suggesting in the era of the mechanical reproducibility of the vector, it makes possible a kind of democratizing of perception, and along two axes. The vector becomes cheaper, less tied to exclusive rituals. Copies can be made for everybody. At the same time, the vector becomes a **transopticon**.

In principle at least, the scale of perception can be massively expanded. Different scales can be combined. Different time series can be organized, which expand or contract temporal perception. In short, montage means a vast expansion of temporal and spatial scales, of points of view, of possible networks of sense. Benjamin described the potentials of the Internet long before it existed.

Benjamin was saying in effect that the transformation of the techno-economic base, the mode of production of perception, would change perception itself. And with this crude, techno-Marxist insight, he was absolutely right. Only the transformation of the means of production is, as he was well aware, a site of struggle rather than a conveyor belt. The ruling class is not about to cede the socialization of the means of perception to popular forces without a fight, even if the maintenance of relations of private property in the domain of the production of perception requires a transformation of the composition of the ruling class itself, and a refashioning of its ideological superstructures.

And so, in short, no more ritual of praying at the altar to the Father. And no more Great Dictators offering the vanity of their own mortal visage in His place. In place of the Father and Big Brother, the little sisters. Interestingly, they are not the daughters of the Father. Their origins, if they need have any at all, are every-day. (Every now and then, a back-story about the famous model with her ordinary middle-aged parents. The story might juxtapose portraits of the model with her family, a regular woman with her regular folks, with pictures of her at work, as a model, invoking The Girl. The poses, the styling, the light, the framing – all will be significantly different.[18] Her other "parents" are unseen except by their handiwork: the stylist, make-up artist, photographer, photo-editor, and so on.) The Girl is a belated retrieval of the value of provenance, and with it whole hierarchies of ownership and property, in an overdeveloped world that long ago shot past the need for such things.

So while desire was the great theme of the late twentieth century, it ended up becoming nothing more than that which a new kind of currency – a living money – denominates. Not that there can't be wants and needs; yens and yearnings. Not that the everyday isn't full of moments for sexual hydraulics, for affect and intimacy, or for seduction and surfaces. Only that the means are at hand to produce all of the above, whether in the most embodied or the most stylized forms, at least partly outside of commodified desire.

By the beginnings of the twenty-first century, the instinct of many of the second-wave feminists was to be wary of "girl power," and rightly so. The Girl stands for the slogan that the political is personal. It is about the freedom of desire to encase itself in the brands of its choice. So-called "empowerment" really meant credit cards. The problem was that retreating to an authenticity of the body – a refusal of seduction, or the insistence on difference – just didn't work. It's hard to make a stand on the body, or on its adequate representation, or on a practice of *écriture féminine*, when all of these things are already caught up in the vectoral.[19] Third nature takes the cleavings of gender and distributes them all over the place. The antipodes of gender becomes an antipodality at work and at play, in any and every relation. Gender difference as the minimal unit of meaning becomes the guarantee of the possibility of meaning wherever a more rigorous game of algorithmic values can't be secured.

Judith Butler made progress by insisting on the impossibility of a concordance of the body with what it is supposed to signify.[20] But this openness to the performative quality of gender stops short of its detachment from subjects and distribution throughout the entire perceivable world.[21] The Girl is in a way subtracted from gender as difference and made to play as the token of a different kind of difference: living money, the evaluation not even of things, but of market opportunities.

This is why the interface of the drag queen doesn't really work to undo the apparent naturalness of gender. The drag queen has nothing to do with gender. She is all about The Girl. The drag queen is the indication that not just (technically!) male bodies but anything at all can be the support for the special effects of Girlness. Even in the exaggerated form of drag, her effect works. She adds the provenance of living money to signs and things assembled and performed. The Girl can be a man, but then The Girl can be a robot, or even just the sign of a robot. The Svedka fembot is even available as a Halloween costume, so that a (technically!) real woman might masquerade as a robot pretending to be The Girl.

None of this ought to mean all that much when put up against the politics of domestic violence, rape, abortion, wage equality, sexual harassment in the workplace or on the street – the list goes on. Except that The Girl is one of the things that stands in the way of there even being a politics within which such things could be the stakes. The Girl as living money of desire occludes the space for imagining a politics of wants and needs. But not only that: what if The Girl also effaced the possibility of another kind of aesthetics, or rather of another **aesthetic economy**, including that of seduction, that was actually based on the lack of provenance of the digital image, on the seemingly infinite flexibility of the vector within daily life?

A "social networking" site like Facebook is a sort of platform for extracting a rent from what used to be called blogging. The rent takes two forms. First, there's the advertising revenue, but second, there's a kind of information rent. Users pay with their information, and that information fuels the development of the business. As of 2011, Facebook was the dominant social networking platform in the United States, with a notional value of billions. (By the time you read this, who knows?)

Part of its success was due to the American college-culture nature of its governing metaphor – the "facebook." Its proprietors did not too strongly insist that its users be, in some sense, true to themselves, but certain common practices of self-presentation took hold. Everyone's page looks more or less the same, and most people present themselves as some version of themselves. Facebook eclipsed MySpace, at least among users who were, or aspired to be, presentably middle class. MySpace had a lingering popularity among military service personnel, and among gay and lesbian youth and young people of color.[22] (This is, of course, just in the United States. Elsewhere in the world other social networking platforms occupied the dominant and supplemental positions.)

A quite particular niche was occupied, at least in the United States, by another site: Tumblr. Started in 2007, its interface works nicely with short posts that are heavy on pictures. It's easy to repost pictures from one person's Tumblr to another. Its New York-based proprietors seem not to care about the authenticity of the identities its users create. Nor are they so bothered by material that Facebook would find obscene.

People use Tumblr for all sorts of things. One thing its qualities as a vector lend themselves to is the construction of anonymous or pseudonymous identities who share and comment on images of their desires. Needless to say, there's a furious trading in images of The Girl, a cutting and pasting of every possible permutation of her and what is proximate to her. The Girl finds herself juxtaposed to fashion, naturally, but also to porn, to the confessional, to everyday life. Sometimes she remains attached to the commodities over which she presides, but sometimes she gets a divorce from them.

Here is a whole other economy, of thefts and gifts, in which The Girl participates. It will never make her go away, but perhaps at least it is a small nudge toward making her join the living dead, or that phantasmagoria that stalks the everyday without commanding it. In the great materialist poets, from Lucretius to Leopardi to Marx, the Gods are still present, but they just look on. It is they who are caught in the spectacle of us; not us who are caught in the spectacle of them.

18

Shit is Fucked Up and Bullshit

Zuccotti Park, New York

I'm a worker. I go to work every weekday. I get paid. Most of that money goes to support my family. There's a little left over for fun. There's some for small acts of generosity. This makes possible a pretty good life. Will my students get to have that life? Or my kids?

In his novel *Dead Europe*, Christos Tsiolkas imagines a man exiled from his country, who dies in another land. On his tombstone are three words: worker, father, husband.[1] Husband is a bit too patriarchal for me. Perhaps mine would say: worker, father, lover. Lover, in different ways, of different people: my partner, my kids. But a lover too, in another way, of my class. The class – or is it classes? – of people who work, with some part of their bodies. People who work with eyes and hands and backs and voices, and so on.

I take pride in my work. Sure, there are good days and bad days. Nobody gives "110 percent." When you hear that sort of bullshit you know it's coming from people who aren't workers. It's the language of the Donald Trump types, who managed not to squander an inheritance and think that makes them a genius. They're so proud of themselves and have no barriers to telling you about it. The pride of the worker is mostly silent. You get up, go to work. You get up, go to work again. Until you can't get up any more. That's all there is to it.

With luck, you get to work at something that won't kill you, and that you might even like. I got lucky. I like my work. I like teaching. I like writing. I have a secure job, doing something I like. This is not something my people took for granted. On the other hand, I refuse to see this through the reactionary language of "privilege." To have work, security, a little left over at the end of the week. This is not privilege. It's a right.

When a small band, some anarchist, some not, marched on Wall Street on September 17, 2011, they played a cat-and-mouse game with the police for a few blocks, then took over Zuccotti Park. And there they stayed, gathered around a brilliant slogan, of obscure origins: WE ARE THE 99 PERCENT. Of course we're the 99 percent of the 1 percent of the planet, but let's not get sidetracked back into the language of privilege. The slogan is all about the remainder, about what is left out. It's a way of saying: we are not the ruling class. Our solidarity, that fragile thing, orbits what it is not.

Maybe it's an Australian thing, or part of an almost extinct antipodean way of thinking, but to be doing well is not something to take too much personal pride in. You can always "fall back" so don't "sell tickets on yourself." Let's recall, just for a minute, that the late Steve Jobs, legendary former CEO of Apple, was adopted. The story is usually told from his point of view – how remarkable his success is, given that he was adopted. Nobody stops to think about the extraordinary act of generosity of the people who chose to provide the enormous, thankless labor of being his parents. The success of Steve Jobs comes from a lot of things – but one of them is "communism."

I'm no Steve Jobs, but I am doing all right for myself. Things happened in my life that taught me how much work it takes for anybody to even get by at all. I can walk because a now-famous surgeon, by trial and error, worked out how to hack my club feet into something that would support bipedal life. Three months in a hospital bed at the age of seven will impress upon you just how many people it takes to make a world where that doctor can operate on that child. The nurses, the kitchen staff, the lady who came to mop the floor. My older brother and sister bringing me books and toys.

They were worried how I would stand up to institutional life, I think. But I wasn't the kid who screamed all night for his mother. My mother was dead. Since the age of six I spent the afternoons after school at the house of a childhood friend. My family was

not close to that child's family, but they had me over every after-
noon anyway, until my big brother could come and get me. And
all things considered, regardless of what had happened, I had a
pretty good childhood. It was good, once again, because of something one could call communism. Because people did things for
each other and made a "community." All they had in common,
in this case, was caring for a child.

So I got by. I emigrated. Found work in a new country. Fell in
love, got married, had kids. Life goes on. I do my job. For me to
do it the guys in gray overalls have to keep the building running.
The women behind the desks have to push paper and quietly
network with each other to do the social maintenance. Not to
mention the MTA employees who keep the subway running to get
me to the New School. Or the people who run the cafes all over
the neighborhood where I actually get work done. We depend on
each other. If I forget my wallet, the guy in the cafe serves me
anyway. He trusts me to pay next time.

Not everybody wants the same things. Negotiating how to
accommodate different versions of the good life is one of the great
challenges of the times. Still, it's surprising how common certain
core desires are. A lot of people want something like the life I am
describing – at least for a start. To love and be loved. To belong
somewhere, with others. To work at something that seems worth
working at. To not have all this taken away.

And it could be taken away. Could my family survive a medical
emergency? The untimely death of either me or my partner? How
would my family get by? Would the apartment have to be sold?
Would the debts mount beyond the point where they could ever
be paid back? What if there were no work? It can keep you up at
night. And there's no comfort in the fact that living hand to
mouth, without proper medical care, under looming waves of
debt, is the life lived now by millions of Americans.

Theodor Adorno put it well: "There is tenderness only in the
coarsest demand: that no-one should go hungry any more."[2] That
children go hungry, that they will be cold and starving, and uncared
for this winter, right here in New York, condemns every fine word
said in favor of the current social order by the sockpuppets whose
fine, well-paid job it is to find excuses for it.

I have never cared all that much about equality. I don't want
to bring anyone down. I find it mildly comic that some people,

even people I know, don't feel motivated or valued unless they have been showered by great gushes of money. I saw contemporaries of mine take truly awful, soul-crushing jobs that held no promise other than that one day they would be fabulously wealthy. Some made it; some didn't. I have compassion for the successful ones, who, having come into money, have no idea what to do with it. They buy big houses. Take endless vacations. Buy "contemporary art." Become patrons of something or other. Sometimes these things seem to be all they have, and all they can talk about. I don't see anything to envy in that.

On the other hand, I know too many people who also do awful jobs who hardly get paid at all. They juggle bills. They screen their phone calls. They cross their fingers and hope for the best. Money is a problem for these friends of mine, but it isn't really a desire. They want it to stop being a problem so they can do things that are more interesting. Make art, or have time for friends, or teach their kids the language of their homeland. These are the things that seem so tenuous and impossible.

There's a Tumblr blog called *We Are the 99 Percent*, on which people hold up home-made signs that tell their stories. The stories are mostly about two things: debt and jobs. Most people don't really care all that much about what the 1 percent has. They are not concerned about someone else's wealth; they are concerned about everyone else's impoverishment. They are concerned about going hungry. This Tumblr is mostly anonymous, but it is not about desires, it is about needs.

The promise of all those fine words, of deregulation, of financialization, was that things would get better for everybody. It didn't. It seems to come as something of a surprise to the sockpuppets that anyone actually believed any of the promises. The promises were just ways to make us all feel better. In reality, the 1 percent expects its cut no matter what. And all the talk about "rewarding risk" was also not supposed to be believed by anybody either. It's the 99 percent who take the risks. The 1 percent expects its bad bets to be covered by the rest of us.

When Occupy Wall Street erupted, nobody was still quite ready to call the 1 percent what they are: a ruling class. Nor were they quite ready to identify what kind of ruling class they are: a rentier class. It's not important. It is only ever a minority who are attracted to an analytical language to explain their circumstances. Popular revolts run on affect, and affect runs on images and stories. Still, the instincts of Occupy Wall Street have been pretty keen. It has identified its own problems: jobs and debt. It has provisionally identified the problem causing their problems: the 1 percent.

The idea of a rentier class can be traced back to David Ricardo. Joan Robinson had a keen analysis of it in her *The Accumulation of Capital*.[3] That's an old book, but its language has hardly been bettered. A rentier class owns some kind of property that everyone else needs in order to invent or create or build anything else. The original rentier class of Ricardo's day owned the land. If land was the choke-hold on the rise of industry, these days it's capital itself. The part of the surplus diverted to an unproductive ruling class isn't rent any more, it's interest.

My personal minimum demand for Occupy Wall Street could be: PUT THE RULING CLASS BACK IN CHARGE! Despite the violence of the class struggle that characterized the United States in its great period of growth and dynamism – from the nineteenth-century robber barons to the rise of Fordism – most of that period is dynamic and forward-looking. The old ruling class built something.

The railways were built over the bones of thousands of Chinese workers. But they were built. The iPhone was built on the backs – once again – of a small army of Chinese workers. But they were built, and they are a damned sight more impressive than the Bakelite rotary phone I remember from my childhood home. The railways and the tech industry had their bubbles. But at least in the aftermath of those exuberant parties there were pools of skilled labor, bits of infrastructure, new techniques lying around waiting for more productive employment. But after the housing bubble of 2008? What was left but the rotting carcass of suburbs nobody needs, and a great pile of debt that working people had to shoulder to keep the rentier class in rent? The rentier class makes even those murdering thugs and thieves, the robber barons, look good.

What makes our current rentier class worse than the robber barons is that they are not even building anything. They are not interested in biopolitics. Their MO is "thanopolitics." They have no interest in the care and feeding of populations. All they care about is extracting the rent. It doesn't matter to them if we get sick, if we can't read, if we are not being raised up and developed to our full capacity. We're just peons. We owe the 1 percent the vigorish (as loan sharks call it) not because they're going to invest it in anything useful and productive. We just owe it. Or else.

There are three components to this struggle. The Marxists are right. It's a class struggle, and us workers have been losing it. When the rise in the rate of productivity slowed down in the seventies, class struggle in the workplace became heated but futile.[4] Wage rises out of line with the rate of improvement in productivity led to inflation, as businesses just passed on the costs. What broke the cycle was not so much some new breakthrough in productive efficiency, as shipping the work off to newly available pools of cheap labor – the symbol of which is China.

The problem is that there's a mismatch between the rise of productive capacity in the underdeveloped world and a decline in real wages in the **overdeveloped** world. The gap was covered, among other things, by rising levels of indebtedness. To have a "middle-class" life in America now means at least two people in a household have to work full time and hope or pray that no disaster – medical or otherwise – befalls them.

The ruling class in the United States is less and less one that makes things, and more and more one that owns information and collects a rent from it. Sometimes this is productive, in that it at least designs new things and creates new markets for them. Apple and Google: the **aesthetic economy** at its finest. But in other respects the ruling class becomes one that just seeks rent without really doing much to earn it.

Apple and Google employ engineering and design and even cultural talent to make things people get to use in their everyday lives. But a lot of that talent gets employed to make pilotless drones and other weapons of mass destruction for the Pentagon. In an age of permanent austerity where the state disinvests from everything, the siphoning of talent into the toys of war is still somehow sacrosanct. Occupy DC protesters forced the National Air and Space Museum to shut down temporarily on October 8, 2011, because the museum was hosting an exhibition about the drones. Shutting the museum was apparently preferable to having them enter the museum with signs that said DRONES KILL KIDS.[5] This event was a small sign of the occupation joining the dots between the different forms of the ruling power.

One branch of our emergent ruling class in the overdeveloped world at least still designs and markets things, but it doesn't really make them. Another branch makes things, but they are designed to kill people. Still another branch makes its money out of money – the vector perfected. Its game is financialization. It's the expansion of the scale of social relations that take a financial form, from the insinuation of commercial credit into everyday life at one scale to the global financial trading infrastructure on the other. Is this ruling class really capitalist any more? Perhaps we could call it **vectoralist**. It collects a rent by controlling the vectors along which information shuttles, not to mention that information itself.

Occupy Wall Street targets one of these three branches of the ruling class with clear and powerful images and stories – the financial wing of vectoral power. It's a perspective from which to start thinking about the other branches of power in the United States – and elsewhere. But perhaps it might take a bit of an update on the old Marxist diagram of class forces. This is not your grandparents' ruling class. Take my home town: it used to be a steel town, which of course means it was near coalmines and on a working port. It still has coalmines, but the coal is shipped to China. The land where the old steel mill was is fallow, and the port now houses office blocks for the regional offices of insurance companies and the like. Perhaps we need to extend and refine – rather than overturn – granddad Karl's analysis of what was once capitalism, to understand what these familiar landscapes of the overdeveloped world are all about.

A powerful alternative analysis can be found in David Graeber's monumental *Debt: The First 5000 Years*.[6] He makes debt, rather than work, the central category of analysis. After a quick debunking of Adam Smith's originary myth of "barter," and through careful use of ethnographic and historical material, he shows that credit came before money. Most people, most of the time, have managed careful relationships of debt and credit. From time to time these become lopsided, debt becomes the permanent indebtedness of the peon. The peons revolt. The ruling order declares a debt jubilee. Life returns to some pattern of stability and integrity.

Money in the form of "coinage" arises out of warfare. Soldiers are by definition not creditworthy. They need to be paid in something that seems more tangible than a promise. With soldiers, a ruling class can conquer territory, enslave populations, and not least impose a cash economy on its subjects in which taxes have to be paid in coin. The necessity to come up with the cash then drives everyone at least partly into the cash economy.

Like anyone with a solid grounding in ethnography, Graeber sees all social formations as hybrid structures, not reducible to the simple-minded abstractions of the economists – or for that matter the political philosophers. At the risk of caricature, this complexity has at least three components: communism, exchange, and hierarchy. Debt works differently in all three.

Communism knows no debt. The one to whom one extends generosity is not the other. That one is one of "us" and as we hold ourselves to be "in common" there's no externality with whom to be in credit or debit. Hierarchy has asymmetric debts. Those below owe something tangible to those above; those above repay that debt with something symbolic. The peasant owes this or its equivalent in coin. The lord or the bishop – as Raoul Vaneigem would say – owes a debt only to the totality.[7] His debt is to the "order" he upholds.

Exchange is not among "us," it is with the "other." There are two kinds of exchange and hence two kinds of debt that exchange creates. One can be quantified. Debts of this kind can be canceled on repayment. But there is another kind of debt, the debt of gift exchange. It is always qualitative. Paying it back is something of an art form. You can't pay it back too quickly, or in too exact an amount. The whole point of the gift as debt is that it can't be canceled on repayment. There is always some incommensurability between one gift and another. Gifts are stratagems for binding people through time.

Graeber draws on a rich tradition which sees money in the form of coinage as foundational social practices on which both philosophy and religion developed both their theories and their practices. Whether for Buddhist temples or Christian monasteries, the withdrawal of gold and silver from circulation to make idols of the saints converts one form of measuring debt into quite another. Our founding categories are caught up in a series of metaphors drawn from ancient amazement at how money works.

The period since the seventies, since the breakdown of Fordism, represents something of a break in Graeber's narrative. Until then most histories oscillate between money as coinage and money as debt, accounted without coins between people in more stable relationships. Coinage and debt payable in coins usually coincides with the kind of state apparatus that uses coins to finance wars to acquire slaves to make more coins to finance more wars, and so on. In other words, situations which foreclose the dense web of social relations – communism, exchange, even hierarchy – which prevail in more stable periods.

The key moment in this narrative is Nixon taking the United States off the gold standard, in order to finance the Vietnam War while continuing to pacify populations at home with state largesse.[8] But Graeber doesn't linger much on what made this possible. He pays attention to early technologies for recording and transmitting information that might work to support all kinds of debt relations. But he stops paying attention to this material dimension as his story gets closer to the present. The missing piece is what I call the vectoral. The underlying story in Graeber's masterful book is the steady improvement, and occasional leaps in development, of the means of recording and transmitting information – the vectoral. Nixon had his reasons, but what he realized was an inevitable break between the transmission of information and the way it is embedded in materiality.

Still, Graeber's work is a useful parallel to the Marxist tradition and its focus on labor. Clearly debt is the other constant in the popular sentiment behind Occupy Wall Street. It's just unfortunate that in *Debt: The First 5000 Years* Graeber so gingerly treats the boundaries between his own perspective and the Marxist one. It is present, barely acknowledged, in the text and the footnotes. There's a space between these two perspectives that Graeber is perhaps constitutionally incapable of "occupying."

I want to suggest there are actually three perspectives one needs to put together to understand the occupation. The third can help traverse the **antipodal** relation between the other two. The first is classically Marxist, and is about labor. The second is anarchist, if of an original kind, and is about debt. The third was pointed out by Gar Alperovitz, and in his terms is about the privatization of the knowledge economy.[9]

An analysis in the journal *Occupy!* of the *We Are the 99 Percent* Tumblr shows that the words "jobs" and "debt" are the two most frequent salient terms in people's handwritten notes about their lives and what makes them part of the 99 percent.[10]

Also in the top 10 are "college" and "student" and "school." A few things to note here: first, one of the big issues, and not just for young people, is student debt. The 2008 recession made paying back such loans very difficult for many people. Those defaulting on student loans have few of the legal protections afforded other kinds of defaulters. Trying to get a piece of the "knowledge economy" through study is just not a sure thing any more. This was the "downside" to the privatization of the commons of knowledge.

Second: it's worth paying attention not just to the content of the *We Are the 99 Percent* Tumblr but the form. The Internet is old news. It's hardly "new media" any more. But one can forget that something like a Tumblr is a tool that simply wasn't available to an early era of social movements. If since Nixon the 1 percent used the vector to untether the financial wing of the vectoral class from anything as tangible as a gold reserve, then social movements too have consistently learned how to occupy whatever abstract means of communication are at their disposal.

Marx said that the people make history, but not with the means of their own choosing. A corollary is that the people make meaning, but not with the media of their own choosing. Occupy Wall Street not only "occupied" Zuccotti Park. It also occupied an abstraction. In Henri Lefebvre's terms it took the struggle out of mere language and onto a more properly symbolic terrain. Or, as the Situationists would put it, what transpired is a brilliant example of *détournement*. Both an actual place in the city of New York and the symbolic place it occupies in the global spectacle as a symbol have been appropriated as if they were common property, as if they belonged to us all. That's the essence of *détournement*: that both the space of the city and the space of culture always and already are a commons.[11]

The third component to analysis, then, alongside work and debt, is the struggle over the means of inventing and communicating, a struggle over information, knowledge, culture, and science, over the "general intellect" if you like. Only it is not just about "intellect" as ideas in people's heads. It is about the form of the relations which interface human and machine intelligence together. It is not just about ownership and control of these means, although that is crucial. It is about the design of these very means themselves. Or sometimes the redesign. The people hack tech, but not with the tools of their own choosing. Sometimes you have to kludge together whatever you can. "Occupying" Tumblr might not be a bad example.

So: the ruling class has at least three components. One is financial; one military; one in the business of the control of a consumer economy of things through intellectual property. Occupy Wall Street identified one aspect of it – financialization and debt. To talk about jobs one would have to talk about how the resources of the state are now directed far more to maintaining the military wing of the vectoral class, while the idea that the state could invest in anything that might provide jobs for anyone else somehow became unthinkable.

Perhaps it's because pilotless drones are so sublimely useless for feeding the hungry that subsidizing them is acceptable. It would condemn to nonsense the whole reigning ideology to point out that states frequently use public money, and quite successfully, to secure investment and create jobs that the private sector might provide but is for some reason incapable of creating. This was, after all, how both the railways and the Internet got built. A lot of private interests were involved in both cases, but underwritten by public investment and authority.

As for the third component of the ruling class, it is hard to get a critical perspective going on Apple or Google when those are the best examples anyone can point to of new kinds of investment, product development, and employment. Hackers like Anonymous align themselves with popular movements. Ordinary people with even basic tech skills hack the social media environment to make it a platform to occupy with a revolt. Yet at the same time the "entertainment" wing of our military–entertainment complex pressed on Congress some of the most punitive and restrictive "intellectual property" legislation imaginable. Even the most seemingly "enlightened" wing of the vectoralist class is not our friend.

Financialization is just part of a wider "vectoralization" in which all social relations are caught in a threefold vice. Relations of culture and commons are replaced by intellectual property. Relations of obligation and gift are replaced by consumer debt. Relations of trust and community are replaced by security surveillance. The danger is threefold, and Wall Street is just the most visible part of it.

To the Marxist and "anarchist" forms of analysis I want to add a third, which for want of a better term I'll call post-Situationist. The theory and practice of the Situationist International have been absorbed in different ways into both the Marxist and anarchist perspectives. Debord's famous book *The Society of the Spectacle* can be read, if somewhat partially, as an Hegelian-Marxist classic. As Graeber notes elsewhere, the anarchist milieu in the United States is steeped in Situationist literature.[12] Yet I think there are other ways of reading this legacy.

The first Situationist tenet of relevance comes from Raoul Vaneigem: "People who talk about revolution and class struggle without referring explicitly to everyday life, without understanding what is subversive about love and what is positive in the refusal of constraints, such people have a corpse in their mouth."[13] Hence the significance of the stories on Tumblr, on the taking of space in Zuccotti Park, of the generosity of so many people in making the occupation a reality. Enough said.

The second comes from René Viénet: "our ideas are on everybody's minds."[14] Boredom and revolt are always present, and lacking nothing but a pretext. The theoretical elaboration always comes after, not before, the revolt itself. If a theory is any good, it provides a language for what the movement already knows. Or, in short, the intellectual's role is an adjunct one. The Leninist fantasy of "leading" a movement is mostly a farcical repeat. (Not to mention nostalgia, if not for Big Brothers, then for Funny Uncles and their bad jokes.)

The third tenet is, of course, Debord: "the whole of life presents itself as an immense accumulation of spectacles."[15] Or, in short, we live inside an **aesthetic economy**, not a political one. One has to question whether politics even exists. Is it not a special effect of the spectacular organization of appearances? Of course: exploitation exists, oppression exists, unnecessary suffering exists. But one cannot take it for granted that there is axiomatically a "politics." Its very possibility has to be invented. This is a less well-known lesson of Debord's famous text.

A fourth tenet might come from the even less well-known writings of Asger Jorn.[16] The tragedy of the commodity economy for Jorn is that it separates form from "content" – indeed, it creates "content" where none otherwise exists. The commodity economy makes concrete a "tin can philosophy" where so many identical cans are filled with equivalent quantities of seemingly formless goop – tomato soup, for example. Jorn, the artist, the maker of new forms, finds this devaluing. In the great romantic tradition of William Morris, he wants to restore the role of the creation of form to the center of collective human endeavor.

This would mean an alliance of the interests of those who labor to make forms and those who labor to fill them with content: artists and workers, in short. Scientists, designers, artists, hackers – the form-makers – are artificially separated as a class from labor. The distinctiveness of Jorn is to understand this in class terms. While "tin can philosophy" might seem archaic in a world that prizes artisanal organic cheeses and other yuppie wonders, consider this: what if the iPad were just a soup can? What if the problem with the vectoral as we now have it is that we are supposed to think of the device as just a form to hold "content." Gone is the possibility of the device as configurable, of technological space as something everyone can hack and share.

A fifth tenet is from Situationist practice: the worker's council.[17] This too may seem a bit archaic. While I think of myself as a worker, not everyone does. The practice in Zuccotti Park of the General Assembly revives the structural principles of the councilist tradition and mixes it with some others, learned along the way. The Situationists were "horizontalists" before there was such a term. This surprises people who know only Debord's self-constructed glamor and not the actual practice of the Situationist International and other groups with which it bears a family resemblance.

Finally, one might turn to the Situationists' account of why May '68 in France failed.[18] At least two lessons seem salient. One is the inability of workers to articulate their desires. Our ideas are on everybody's minds, but not the access to language and images with which to communicate. It's a question then of proposing, but not determining, some possibilities. Second, the occupied factories could not communicate with each other or with the student movement. This became less of a problem in what the Situationists called the overdeveloped world. Certain technical and legislative initiatives may yet foreclose what is left of the great vision that was the "Internet." But for now the vector can be occupied.

It's not just because the tools are now available that the tactics of "horizontalism" seem to work.[19] It's that labor is not what it was either. Most jobs in the overdeveloped world require not just the filling of forms but the invention of forms as well. We all hack the workplace, just to make it work at all. We might not know much about factory work, let alone harvesting the fields, but we know how to organize information, people, and things in productive and more or less harmonious ensembles.

Everybody knows. It was so articulately put by the person at Occupy Wall Street whose sign read: SHIT IS FUCKED UP AND BULLSHIT. We know it's broken; we know the sockpuppets have nothing to say. What has frankly to be described as a neo-fascist backlash was already under way even before Occupy Wall Street began. It can only intensify.

The aestheticization of politics that Benjamin detected in fascism has proceeded apace.[20] Perhaps to the point of effacing the political almost entirely, subsuming it within an aesthetic economy. Expect more attacks on reason and science. Expect more demands that someone be made to suffer so some imagined silent majority might feel good about themselves. Expect more pseudo-religious language about spiritual "debts" and "sacrifices," to be made by everyone except the ruling class itself. Expect more "threats" to "security." Expect a few occupiers to become cops and a few cops to become occupiers. That's what neo-fascism looks like.

I have come back to Zuccotti Park to finish writing this book. It is November now. The first snow has come and gone. The police and the occupiers continue to play games with each other. The police tried to take down the medical tent. When that move failed, the occupiers erected a second tent. Now the park is filled with tents. Still, the future of this revolt is uncertain, as it always is within the space and time of the event. By the time you read this maybe nobody will even remember. But one of the reasons **low theory** exists as a form of writing is to be a relay between other pasts and this present. To remind us that while the sockpuppets insist that their shiny world has abolished the irreconcilable differences between classes, it only appears so if one neglects the evidence of one's own senses.

Sitting here in the park, in this spontaneous commons, one can afford at least a little optimism. Perhaps, with luck, the occupation can continue to occupy enough of symbolic space – in part by occupying physical space, in part by occupying the vector – to shift the range of possibilities within the aesthetic economy of the overdeveloped world a few inches leftwards. Perhaps it can put back on the agenda the only worthy goal modernity ever had: the incremental overcoming of unnecessary suffering.

Even if it is defeated, and neo-fascism has its day, the best university is right now open around me. This one is, if not free, then taking donations in kind. The occupation is a living workshop in "communism," but also in the gift economy of exchange. Every day, people buy stuff and convert it back into gifts to total strangers. Every day, people discover solidarity through camping together, cooking together, and picking up the trash. Every day, people take time out from their jobs or caring for their families just to be in an occupied space. All that is as valuable as the General Assembly.

Not a few will have an existential crisis there. In those moments when the cops are not there to confront, and there's nothing to buy – what the hell is one supposed to do? What is one supposed to be? This is the source of the strange psychogeography of occupied space. These spaces are poorly equipped, shoddily built exemplars of something remarkable: that there could be other social relations, besides finance, security, and the commodity. And that if any of this stuff is remotely scalable, then why do we even need this ruling class at all?

19

Last Words and Key Words

If there is a story that sums up what this book is all about, it is this one: "We're not quite sure what happened yet," claimed General Robert Kehler of the US Strategic Command. What was certain was that a computer virus infected the remote "cockpits" at Creech Air Force Base in Nevada, which control pilotless drone aircraft all over the world. Kehler said the virus had entered "from the wild," meaning it was not specifically targeted at the Creech Base installation.

A defense official told the media that the virus was a credential stealer "routinely used to steal login and password data from people who gamble or play games like *Mafia Wars* online."[1] While it is possible the infection happened through the use of hard drives that were infected elsewhere and then connected to the cockpit computers, this does not entirely rule out the possibility that pilots charged with flying armed drones play *Mafia Wars* in their down time on their "office" computers – just like everybody else who has to do drone-like labor in cubicle farms around the planet.

In this story three uses of the vector come together. First, the vector as means of deploying force at a distance – the pilotless drone. Second, the vector as space for creative reappropriation – the virus. Third, the vector as space for games as means to soak up excess boredom – *Mafia Wars*.

All three aspects of the vector appear here in less than ideal forms. There is something sinister about pilotless drones, that new symbol of power which projects itself without risking itself. This kind of killing makes a mafia "hit" look like a sacred act by comparison. *Mafia Wars* is a casual game, successful but banal to anyone with an interest in the aesthetics of games. The virus is a routine hack, neither creative nor aimed at anything of worth besides stealing logins, no doubt to be used to set up zombie server farms to send out spam or something even less interesting.

Still, the coincidence of these three aspects of the vectoral gives pause for thought, as it is not a bad emblem of the shape of an emerging world. Like any new world, this one confronts us with the problem of description. Its contours and forms are not quite what we are familiar with. It appears as either radically other or is all too quickly assimilated to the familiar. What seems other can really just be a shade of difference; what seems familiar can actually be very, very strange. The event more often than not reveals mistakes of both kinds.

One way of proceeding then is to work on language, on making language itself both strange and familiar in new ways, trying to fit the contours of the strange and familiar within language to the contours of the strange and familiar in the world observed in the wake of weird global media events, be they big or small. What follows here, by way of a conclusion, is a summary of the language created over the course of *Telesthesia*. William Blake preferred to create his own "system" to being enslaved by someone else's. In the same spirit I don't advocate adopting these terms, but rather the creation of new ones, when and where they appear to describe this impending world.

Abstraction: The plane upon which concrete particulars can be arrayed in relation to each other. Language is an abstraction; phonemes are concrete. A road or rail or flight-path infrastructure is an abstraction. The vehicles and their paths are concrete. The telegraph is an abstraction; so too is the Internet. Abstractions are not concepts or ideas. They are real. They are more real than the concrete, as they are the condition under which concrete particulars can be related to each other.

Addressable: The locating of a place or a thing or information so that it can be reliably retrieved from that location, or so that something can be sent to that location. The postal system is based on making physical space addressable. So too does global positioning. Computers have memories that are addressable. Chunks of information can be stored and retrieved even though they do not necessarily occupy a particular physical address.

Aesthetic economy: A materialist analysis of the power of perceptions and the perceptions of power. It understands both economic and cultural matters through the same lens: namely, the material form of their relations and the forms of property imposed upon them.

Antipodality: The experience of being neither here nor there. An antipode is the other foot. It presupposed a pair of poles and a relation between them. Antipodality is the tendency for this relation between poles to become unanchored from particular places and to become a general condition. Australia and New Zealand are the antipodes in relation to Britain as the metropole, but antipodality can come into being between any two points, even points that are in motion, provided there is a means to make a relation between them.

Cellspace: Mobile telephony makes cellspace perceivable as an abstract terrain of addressable nodes, both in physical space and computer space, in which data and commands can be routed in principle between any addressable spaces. Its advance on cyberspace is that its physical nodes become almost as freely addressable as its computer space. Its nodes can be fully mobile, so long as the network of cells which manage data flow and current physical address don't fail. Cellspace, incidentally, records the telemetry of mobile bodies equipped with transmitting devices. It thus greatly expands the available data on the state and location of objects or subjects, further incorporating them in game space.

Cyberspace: The Internet makes cyberspace perceivable as an abstract terrain of addressable spaces, both in physical space and computer memory, in which data and commands can be routed in principle between any addressable spaces.

Gamer: A kind of interface that perceives its relation to others as one of rivalry based on a measurable score, and which treats its relation to its environment as a challenge in which its success or failure is measurable.

Game space: The making over of the world as a field in which any and every relation can yield a value in a game, with no remainder. A world in which there is nothing outside the playing of games. Game space divides into commodity-space, strategy-space and other such games. The playing field for these tends to encompass the planet.

The Girl: A kind of interface through which the world is perceived as a domestic sphere subject to the authority of beauty. The Girl is a kind of living money that validates the commodity as the repository of what desire desires.

Hacker: A kind of interface that perceives its relation to others as a qualitative rivalry, based on the creation of incommensurable values. Hackers create the new, and in that sense they are a key interface to modernity. They arise in their fully realized form, however, with the expansion of intellectual property laws to cover the whole of creation. While associated with computers, hacking can pertain to any field.

Hacker class: Classes are created by relations of private property, which cleave those who have it from those who don't. The evolution of the property form into "intellectual" property creates new class relations, cleaving the hacker class from the vectoral class.

Hypocritical theory: When it loses its vocation as critical thought in and against the commodity form, critical theory becomes hypocritical theory. It no longer works on the non-identity between what it says and what it does.

Interface: This is the portal between the human and the inhuman. It can make the inhuman world legible to the human (thus calling into being an experience of the human as human). Interfaces can either enable the agency of the human in the inhuman, or vice versa.

Low theory: As opposed to High Theory, low theory does not necessarily play the game of quantifiable recognition within the academy. It experiments instead with the creation of new relations between practices and modes of communication. It may pass through the worlds of scholarship, journalism, politics, aesthetics, and literature, but it is not bound by the rules of any of these. It makes up its own.

Military–entertainment complex: A way of describing a kind of power in which the vector is used to secure both resources and desires. It relies on the same (vectoral) technologies to exert power across space and time through the management of information about that space.

Postcolonial: A spatial figure or trope that poses the question of the relation of the metropolitan powers to their peripheries. First registered as a rejection or reversal of the privileging of the metropole, it also opens up toward a more general questioning of the apparent spatial discreteness of metropole and periphery.

Postmodern: A temporal figure or trope that poses the question of the historical trajectory of the modern. First registered as skepticism about the modern, it also opens up the possibility of rethinking its temporal sequences and periods.

Overdeveloped world: Rather than developed and underdeveloped, here the concept of (economic, social) development is turned against itself, and the so-called developed world displaced as the standard. It is a way of reading the postcolonial critique back into narratives of historical stages. It sparks the thought that perhaps the West missed a certain historical juncture where a qualitative break into another way of life may have been possible.

Telesthesia: Perception at a distance, as in the telescope, telegraph, telephone, television, or telecommunications in general. Its key quality is to bring what is distant near, and make what is distant a site of action. It is a property of a class of vectors that have the quality of making information move faster than people or things, thus opening up the terrain of third nature as a terrain of command and control, and eventually of a game space.

Third nature: The collective struggle to wrest freedom from necessity produces a second nature, in which everyday life can take place in a world more concordant with its needs. But the process of producing second nature produces yet more necessities. Third nature is the attempt to overcome the limits of second nature by enclosing it within a layer not of built forms but of media and communications. Nature itself is only ever perceived as a residue, as that from which second and third nature extract themselves.

Transopticon: If the Panopticon imbues its subjects with a sense of being perceived by a central authority or Blg Brother, the transopticon distributes that perception throughout space. It is the sense also that perceptions from different points of view can be composited regardless of their heterogeneous quality.

Vector: One definition of a vector is a line of fixed length but no fixed position. By extension, vector can be thought of as any material form a relation can take which has certain definable qualities but which has no fixed position. For example, roads or telegraph lines have certain properties irrespective of their location. A telegraph line transmits only information, while vehicles traveling on roads can move people, commodities, weapons, or information. The vector is also indifferent to the qualities or meaning of what it transmits.

Vectoral class: A class that secures its power as intellectual property and as control of the information vector. It may be conceived either as a fraction of the ruling class or, more provocatively, as a new ruling class entirely. It has two fractions: one uses the vector to dominate the movement of commodities; the other the movement of resources. Or, in short, both fractions use third nature to control second nature and nature, respectively, through the games of commodity-space and strategy-space.

Vulture industry: The culture industries mass-produced culture as a commodity, thus imbuing culture itself with the very form of the commodity. But at least the culture industry went to the trouble of making something to be consumed. The vulture industries retreat from making culture to controlling the vector of its distribution and extracting a rent from its use. The rise of the vulture industries is in part a tactical acknowledgment that culture has been partly resocialized by digital sharing. But it is in part also a new attack on the common cultural realm.

Weird global media event: Something of significance that appears to happen in a particular place, but which actually takes place along the vectors which connect that place to a world. The world called into being by the event is not global in the sense of universal, but rather it invokes *a* world. Its weirdness stems from some unexpected novelty in where and how it happens.

Notes and References

Chapter 1 How to Occupy an Abstraction

1 A. D. Wissner-Gross and C. E. Freer, "Relativistic Statistical Arbitrage", *Physical Review*, E 82, 056104, 2010.
2 There was a "Declaration of the Occupation" which was "approved by consensus on September 29, 2011." See the *Occupied Wall Street Journal*, c. September 30, 2011; at: <http://www.occupiedmedia.us>.
3 I am thinking here of Doug Henwood and Jodi Dean, who wrote insightful critical pieces at the time. These paragraphs on the occupation were originally intended in part as comradely discussion on these points.
4 Jane Mayer, "The Billionaire Brothers Who Are Waging a War Against Obama," *New Yorker*, August 30, 2010; at: <http://www.newyorker.com; Frank Rich, "Billionaires Bankrolling the Tea Party," *New York Times*, August 28, 2010; at: <http://www.nytimes.com>.
5 Paul Krugman, "Panic of the Plutocrats," *New York Times*, October 9, 2011; at: <http://www.nytimes.com>.
6 Erika Fry in *Columbia Journalism Review*, September 29, 2011; at: <http://www.cjr.org>.
7 See Ezra Klein's interview with David Graeber, in *Washington Post Wonkblog*, October 3, 2011; at <http://www.Washingtonpost.com>. Not a few leading anarchist figures considered the occupation too reformist to be of interest.

8 For a representative statement of the trends critiqued here, see Costas Zouzinas and Slavoj Žižek (eds), *The Idea of Communism*, London: Verso, 2010.

9 *The John Gambling Show*, WOR News Talk Radio 710, September 30, 2010; at <http://www.Wor710.com>.

10 *Register of Debates in Congress*, vol. 8, col. 1325, 1832. Emphasis added.

11 A remarkable document, nonetheless: Nadia Idle and Alex Nunns (eds), *Tweets from Tahrir*, New York: O/R Books, 2011.

12 See Tom McDonough (ed.), *The Situationists and the City*, London: Verso, 2010, and also the opening chapters of McKenzie Wark, *The Beach Beneath the Street*, London: Verso, 2011.

13 See, for example, Homi Bhabha, *The Location of Culture*, London: Routledge, 1994; Gilles Deleuze and Felix Guattari, *A Thousand Plateaus*, Minneapolis, MN: University of Minnesota Press, 1987; Donna Haraway, *Simians, Cyborgs and Woman*, New York: Routledge, 1990.

14 See, for example, Paul Gilroy's excellent *The Black Atlantic: Modernity and Double Consciousness*, Cambridge, MA: Harvard University Press, 1993.

15 On the speculative method, see Gillian Rose, *Hegel Contra Sociology*, London: Verso, 2009.

16 Clifford Geertz, *The Interpretation of Cultures*, New York: Basic Books, 1977, p. 23. Emphasis changed.

17 George Trow, *In the Context of No Context*, New York: Atlantic Monthly Press, 1997.

18 On the transatlantic creation of French Theory, see François Cusset, *French Theory*, Minneapolis, MN: University of Minnesota Press, 2008; on the internal structure of French higher education from which it sprang, see Pierre Bourdieu, *Homo Academicus*, Stanford, CA: Stanford University Press, 1990.

19 See Reda Bensmaïa, *The Barthes Effect: The Essay as Reflective Text*, Minneapolis, MN: University of Minnesota Press, 1987. The vector along which low theory slides between France and the anglophone world was the journal and imprint Semiotext(e). See Chris Kraus and Sylvère Lotringer (eds), *Hatred of Capitalism: A Semiotext(e) Reader*, Los Angeles, CA: Semiotext(e), 2001.

20 On Bernard Smith, see Peter Beilharz, *Imagining the Antipodes*, Cambridge: Cambridge University Press, 2002. For a recent collection of Meaghan Morris essays, see *Identity Anecdotes: Translation and Media Culture*, London: Sage, 2006.

21 Tara Brabazon, *Tracking the Jack*, New South Wales: University of New South Wales Press, 2000, inscribes the New Zealand version

of the antipodes into the concept. And why not the Cocos Islands as well? See John Kinsella, *Post-Colonial*, Brisbane and Chiang Mai: Paper Tiger Media, 2009.

22 Mark Gibson, *Culture and Power: A History of Cultural Studies*, Oxford: Berg, 2007, p. 183.

23 Suetonius, *The Twelve Caesars*, translated by Robert Graves, London: Penguin, 2007, p. 18.

24 See Bernard Stiegler, *Pour une nouvelle critique de l'économie politique*, Paris: Editions Galilée, 2009.

25 Molly Wright Steenson, "Interfacing with the Subterranean," *Cabinet*, spring 2011; at: <http://www.cabinetmagazine.org>.

Chapter 2 Fresh Maimed Babies

1 On how the child/adult construct works in media culture, see Kate Crawford, *Adult Themes*, Sydney: Pan Macmillan, 2006.

2 This was written before Zbigniew Libera's work *Lego Concentration Camp Set* appeared at a show at the Jewish Museum in New York entitled *Mirroring Evil: Nazi Imagery/Recent Art*, 2002.

3 Michel de Montaigne, "On Cruelty," in *Complete Essays of Montaigne*, translated by Donald Frame, Stanford, CA: Stanford University Press, 1957, p. 306ff.

4 Phillip Knightley, *The First Casualty*, London: Pan Books, 1989; an interesting collection of case studies on television and war is provided in Bruce Cumings, *War and Television*, London: Verso, 1992.

5 I am sometimes credited with coining this term, but I got it from Brenda Laurel at *Siggraph* in Orlando in 1991. It's not clear where it originated. See James Der Derian, *Virtuous War: Mapping the Military–Industrial–Media–Entertainment Network*, 2nd edn, New York: Routledge, 2009.

6 John R. MacArthur, *Second Front*, New York: Hill & Wang, 1992.

7 Hannah Arendt, *Eichmann in Jerusalem: A Report on the Banality of Evil*, New York: Penguin, 1994, p. 252.

8 John Pilger, *Distant Voices*, London: Vintage, 1995, p. 177.

9 Dilip Hiro, *Desert Shield to Desert Storm*, London: HarperCollins, 1992, p. 154.

10 Slavoj Žižek, "Eastern Europe's Republics of Gilead," *New Left Review*, 183 (September 1990): 53–4.

11 Edward Said, *Orientalism*, Harmondsworth: Penguin Books, 1985; see also his books *Covering Islam*, New York: Vintage, 1997; and *Culture and Imperialism*, London: Chatto & Windus, 1993.

12 Mohamed Hekial, *Illusions of Triumph*, London: HarperCollins, 1992, pp. 160, 167; Akbar Ahmed, *Postmodernism and Islam*, London: Routledge, 1992, p. 238.
13 *Telegraph Mirror*, November 27, 1993, p. 1.
14 See Emily Apter, *Feminizing the Fetish*, Ithaca, NY: Cornell University Press, 1993.
15 See Catharine Lumby and Duncan Fine, *Why Television is Good for Kids*, Melbourne: Pan Macmillan, 2006.
16 Jean Baudrillard, *The Ecstasy of Communication*, New York: Semiotext(e), 1988.

Chapter 3 Neither Here Nor There

1 Benedict Anderson, *Imagined Communities*, London: Verso, 1983.
2 For more detailed studies of the vectoral infrastructure, see Lisa Parks, *Cultures in Orbit: Satellites and the Televisual*, Durham, NC: Duke University Press, 2005; Brian Larkin, *Signal and Noise: Media, Infrastructure and Urban Culture in Nigeria*, Durham, NC: Duke University Press, 2008. My thanks to New School colleague Shannon Mattern for illuminating this body of work for me.
3 Manuel Castells, *The Informational City*, Oxford: Blackwell, 1989.
4 See the title story in Frank Moorhouse, *The Coca-Cola Kid*, Sydney: Angus & Robertson, 1985.
5 Raymond Williams, "Base and Superstructure in Marxist Cultural Theory," in *Problems in Materialism and Culture*, London: Verso, 1980, pp. 31–50.
6 Bernard Stiegler, *For a New Critique of Political Economy*, Cambridge: Polity, 2010, p. 33.
7 See Christiane Paul, *Digital Art*, London: Thames & Hudson, 2008; Rachel Greene, *Internet Art*, London: Thames & Hudson, 2004.
8 On the everyday, see Michel de Certeau, "Montaigne's 'Of Cannibals': The Savage 'I,' " in *Heterologies: Discourse on the Other*, Minneapolis, MN; University of Minnesota Press, 1986, p. 67ff.
9 G. W. F. Hegel, *The Philosophy of History*, Buffalo, NY: Prometheus Books, 1991, p. 90.
10 James Carey, "Technology and Ideology: the Case of the Telegraph," in *Communication as Culture*, New York: Routledge, 2009, p. 155ff.
11 Charles Taylor, *Hegel*, Cambridge: Cambridge University Press, 1991, p. 535ff; see also Guy Debord, *The Society of the Spectacle*, Detroit, MI: Black & Red, 1983, epigrams 186–8.

12 See McKenzie Wark, "From Fordism to Sonyism: Perverse Readings of the New World Order," *New Formations*, 16 (1992): pp. 43–54.

13 Compare Bernard Smith's neglected masterpiece *European Vision and the South Pacific*, Oxford: Oxford University Press, 1989, with Michel Foucault's *Discipline and Punish*, Harmondsworth: Penguin Books, 1977.

14 Paul Foss, "Theatrum Nondum Cogitorum," in *The Foreign Bodies Papers*, Local Consumption Series 1, Sydney, 1981, pp. 15–38.

15 Geoffrey Blainey, *The Tyranny of Distance: How Distance Shaped Australia's History*, Melbourne: Macmillan, 1986.

16 Bernard Smith, *European Vision and the South Pacific*, Oxford: Oxford University Press, 1989. See also Peter Beilharz, *Imagining the Antipodes: Culture, Theory and the Visual in the Work of Bernard Smith*, Cambridge: Cambridge University Press, 1997.

17 Martin Heidegger, *The Question Concerning Technology*, New York: Harper and Row, 1977, pp. 26–7.

18 See Paul Carter, *The Road to Botany Bay*, New York: Knopf, 1988.

19 Gilles Deleuze and Felix Guattari, *Anti-Oedipus: Capitalism and Schizophrenia*, London: Athlone Press, 1984, p. 321.

20 William Shawcross, *Murdoch*, Sydney: Random House Australia, 1992; Manuel De Landa, *War in the Age of Intelligent Machines*, New York: Zone Books, 1991.

21 See Ross Gibson's essays, especially his reading of Mad Max in *South of the West*, Bloomington, IN: Indiana University Press, 1992.

22 Toby Miller et al., *Global Hollywood: No. 2*, London: British Film Institute, 2008.

23 Roland Robertson, *Globalisation: Social Theory and Global Culture*, London: Sage Books, 1992.

24 McKenzie Wark, *Virtual Geography: Living With Global Media Events*, Bloomington, IN: Indiana University Press, 1994.

25 See "Address to Revolutionaries of Algeria and all Countries," in Ken Knabb (ed.), *Situationist International Anthology*, p. 191; *Internationale Situationiste*, 10 (March 1966): 46: "surdéveloppement irrationel." Paul Gilroy also uses the term. See *The Black Atlantic: Modernity and Double Consciousness*, Cambridge, MA: Harvard University Press, 1993, p. 42.

26 Roland Munck, *Globalization and Contestation: The New Great Counter Movement*, New York: Routledge, 2006.

27 Eric Michaels, *For a Cultural Future: Francis Jupurrurla Makes TV at Yuendumu*, Sydney: Artspace Art & Criticism Monograph Series, 1987.

28 Tim Rowse, "Enlisting the Warlpiri," *Continuum*, 3/2 (1990): 174–200.

Chapter 4 Speaking Trajectories

1 See any of the annual editions of *Best American Essays*, New York: Houghton Mifflin Harcourt.

2 *Roland Barthes by Roland Barthes*, New York: Noonday, 1989, pp. 83–5. To the extent that Morris engages with other authors by writing with them, then her relation to Barthes can be tracked through. See "Metamorphoses at Sydney Tower," *New Formations*, 11 (1991): 5–18.

3 Meaghan Morris, "Panorama: The Live, the Dead and the Living," in Paul Foss (ed.), *Island in the Stream: Myths of Place in Australian Culture*, Sydney: Pluto Press, 1988, p. 162.

4 *Financial Review*, February 8, 1988 at <http://www.afr.com>.

5 Meaghan Morris, "At Henry Parkes Motel," in John Frow and Meaghan Morris (eds), *Australian Cultural Studies: A Reader*, Champaign, IL: University of Illinois Press, 1993, pp. 241–75.

6 On the problem of reconnecting cultural studies to some sense of economic discourse and economic processes, see McKenzie Wark, "Fashioning the Future," *Cultural Studies*, 5/1 (1991): 61–76.

7 What Morris has in common with Baudrillard is a concentration on solutions to contemporary critical problems at the level and through the techniques of rhetoric. The similarity begins and ends there. Where Baudrillard sets up pairs of terms which then contaminate each other, flipping over into their opposites, demonstrating the futility of classical critical strategies in a postcritical world, Morris's essays set up rhetorical categories which form a series, along which analysis self-consciously slides. See her essay on Baudrillard, "Room 101 Or a Few Worst Things in the World," in *The Pirate's Fiancée*, London: Verso, 1988, pp. 187–222.

8 Morris's interest in Lyotard can be traced in "Postmodernity and Lyotard's Sublime," in *The Pirate's Fiancée*, pp. 223–40.

9 Morris, "Panorama: The Live, the Dead and the Living," in Paul Foss (ed.), *Island in the Stream: Myths of Place in Australian Culture*, Sydney: Pluto Press, 1988, p. 186.

10 Meaghan Morris, "Identity Anecdotes," in *Camera Obscura*, 12 (1984): 42.

11 Paul Carter, *The Road to Botany Bay*, New York: Knopf, 1988.

12 Ghassan Hage, *White Nation: Fantasies of White Supremacy in a Multicultural Society*, Sydney: Pluto Press, 2008.

13 Morris, "Identity Anecdotes," in *Camera Obscura*, 12 (1984): 44.

14 Meaghan Morris, contribution to "The Spectatrix" special issue of *Camera Obscura*, 20–21 (1990): 241–5.

15 See, for example, John Fiske, *Television Culture*, London: Methuen, 1987, ch. 10.
16 Cf. Morris, "A Small Serve of Spaghetti," *Meanjin*, 69/4 (2010): 98–106.
17 Michel de Certeau, *The Practice of Everyday Life*, Berkeley, CA: University of California Press, 1988. Morris discusses de Certeau in "At Henry Parkes Motel," in John Frow and Meaghan Morris (eds), *Australian Cultural Studies: A Reader*, Champaign, IL: University of Illinois Press, 1993, pp. 241–75.
18 Ross Gibson, *South of the West*, Bloomington, IN: Indiana University Press, 1992.
19 Geoffrey Blainey, *The Tyranny of Distance: How Distance Shaped Australia's History*, London: Macmillan, 1977.

Chapter 5   Cruising Virilio's Overexposed City

1 Le Corbusier, *The City of Tomorrow*, London: The Architectural Press, 1978, pp. 179–90.
2 Paul Virilio, "The Overexposed City," in *Zone*, 1/2 (1987), pp. 14–21 (hereafter OC). Also in *Third Degree*, 1, Sydney, 1985.
3 Gilles Deleuze and Felix Guattari, *A Thousand Plateaus*, London: Continuum, 2004, pp. 225–6.
4 OC, pp. 17, 20–1.
5 Paul Virilio and Sylvere Lotringer, *Pure War*, New York: Semiotext(e) Foreign Agents Series, 1983, pp. 34–5; (hereafter *PW*).
6 "Space, Time & the City" in *Lotus International*, 51 (1987): 3–62.
7 *PW*, p. 34; cf. OC, p. 19.
8 OC, p. 25.
9 *PW*, p. 34; cf. OC, p. 23.
10 OC, p. 23.
11 Quoted in Hal Foster, "(Post)Modern Polemics," in *New German Critique*, 33 (fall 1984): 68.
12 Robert Venturi, Denise Scott Brown, and Steven Izenour, *Learning From Las Vegas* (rev. edn), Cambridge, MA: MIT Press, 1986, p. 151.
13 OC, p. 29.
14 from J. G. Ballard's famous 1974 preface to his novel *Crash!*, London: Triad/Panther Books, 1985; also in the special issue on Ballard, of *Re/Search*, 8/9 (1984): 96–8.
15 Umbro Apollonio (ed.), *Futurist Manifestos*, London: Thames & Hudson, 1973, p. 22.
16 *PW*, p. 40; cf. Paul Virilio, *Speed and Politics*, New York: Semiotext(e) Foreign Agents Series, 1986.

17   See Erkki Hutamo and Jussi Parikka (eds), *Media Archaeology*, Berkeley, CA: University of California Press, 2011.
18   *PW*, p. 33.
19   Aldo Rossi, *The Architecture of the City*, Cambridge MA: Opposition Books, 1984.
20   I am indebted to Ross Gibson's reading of this film. See *South of the West*, Bloomington, IN: Indiana University Press, 1992.
21   In *Impulse*, 12/4 (summer 1986): 35–7.
22   Paul Virilio and Sylvere Lotringer, *Crepuscular Dawn*, Los Angeles, CA: Semiotext(e), 2002.

Chapter 6   Architectronics of the Multitude

1   Michel de Certeau, *The Practice of Everyday Life*, Berkeley, CA: University of California Press, 2002.
2   Paolo Virno, *The Grammar of the Multitude*, New York: Semiotext(e), 1994, p. 35.
3   Gang of Four, *Entertainment!*, Warner Bros, 1979.
4   Karl Marx, *Capital*, vol. 1, chap. 33; at <http://www.marxists.org>.
5   Kent Russell, "American Juggalo," *N+1*, 12 (2011) at: <http://www.nplusonemag.com>.
6   See David Brooks, *On Paradise Drive*, New York: Simon & Schuster, 2004; and Curtis White, *The Middle Mind*, San Francisco, CA: HarperCollins, 2003.
7   While Harold Innis does not quite write in these terms, the concept is essentially his. See *The Bias of Communication*, 2nd edn, Toronto: University of Toronto Press, 2008.
8   See McKenzie Wark, *A Hacker Manifesto*, Cambridge, MA: Harvard University Press, 2004.
9   In coining the term, Foucault explicitly links biopolitics to population, although this perspective is often lost in the subsequent literature. See Michel Foucault, *The Birth of Biopolitics*, London: Palgrave, 2008, p. 21.
10 See Jean Baudrillard, *For a Critique of the Political Economy of the Sign*, St Louis, MO: Telos Press, 1981.
11 Ross Perlin, *Intern Nation*, London: Verso, 2011.

Chapter 7   Weird Global Media Event and Vectoral Unconscious

1   *Daily Mail*, May 27, 2010; at: <http://www.dailymailco.uk>.
2   See McKenzie Wark, *Virtual Geography*, Bloomington, IN: Indiana University Press, 1994.

3   Jarett Kobek, *ATTA*, Los Angeles, CA: Semiotext(e), 2011. It is a fictional account of the life of 9/11 pilot Mohammad Atta, but based on solid documentary evidence about his life. It is a brilliant and alarming evocation of the terrorist structure of feeling. In Kobek's version, Atta is destroying only the abstract space. He has entirely forgotten the quotidian dimensions of concrete space, to which his architect training makes him quite sensitive.

4   The classic study of these kinds of events is Daniel Dayan and Eilhu Katz, *Media Events: The Live Broadcasting of History*, Cambridge, MA: Harvard University Press, 1994.

5   "Royal Wedding Satire Ban," April 28, 2011, at: <http://www.abc. net.au.>.

6   Theodor Adorno, *Minima Moralia*, London: New Left Books, 1974, p. 57.

7   The lightning metaphor is borrowed from Georges Bataille, *Visions of Excess*, Minneaoplis, MN: University of Minnesota Press, 1985, p. 78. Needless to say, Bataille had something else in mind.

8   Neal Stephenson, *Reamde*, New York: William Morrow, 2011, is a quite terrible novel about terrorism, but which does contain a very interesting account of the geopolitics of air traffic control. Interestingly, it's about a private jet as a terrorist vector, rather than commercial ones.

9   Tom Standage, *The Victorian Internet*, New York: Walker & Co, 2007. I am particularly indebted to the fine essay by James Carey in *Communication as Culture*, New York: Routledge, 2008.

10 Martin Heidegger, *The Question Concerning Technology*, New York: Harper & Row, 1977, p. 17.

11 Not Walter Benjamin's angel, but Heiner Müller's: *Germania*, New York: Semiotext(e), 1990.

12 Jodi Dean, *Aliens in America*, Ithaca, NY: Cornell University Press, 1998, p. 14.

13 Jane Bennett, *Vibrant Matter: A Political Ecology of Things*, Durham, NC: Duke University Press, 2009.

14 Alex Callinicos, *Bonfire of Illusions: The Twin Crises of the Liberal World*, Cambridge: Polity, 2010, p. 34.

15 S. M. Amadae, *Rationalizing Capitalist Democracy: The Cold War Origins of Rational Choice Liberalism*, Chicago, IL: University of Chicago Press, 2003, p. 83ff.

16 Paul Krugman, *The Return of Depression Economics*, New York: Norton, 2008.

17 *New York Times*, November 8, 2007; at: <http://www.nytimes. com>.

18 Gary Shteyngart, *Super Sad True Love Story*, New York: Random House, 2011.

19　Alan Rusbrigger et al., *Phone Hacking*, London: *Guardian* Shorts, 2011.
20　Jason Vest, "The Dubious Genius of Andrew Marshall," *American Prospect Online*, February 15, 2001; at: <http://www.prospect.org>.
21　Andrew Pollack, "Building the Military–Entertainment Complex," *New York Times*, October 10, 1997; at: <http://www.nytimes.com>.
22　Jean Baudrillard, "Du Miroir & De L'écran," *Critical Secret*, 10 (2003); at: <http://www.criticalsecret.com>.
23　Peter Finn, "A Future for Drones: Automated Killing," *Washington Post*, September 19, 2011; at: <http://www.washingtonpost.com>.
24　Matt Taibbi, *Griftopia*, New York: Speigel and Grau, 2010, p. 32.
25　"GPS Tool Will Help Immigrants Cross Border," *Orange County Register*, November 20, 2009; at: <http://www.ocregister.com>.

Chapter 8　Securing Security

1　Phil Kline, *Zippo Songs: Airs of War and Lunacy*, New York: Cantaloupe Music, 2004. The slogan is usually held to have started with the Army's 9th Division, painted on the headquarters of its helicopter unit. I am indebted also to an unpublished thesis by Michael Corey.
2　Bernard Stiegler, *For a New Critique of Political Economy*, Cambridge: Polity, 2010.
3　Konrad Becker, *Tactical Reality Dictionary*, Vienna: Editions Selene, 2002, p. 10.
4　Joseph Schumpter, *Capitalism, Socialism and Democracy*, London: Taylor & Francis, 2003, pp. 104–5.
5　Paul Virilio, *Pure War*, New York: Semiotext(e), 1983, pp. 95–8.
6　*New York Times*, September 24, 2011; at: <http://www.nytimes.com>.
7　Naomi Klein, *Shock Doctrine: The Rise of Disaster Capitalism*, New York: Picador, 2007.
8　Marshall McLuhan, *Understanding Media*, Cambridge, MA: MIT Press, 1994, p. 12.
9　Guy Debord, *Comments on the Society of the Spectacle*, London: Verso, 1998.
10　C. J. Chivers, "The Orange Revolution: Ukraine's Inner Battle," *New York Times Multimedia*, February 9, 2005; at: <http://www.nytimes.com>.
11　David Harvey, *New Imperialism*, Oxford: Oxford University Press, 2003, p. 17.

12 Jonathan Neale, "Afghanistan: The Case Against the Good War," *International Socialism*, October 2008; "The Long Torment of Afghanistan," *International Socialism*, winter 2001; at: <http://www.isj.org.uk>.

13 Giorgio Agamben, *Means Without End: Notes on Politics*. Minneapolis, MN: University of Minnesota Press, 2000, p. 87.

Chapter 9 Game and Play in Everyday Life

1 Donald L. Bartlett and James B. Steele, "Has Your Life Become a Game of Chance?," *Time*, February 2, 2004, p. 42.

2 Sam Brenton and Reuben Cohen, *Shooting People: Adventures in Reality TV*, London: Verso, 2003, p. 9.

3 General H. Norman Schwarzkopf, *It Doesn't Take A Hero*, New York: Bantam Books, 1993, p. 37.

4 Slavoj Žižek, *The Fragile Absolute*, London: Verso, 2000, p. 77.

5 George Perec, *W, or, The Memory of Childhood*, New York: David Godine, 2003.

6 Bernard DeKoven, *The Well Played Game*, Garden City, NY: Anchor Books, 1978, p. 9.

7 Henri Lefebvre, *Critique of Everyday Life*, Vol. 2, London: Verso, 2002.

8 Jacques Derrida, *Disseminations*, Chicago, IL: University of Chicago Press, 1983.

9 Brian Massumi, *Parables for the Virtual*, Durham, NC: Duke University Press, 2002.

10 Armin Medosh (ed), *Dive*, Liverpool: Virtual-CentreMedia.Net, 2003, p. 30.

11 Steven Shaviro, *Connected*, Minneapolis, MN: University of Minnesota Press, 2003, p. 43.

12 Jackson Lears, *Something for Nothing: Luck in America*, New York: Penguin, 2004.

13 See McKenzie Wark, *Gamer Theory*, Cambridge, MA: Harvard University Press, 2007.

14 Orson Scott Card, *Ender's Game*, New York: Tor Books, 2003.

15 Sven Lindqvist, *A History of Bombing*, New York: New Press, 2003.

16 Henry Jenkins, *Convergence Culture*, New York: New York University Press, 2008.

17 Gabriella Coleman, "The Anthropology of Hackers," *The Atlantic*, September 21, 2011; at: <http://www.theatlantic.com>.

18 Georges Bataille, *Theory of Religion*, New York: Zone Books, 1992.

19 Graham Parker, "Specters of Marks," in *Fair Use*, London: Bookworks, 2005, pp. 3, 5.
20 David Graeber, *5000 Years of Debt*, New York: Melville House, 2011.
21 Peter Hopkirk, *The Great Game: The Struggle for Empire in Central Asia*, Tokyo: Kodansha, 1992.
22 David Sudnow, *Pilgrim in the Microworld*, New York: Warner Books, 1983.
23 Bernard Suits, *The Grasshopper: Games, Life and Utopia*, Toronto: University of Toronto Press, 1978.
24 Alexander Galloway and Eugene Thacker, *The Exploit: A Theory of Networks*, Minneapolis, MN: University of Minnesota Press, 2007, p. 157.
25 Ian Bogost, *Unit Operations: An Approach to Videogame Criticism*, Cambridge, MA: MIT Press, 2008, and Ian Bogost, *Persuasive Games*, Cambridge, MA: MIT Press, 2010. See also Miguel Sichart, "Against Procedurality," *Game Studies*, 11/3 (December 2011), at: <http://www.gamestudies.org>.

Chapter 10   The Gift Shop at the End of History

1 Terry Eagleton, *After Theory*, New York: Basic Books, 2003, p. 60.
2 Walter Benjamin, "The Destructive Character," *Selected Writings 1931–1934*, Cambridge, MA: Harvard University Press, 1999, p. 541ff.
3 Fredric Jameson, *A Singular Modernity*, London: Verso, 2002, p. 35.
4 Guy Debord, *In Girum Imus Nocte Et Consumimur Igni*, London: Pelagian Press, 1981, p. 24.
5 Georg Lukács, *History and Class Consciousness*, London: Merlin Press, 1971, p. 199.
6 Henry Flynt, *Blueprint for a Higher Civilization*, Milan: Multiphla Edizioni, 1975, p. 185.
7 Raoul Vaneigem, *A Cavalier History of Surrealism*, Edinburgh: AK Press, 1999.
8 This remark, and a later one by Fredric Jameson, were made at the conference on *Modernity ≠ Contemporaneity: Antimonies of Art and Culture after the Twentieth Century*, Pittsburgh, PA: University of Pittsburgh, November 4–6, 2004. This chapter is drawn from my contribution to the event. An earlier version is included in Terry Smith et al., *Antimonies of Art and Culture*, Durham, NC: Duke University Press, 2008. My thanks to the organizers and editors.

9 But then in the Deleuze and Guattari of *Anti-Oedipus* one finds something miraculous. Another historical narrative awaits, one that carries the struggle on, into another time, into other spaces. Gilles Deleuze and Felix Guattari, *Anti-Oedipus*, London: Continuum, 2003, p. 153ff.

10 Bruno Latour, *We Have Never Been Modern*, Durham, NC: Harvard University Press, 1993.

11 See McKenzie Wark, *Spectacles of Disintegration*, London: Verso, 2012.

12 Guy Debord, *Oeuvres*, Paris: Gallimard, 2006, p. 1598.

13 Karl Marx and Friedrich Engels, "Manifesto of the Communist Party," *The Revolutions of 1848: Political Writings, Volume 1*, ed. David Fernbach. Harmondsworth: Penguin, 1978, pp. 86, 98.

14 Critical Art Ensemble, *The Electronic Disturbance*, New York: Autonomedia, 1994, pp. 16–17. See also Critical Art Ensemble, *The Molecular Invasion*, New York: Autonomedia, 2002.

15 Naomi Klein, *No Logo*. London: HarperCollins, 2000, p. 35.

16 Gregory Bateson, *Steps Towards An Ecology of Mind*. New York: Ballantine Books, 1972.

17 Antonio Negri, *The Politics of Subversion: A Manifesto for the Twenty-First Century*. Cambridge: Polity, 1989, p. 203.

18 Alexander Galloway and Eugene Thacker, *The Exploit*, Minneapolis, MN: University of Minnesota Press, 2007, p. 97.

Chapter 11 From Intellectual Persona to Hacker Interface

1 Paul Valéry, *The Outlook for Intelligence*, Princeton, NJ: Princeton University Press, 1989, p. 23.

2 Fredric Jameson, *A Singular Modernity*, London: Verso, 2002, p. 29.

3 Georg Lukács, *History and Class Consciousness*, London: Merlin, 1971, p. 110.

4 Simon Critchley, *Ethics, Politics, Subjectivity*, London: Verso, 1999, p. 139.

5 Gayatri Chakravorty Spivak, *A Critique of Postcolonial Reason*, Cambridge, MA: Harvard Univesity Press, 1999.

6 See, for example, Alain Badiou, *The Communist Hypothesis*, London: Verso, 2010.

7 Richard Barbrook, *Imaginary Futures*, London: Pluto Press, 2007.

8 Vandana Shiva, *Protect or Plunder?: Understanding Intellectual Property Rights*, Bangladesh: Bangladesh University Press, 2001, p. 3.

9 See Dominic Pettman, *Love and Other Technologies*, New York: Fordham University Press, 2006.

10 Guy Debord, *Panegyric, Volumes 1 and 2*, London: Verso, 2004, p. 66.

11 Antonio Gramsci, *Selections from the Prison Notebooks*, London: Lawrence & Wishart, 1982, p. 9.

12 Adilkno, *Media Archive*, New York: Autonomedia, 1998, p. 48.

13 Richard Stallman, *Free Software, Free Society*, Boston, MA: GNU Press, 2002, p. 15.

14 Arthur Kroker and Michael A. Weinstein. *Data Trash: The Theory of the Virtual Class*. New York: St Martin's Press, 1994, p. 6; at: <http://www.salon.com>.

15 Courtney Love, "Courtney Love Does the Math," *Salon*, June 14, 2000.

16 McKenzie Wark, *A Hacker Manifesto*, Cambridge, MA: Harvard University Press, 2004, §389.

Chapter 12   Disco Marxism vs Techno Marxism

1 Randall Stross, "When a Video Game Stops Being Fun," *New York Times*, November 21, 2004; at: <http://www.nytimes.com>.

2 Julian Dibbell, "The Unreal Estate Boom," *Wired*, 11/1, January 2003; at: <http://www.wired.com/wired/archive/11.01/gaming.html>.

3 McKenzie Wark, *A Hacker Manifesto*, Cambridge, MA: Harvard University Press, 2004, §002.

4 Jacques Derrida, *Specters of Marx*, New York: Routledge, 1994, p. 32.

5 David Ricardo, *Works and Correspondence*, edited by Piero Sraffa and Maurice Dobb, Cambridge, MA: Cambridge University Press, 1973; Maurice Dobb, *Theories of Value and Distribution Since Adam Smith*, Cambridge, MA: Cambridge University Press, 1973.

6 Karl Marx, *Capital*, vol. 1, ch. 6; at: <http://www.marxists.org>.

7 Slavoj Žižek, "The Lesson of Rancière," in Jacques Rancière, *The Politics of Aesthetics*, London: Continuum, 2005, p. 75.

8 Simon Critchley, *Infinitely Demanding*, manuscript, 2005, ch. 5, p. 4.

9 Ibid., ch. 5, p. 3.

10 Michael Hardt and Antonio Negri, *Multitude*, New York: Penguin Books, 2004, p. 108.

11 Ibid., p. 113.

12 Ibid., p. 185.

13 Ibid., p. 188.

14 Originally formulated jointly with Michael Weinstein, *Data Trash: The Theory of the Virtual Class*, Montreal: New World Perspec-

tives, 1994. For context, see Marielouise Kroker and Arthur Kroker, *Life in the Wires: The C Theory Reader*, Victoria, Canada: New Worlds Press, 2004.

15 Arthur Kroker, *The Will to Technology and the Culture of Nihilism*, Toronto: Toronto University Press, 2004, p. 126.
16 Ibid., p. 128.
17 Ibid., p. 129.
18 Ibid., p. 134.
19 Ibid., p. 137.
20 Ibid., p. 139.
21 Michael Hardt and Antonio Negri, *Multitude*, New York: Penguin Books, 2004, p. 185.
22 Lawrence Lessig, *Free Culture*, New York: Basic Books, 2004.
23 See Flo Conway and Jim Siegelman, *Dark Hero of the Information Age: In Search of Norbert Wiener, The Father of Cybernetics*, New York: Basic Books, 2005.

Chapter 13   The Vectoral Class and Its Antipodes

1 "Google Search Goes to Sea," *New York Times*, September 29, 2008; at: <http://www.nytimes.com>.
2 Michel Aglietta, *A Theory of Capitalist Regulation*, London: Verso, 2001.
3 Naomi Klein, *No Logo*, London: HarperCollins, 2000, p. 35.
4 McKenzie Wark, *A Hacker Manifesto*, Cambridge, MA: Harvard University Press, 2004, §126.
5 Evgeny Pashukanis, *The General Theory of Law and Marxism*, Piscataway, NJ: Transaction Publishers, 2001.
6 James Boyle, *Shamans, Software & Spleens*, Cambridge, MA: Harvard University Press, 1996.
7 Mauss, Marcel. *The Gift*. New York: Norton, 1990, p. 67.
8 John Frow, *Time and Commodity Culture*, Oxford: Oxford University Press, 1997.

Chapter 14   From Disco Marxism to Praxis (Object Oriented)

1 *Daily Mail*, December 9, 2011; at: <http://www.dailymail.co.uk>.
2 Simon Critchley, *Ethics, Politics, Subjectivity*, London: Verso, 1999, p. 139.
3 Simon Critchley, *Infinitely Demanding*, manuscript, 2005, ch. 1, p. 1.
4 Simon Critchley, *Ethics, Politics, Subjectivity*, London: Verso, 1999, p. 148.

5 Simon Critchley, *Infinitely Demanding*, manuscript, 2005, ch. 1, p. 3.

6 Guy Debord, *Panegyric*, London: Verso, 1998.

7 Ernesto Laclau, *Emancipation(s)*, London: Verso, 1996, pp. 80–1.

8 Gilles Deleuze and Felix Guattari, *What Is Philosophy?*, London: Verso, 1994.

9 Gilles Deleuze and Felix Guattari, *Anti-Oedipus*, London: Athlone Press, 1984.

10 Simon Critchley, *Infinitely Demanding*, manuscript, 2005, ch. 5, p. 4.

11 McKenzie Wark, *A Hacker Manifesto*, Cambridge, MA: Harvard University Press, 2004, §1.

12 Jacques Derrida, *Specters of Marx*, New York: Routledge, 1994, p. 170.

13 Simon Critchley, *Ethics, Politics, Subjectivity*, London: Verso, 1999, p. 150.

14 Ibid., p. 149.

15 Gregory Bateson, *Steps to an Ecology of Mind*, Chicago, IL: University of Chicago Press, 2000, p. 459.

16 Pete Engardio and Bruce Einhorn, "Outsourcing Innovation," *Business Week*, March 21, 2005, p. 94.

17 McKenzie Wark, *A Hacker Manifesto*, Cambridge, MA: Harvard University Press, 2004, §006.

18 For a primer, see Graham Harman, *Towards Speculative Realism*, London: Zero Books, 2010. I would not claim for a minute to be doing this argument justice.

19 Karl Marx and Friedrich Engels, *Collected Works*, Vol. 1, London: Lawrence & Wishart, 1975, p. 25ff.

20 See John Bellamy Foster, *Marx's Ecology: Materialism and Nature*, New York; Monthly Review Books, 2000.

21 Perry Anderson, *Considerations on Western Marxism*, London: Verso, 1976.

22 Jane Bennett, *Vibrant Matter: A Political Ecology of Things*, Durham, NC: Duke University Press, 2009, p. xiii.

23 Nikolai Bukharin, *Historical Materialism*, London: Routledge, 2010; Lukács' critique is in *Tactics and Ethics*, London: New Left Books, 1972. See Helena Sheehan, *Marxism and the Philosophy of Science*, Amherst, NY: Humanities Press, 1993.

24 See A. A. Bogdanov, *Red Star*, Bloomington, IN: Indiana University Press, 1984.

25 Timothy Morton, *Ecology Without Nature*, Cambridge, MA: Harvard University Press, 2009.

26 V. Gordon Childe, *What Happened in History*, Harmondsworth: Pelican, 1975.

27 A. A. Bogdanov, *Essays in Tektology*, Seaside, CA: Intersystems Publications, 1980.

28 Reza Negarastani, *Cyclonopedia*, re.press, Melbourne, 2008.

29 See Andrew Brown, *The Sage of Science*, Oxford: Oxford University Press, 2007.

30 See the contributions to the *Designing Geopolitics Symposium*, CalIT2, June 3, 2011; at: <http://www.calit2.net>.

Chapter 15   Considerations on a Hacker Manifesto

1 Mark Hachman, "Negroponte: 'We': Throw OLCPs Out of Helicopters," *PCMag*, November 2, 2011; at: <http://www.pcmag.com>.

2 See the classic presentation by Michel Aglietta, *A Theory of Capitalist Regulation*, London: Verso, 2001.

3 See Stewart Home, *Blood Rites of the Bourgeoisie*, London: Book Works, 2010.

4 William Gibson, *Spook Country*, New York: Putnam, 2007.

5 To paraphrase Guy Debord, *Society of the Spectacle*, New York: Zone Books, 1994, §17.

6 Julian Dibbell, *Play Money*, New York: Basic Books, 2006.

7 Andrew Ross, *Nice Work if You Can Get It*, New York: New York University Press, 2010, p. 175.

8 Christine Harold, *Ourspace: Resisting the Corporate Control of Culture*, Minneapolis, MN: University of Minnesota Press, 2004, p. 24. There is of course no such thing as "situationism."

9 Cf McKenzie Wark, "Copyright, Copyleft, Copygift," *Open*12, 2007; at: <http://www.skor.nl>.

10 Peter Linebaugh and Marcus Rediker, *The Many Headed Hydra*, Boston, MA: Beacon Press, 2001.

11 "The New Rebels," *Spiegel Online Internatonal*, September 19, 2011; at: <http://www.Spiegel.de>.

Chapter 16   After Politics: To the Vector, the Spoils

1 This chapter was originally from a dialogue with Michael Walzer, "Does the Internet Change Politics?," *Dissent*, May 19, 2009; at: <http://www.dissentmagazine.org>.

2 A term coined, to the best of my knowledge, by David Bennahum.

3   Joshua Meyrowitz, *No Sense of Place*, New York: Oxford University Press, 1983.

4   Michael Rogin, *Ronald Reagan: The Movie*, Berkeley, CA: University of California Press, 1987.

5   See Jeffrey Goldfarb, *The Politics of Small Things*, Chicago, IL: University of Chicago Press, 2007.

6   Here "affect" is used in an unsophisticated sense. See Melissa Gregg and Gregory Seigworth, *The Affect Theory Reader*, Durham, NC: Duke University Press, 2010.

7   Simon Critchley, "The American Void," *Harper's*, November 2008; at: <http://www.harpers.org>.

8   On the practice of politics in the age of cellspace, see Markos Mouliisas Ziniqa, *Taking On the System*, New York: Penguin, 2008.

9   Frances Fitzgerald, "Come One, Come All," *New Yorker*, December 3, 2007; at: <http://www.newyorker.com>.

10 Gabriel Sherman, "The Elephant in the Green Room," *New York Magazine*, May 22, 2011; at: <http://www.nymag.com>.

Chapter 17   The Little Sisters Are Watching You

1   Michael Gross, *Model: The Ugly Business of Beautiful Women*, New York: Harper, 2003.

2   Imaginal as defined by Chiara Bottici and Benoit Challand, *The Politics of Imagination*, London: Birkbeck Law Press, 2011. The imagination is usually thought of as an individual faculty, and the imaginary leaves no room for subjective agency at all. The imaginal, in the spirit of Castoriadis, is both agency and structure.

3   "Premieres matériaux pour une théorie de la Jeune-Fille," *Tiqqun: Organe Conscient du Parti Imaginaire*, Paris, 1999, p. 101.

4   Jean Baudrillard, *America*, London: Verso, 1988, p. 33.

5   "Help Children in Africa," *Mail Online*, July 10, 2010; at: <http://www.dailymail.co.uk>; "Supermodel Vows to Stay Naked . . . ," September 8, 2009; at: <http://www.aidwatchers.com>.

6   Guy Debord, *Society of the Spectacle*, New York: Zone Books, 1994, §12.

7   See T. J. Clark, *The Painting of Modern Life*, Princeton, NJ: Princeton University Press, 1999.

8   Sasha Grey, *Neü Sex*, Brooklyn, NY: Vice, 2011.

9   Jean Baudrillard, *Seduction*, London: Palgrave, 1991, p. 15.

10 Ibid, p. 26.

11 Laura Kipnis, *Against Love: A Polemic*, New York: Vintage, 2004.

12 "Premieres matériaux pour une théorie de la Jeune-Fille," *Tiqqun: Organe Conscient du Parti Imaginaire*, Paris, 1999, p. 105; Alexandre Kojève, *Introduction to the Reading of Hegel*, Ithaca, NY: Cornell University Press, 1969.

13 Pierre Klossowski, *Le monnaie vivante*, Paris: Rivages, 1997.

14 "Premieres matériaux," p. 111.

15 Cornelius Castoriadis, *Figures of the Thinkable*, Stanford, CA: Stanford University Press, 2007, p. 71ff. Castoriadis writes here of a decline in imaginal power, but having abandoned a class analysis he has no account of why it should decline. Imagination is like the weather; it just fluctuates. Perhaps one might get further by imagining it not as a constant, but as a flow that can be directed toward institutional innovation or into refreshing the cladding of the existing order in the interests of its ruling class.

16 Slavoj Žižek, *The Ticklish Subject*, London: Verso Books, 1999, p. 313ff.

17 Walter Benjamin, *The Work of Art in the Age of Its Technological Reproducibility and Other Writings on Media*, Cambridge, MA: Harvard University Press, 2008.

18 See Lynn Yaeger, "Little Dutch Girl," *New York Times*, September 23, 2011; at: <http://www.nytimes.com>.

19 See Catharine Lumby, *Bad Girls: The Media, Sex and Feminism in the 90s*, Sydney: Allen & Unwin, 1997.

20 Judith Butler, *Gender Trouble*, London: Routledge, 2006.

21 See McKenzie Wark, "Let's Perform," *Meanjin*, 69/4, December 2010: 119–23.

22 danah boyd, "Viewing American Class Divisions Through Facebook and Myspace," *Apophenia Blog*, June 24, 2007; at: <http://www.danah.org>.

Chapter 18   Shit is Fucked Up and Bullshit

1 Christos Tsiolkas, *Dead Europe*, Melbourne: Vintage, 2005.

2 Theodor Adorno, *Minima Moralia*, London: New Left Books, 1973, p. 156.

3 Joan Robinson, *The Accumulation of Capital*, London: Palgrave, 1969.

4 See Alain Lipietz, *Mirages and Miracles: Crisis in Global Fordism*, London: Verso, 1987.

5 *Human Rights Examiner*, October 8, 2011; at: <http://www.examiner.com>.

6 David Graeber, *Debt: The First 5000 Years*, Brooklyn, NY: Melville House, 2011.

7 Raoul Vaneigem, "Basica Banalities," in Ken Knabb (ed.), *The Situationist International Anthology*, Berkeley, CA: Bureau of Public Secrets, 2005. Graeber acknowledges the influence of Vaneigem, glancingly, and only in a footnote. He quite rightly avoids being entangled in the pro-situ world as much as he resists the Marxological one.

8 See Ricardo Parboni, *The Dollar and Its Rivals*, London: Verso, 1982.

9 Gar Alperovitz, "How the 99 Percent Really Lost Out," *Truthout*, October 29, 2011; at: <http://www.truth-out.org>.

10 Mike Konczal, "Parsing the Data and Ideology of the We Are the 99 Percent Tumblr," *Occupy!*, October 2011, p. 28ff.

11 See McKenzie Wark, *The Beach Beneath the Street*, London: Verso, 2011, on both Lefebvre and détournement.

12 David Graeber, *Direct Action: An Ethnography*, Oakland, CA: AK Press, 2009.

13 Raoul Vaneigem, *The Revolution of Everyday Life*, London: Rebel Press, 2001, p. 26.

14 René Viénet, "The Situationists and New Forms of Action Against Politics and Art," in Ken Knabb (ed.), *Situationist International Anthology*, Berkeley, CA: Bureau of Public Secrets, 2006, pp. 273–6.

15 Guy Debord, *Society of the Spectacle*, New York: Zone Books, 1994.

16 Asger Jorn, *The Natural Order*, Aldershot: Ashgate, 2002.

17 See René Riesel, "Preliminaries on Councils and Councilist Organization," in Ken Knabb (ed.), *Situationist International Anthology*, Berkeley, CA: Bureau of Public Secrets, 2006, pp. 348–62. The workers' council tradition pre-dates the Situationists, of course. See Anton Pannekoek, *Workers' Councils*, Oakland, CA: AK Press, 2002.

18 René Viénet, *Enrages and Situationists in the Occupation Movement*, New York: Autonomedia, 1993.

19 See Marina Sitrin, *Horizontalism: Voices of Popular Power in Argentina*, Oakland, CA: AK Press, 2006.

20 Walter Benjamin, *The Work of Art in the Age of Its Technological Reproducibility and Other Writings on Media*, Cambridge, MA: Harvard University Press, 2008.

Chapter 19   Last Words and Key Words

1 Noah Shactman, "Military 'Not Quite Sure' How Drone Cockpits Got Infected," *Wired News*, October 19, 2011; at: <http://www.wired.com>.

Index

Heikal, Mohamed 22
hierarchy 195, 196
Hill & Knowlton, public relations
  company 19–20
history 98, 101–17, 152, 159,
  197
Hobbes, Thomas 58
Hollywood 52, 82, 84
hope 119, 173
horizontalism 200–1
hostages, children 21–2
Huizinga, Johan 92, 95, 100
humanitarian aid 19, 20, 178–9
Hurd, Douglas 21
hybridity 10
hypocritical theory 104, 123,
  125, 130, 148, 206

idealism 31, 32–3
identity 35–7, 42, 87–8, 98,
  186–7
  cultural 47–8, 119
  and difference 43–8, 111–12,
  114, 142, 185
ilinx (vertigo) 92, 96
imagery 33, 102
  see also media imagery
imaginal world 176, 182, 226,
  227
imperialism 32, 41, 44
incentives 145, 146
income distribution 6
Indonesia 107, 108
industry 53, 81–2
  and capitalism 61, 111, 120–1,
  137, 141, 147, 164
  and class relations 123, 194
infanticide 19, 20
information
  and commodification 109–12,
  116, 117, 124–6, 136,
  143–4, 155
  flows 33–4, 37, 72, 75, 108

freedom of 145, 146, 148, 169
knowledge 69, 114, 196
and scarcity 126, 144, 155,
  156, 165
and space 32, 37, 75, 108–9
and time 51, 75–6
see also property rights,
  intellectual property
innocence 18, 20, 21–2, 23
innovation 111, 142, 154
integration 111, 142
intellectuals 121, 124
intelligence, military 33, 86–7
interface 88
  and class relations 130, 197
  and games 93, 99, 100, 102,
  205
  The Girl 177–87, 206
  hacker interface 100, 118–26,
  162, 206
Internet 36, 67, 170, 171, 172,
  173–4, 184, 197, 200
investment 198
iPhone 192
Iraq 19–20, 74, 83, 94, 165
Irma, baby 17–18
irony 44, 53, 173, 180
Islam 85

Jackson, Andrew 7–8
Jameson, Fredric 42, 102, 116,
  118
Jenkins, Henry 96
Jobs, Steve 189
Jorn, Asger 199–200
junkspace 69

Kennedy, President J. F. 66, 68
Kennedy, Ted 172
Khmer Rouge 20–1
Kindle Fire 86
Kipnis, Laura 180
kipple 69